BODIES AS SITES OF CULTURAL REFLECTION IN EARLY CHILDHOOD EDUCATION

Rachael S. Burke
Judith Duncan

Routledge
Taylor & Francis Group

NEW YORK AND LONDON

KH

First published 2015
by Routledge
711 Third Avenue, New York, NY 10017

and by Routledge
2 Park Square, Milton Park, Abingdon, Oxon OX14 4RN

Routledge is an imprint of the Taylor & Francis Group, an informa business

© 2015 Taylor & Francis

The right of Rachael S. Burke and Judith Duncan to be identified as the authors of this work has been asserted by them in accordance with sections 77 and 78 of the Copyright, Designs and Patents Act 1988.

Library of Congress Cataloging-in-Publication Data
Burke, Rachael S.
Bodies as sites of cultural reflection in early childhood education / Rachael S. Burke, Judith Duncan.
    pages cm — (Changing images of early childhood)
    Includes bibliographical references and index.
  1. Early childhood education—Social aspects.   2. Body image.
I. Title.
    LB1139.23.B87 2015
    372.21—dc23
    2014023934

ISBN: 978-1-138-79503-7 (hbk)
ISBN: 978-1-138-79504-4 (pbk)
ISBN: 978-1-315-75871-8 (ebk)

Typeset in Bembo
by Apex CoVantage, LLC

MIX
Paper from
responsible sources
FSC
www.fsc.org   FSC® C013056

Printed and bound in Great Britain by
TJ International Ltd, Padstow, Cornwall

5/9/16

BODIES AS SITES OF CULTURAL REFLECTION IN EARLY CHILDHOOD EDUCATION

Taking the body as a locus for discussion, Rachael S. Burke and Judith Duncan argue not only that implicit cultural practices shape most of the interactions taking place in early childhood curricula and pedagogy, but that many of these practices often go unnoticed or unrecognised as being pedagogy. Current scholars, inspired by Foucault, acknowledge that the body is socially and culturally produced and historically situated—it is simultaneously a part of nature and society as well as a representation of the way that nature and society can be conceived. Every natural symbol originating from the body contains and conveys a social meaning, and every culture selects its own meaning from the myriad of potential body symbolisms.

Bodies as Sites of Cultural Reflection in Early Childhood Education uses empirical examples from qualitative fieldwork conducted in New Zealand and Japan to explore these theories and discuss the ways in which children's bodies represent a central focus in teachers' pedagogical discussions and create contexts for the embodiment of children's experiences in the early years.

Rachael S. Burke is Postdoctoral Fellow at Hiroshima University, Japan. She also conducts independent research in her role as Director of Small Earth Consulting Ltd., New Zealand.

Judith Duncan is Professor of Education, School of Educational Studies and Leadership, at University of Canterbury, New Zealand.

Changing Images of Early Childhood
Series Editor: Nicola Yelland

Books in this forward-thinking series challenge existing practices in early childhood education and reflect the changing images of the field. The series enables readers to engage with contemporary ideas and practices of alternative perspectives which deviate from those theories traditionally associated with the education of young children and their families. Not only do these books make complex theory accessible, they provide early childhood educators with the tools to ensure their practices are backed by appropriate theoretical frameworks and strong empirical evidence.

Titles in the *Changing Images of Early Childhood* series include:

This book is dedicated to our sons, Finn, Gabriel, Angus, and Lucas, who have inspired us to begin, continue, and complete this journey.

CONTENTS

FIGURES

FOREWORD

In this book, Burke and Duncan make a compelling case for a turn in early childhood education research from the mind to the body. The focus on the thinking and the talk of young children and their teachers that has characterised most research in the field needs to be balanced with attention to how preschool teachers and children employ techniques of the body. A focus on embodied practices in turn requires a shift from textual analyses of what children and teachers think and say to video analyses of what they do. This book is one of the first in the field of early childhood education to make this shift.

The bodily turn can be found across the disciplines of sociology, anthropology, philosophy, gender studies, and geography. Some theorists refer to this renewed attention to the body as part of 'the posthuman turn', a term that signals a decentering of the thinking, talking human subject. Some of the work in this new tradition focuses on things, some on animals, and some, like this study, on bodies.

Burke and Duncan put forward a tripartite conceptual framework of the body, as they locate and incorporate (no pun intended) three strands of scholarship on the body that usually are not brought together: a Foucauldian notion of the political control of the body; an anthropological concern with the body and its actions as symbolic; and a sociological concern with techniques of the body and bodily habitus. I find their discussion of the writings on the body of Foucault, Mary Douglas, Marcel Mauss, and Pierre Bourdieu consistently insightful. A great strength of this book is their application of each of these theorists to their fieldwork data. Burke and Duncan demonstrate that preschool programs in both Japan and New Zealand simultaneously discipline the bodies of children and teachers (à la Foucault); deal with purity and impurity (à la Douglas); and display and reproduce culturally characteristic techniques of the body (à la Mauss and Bourdieu).

A virtue of this study is that it presents a comparison of Japanese and New Zealand preschools. Comparative studies of early childhood education and care settings are rare. Most of these, including my own research, use the United States as the 'other' to cultures more exotic to the Anglophone reader. I would bet that North American and European readers of this book will find much in the authors' depiction of New Zealand practices familiar, but also much that is surprising.

These days when early childhood education practitioners in New Zealand, the United States, and other countries look abroad for models of best practice it is most often to Italy, and specifically to the preschools of Reggio Emilia. I have argued elsewhere (2005) that while Japanese preschools may not be as useful a model for practitioners in other countries to copy, they do provide a useful challenge to Western assumptions about what is possible and desirable to do in the education and care of young children. In this book, Burke and Duncan offer example after example of embodied practices of teachers and children in Japanese preschools that confront Western assumptions and expand our repertoire of possibilities.

Their research design is a version of the video-cued, multi-vocal, ethnographic method I developed and have used in various studies of preschools in Japan and elsewhere. I call this version of video research 'multi-vocal diachronic video-cued ethnographic interviewing'. But no one else does. It's more commonly called the 'preschool in three cultures' method or 'video-cued interviewing'. This method is more praised than used because it is so arduous. I have made the claim that making a video of a cultural practice and then using the video as a cue for ethnographic interviewing telescopes and speeds up the traditional year-long process of ethnographic fieldwork. But this is not to say that this method makes ethnographic work faster or easier. The hard work Burke and Duncan put into shooting, editing, and screening the videos bears fruit in the nuance of their analyses.

In this study videos work well in two ways. Although I have emphasised in my studies that the videos in this method are primarily cues for interviewing rather than data, my colleagues and I increasingly have come to appreciate the value of the videos also as data and demonstration (Hayashi & Tobin, 2012). Burke and Duncan's inclusion of still images from their videos coupled with their written descriptions of scenes in the videos work effectively to bring subtle aspects New Zealand and Japanese preschools to life for readers.

This combination of theories of embodiment with visual and ethnographic methods allow Burke and Duncan to challenge the taken-for-grantedness of quotidian life inside early childhood education centres in New Zealand and Japan, and in so doing, make the familiar both strange and beautiful. The reader is left with an appreciation for the resourcefulness and thoughtfulness of the practitioners in their study, who in the best tradition of cultural anthropology are privileged as expert informants.

Joseph Tobin
University of Georgia

References

Hayashi, A., & Tobin, J. (2012). Reframing an ethnography of a Japanese preschool classroom, *Visual Anthropology Review*, *28*(1), 13–31.

Tobin, J. (2005). Quality in early childhood education: An anthropologist's perspective, *Early Education and Development*, *16*(4), 422–434.

ACKNOWLEDGEMENTS

There are many people who have kindly contributed towards making this book a reality. First and foremost, we would like to express our heartfelt gratitude to the staff, children, and parents of the early childhood centres in New Zealand and Japan where fieldwork took place. In order to preserve your anonymity, we will not list your names here, but without your willingness to open up your centres, this project could never have been realised. We thank you so very much for your patience, tolerance, and interest in the midst of busy teaching and family demands.

We are equally grateful for the support shown by members of the New Zealand and Japanese early childhood community in the form of focus group sessions across both countries. Again, we will not go into specifics so that your confidentiality can be maintained, but we are thankful for the way you generously made time for an emerging researcher. Your insightful comments, discussions, and feedback have provided us with precious insights into the worlds you inhabit.

Rachael would like to give her heartfelt thanks to all those who supported her by providing accommodation, food, transportation, information and, above all, their valued friendship during her fieldwork in Japan: Vicky Kobayashi, Hiroyo and Keiji Sato, Katsuhiko and Hitomi Igarashii, Masayuki and Keiko Maeda, Emi Nakamura, Kayoko Suzuki, Hikaru Kawamoto, Shuji Nakano, Kayo and Masanobu Miki, Midori Sasaki, and Caroline Cooley. Rachael is especially grateful to Valerie and Kazuhiko Shimbu for having her stay for the month that she conducted fieldwork in Hokkaido. Rachael would also like to thank Kiyoko Nakano for her assistance in translating subtitles for the edited Japanese version of the film.

We also wish to thank the academic guidance of Dr Graeme MacRae, School of People, Environment and Planning at Massey University, and Nicola Yelland, Victoria University at Melbourne, for supporting our ideas to come alive in this book. We wish to acknowledge the original artwork that was created for the cover of the book by Japanese artist, Yoshiko Onodera, which captured the spirit of our publication: both in topic and in collaboration.

The research reported in this book was financially assisted by a Massey University Doctorate Scholarship, New Zealand Postgraduate Study Abroad Award Programme, and Massey Graduate Research Fund. In addition this book was made possible by funding from the University of Canterbury, and New Zealand Workbridge.

NOTE ON AUTHORS

Rachael S Burke, PhD (Postdoctoral Fellow, Hiroshima University, Japan)

Rachael graduated with a PhD in social anthropology from Massey University, New Zealand, in 2013. Her doctoral thesis examined implicit cultural practice in early childhood education in New Zealand and Japan. Her master of arts thesis was also concerned with aspects of anthropology in Japan through its analysis of socialisation processes in early childhood settings in Hokkaido. Prior to this, Rachael spent six years living and working in rural Japan, where her three children were born and attended kindergarten.

Judith Duncan, PhD (Professor of Education, University of Canterbury, New Zealand)

Judith's research and teaching interests include early childhood education, children's voice, gender and education, education policies and practices, and family support. For over twenty years, she has been involved in research that examines early childhood from multiple and interdisciplinary perspectives, placing central to each research project the perspectives of children and their families. Over the last decade, Judith has been working alongside colleagues in Japan exploring social support for families—in the contexts of children with disabilities, transition to school, community building post-disaster, and cultural perspectives.

GLOSSARY OF KEY TERMS

Terms from the Japanese Context

While there are several ways of writing Japanese in its romanised form, this glossary employs the Hepburn method. The often used double vowels **oo** and **uu** are written with a macron, and become **ō** and **ū** respectively. The same rule applies to the double vowel **aa** which becomes **ā**, whereas as the long **ee** vowel is written as **ei**. Romanised place names commonly use a modified version of the Hepburn system in which long vowels are ignored, hence Tokyo or Hokkaido with no macrons.

Ainu	the indigenous people of Hokkaido
aisatsu	daily greetings
amae	dependency
bacchi	child's word for dirty
baikin	germs
anime	Japanese style of motion-picture animation
bentō	packed (box) lunch
chinchin	penis (colloquial)
enryo	reserve, restraint
furusato	home village, home town or native place
gaijin	foreigner, literally 'outside person'
gambaru	to do one's best, to persevere
genki	lively, energetic
genkan	entrance foyer where one takes off one's shoes
hadashi kyōiku	naked education
hanseikai	self-reflection meeting

hoikuen	early childcare centre
Hokkaido	Japan's northernmost major island
Honshu	Japan's main island where the capital, Tokyo, is situated
irete	shortened form of *nakami ni irete*, "Can I join you?"
itadakimasu	greeting which precedes consumption of food
kanji	Chinese characters adapted into Japanese language
kanyu	fruit-flavoured jelly vitamins made from cod liver oil
katakana	phonetic alphabet used for foreign loan words
kibun-tenkan	technique used by teachers to focus children's attention elsewhere
kodomokai	children's association
kodomo-rashi	childlike
Kōseisho	Ministry of Health and Welfare
kurō	hardship
kyōiku	education
kyōiku mama	education mother
machi no hoiku	caring for children by waiting
manga	Japanese comic books
mimamoru	'wait and see' approach taken by teachers
Mombukagakushō	Ministry of Education, Culture, Science, Sports, and Technology
nintei kodomoen	child-accredited centre
ohayō gozaimasu	good morning
ohirune	naptime
okāsan	mother
okāsan suwari	sitting on one's knees, literally 'to sit like a mother'
onara	fart (colloquial)
onsen	hot spring
oppai	breasts (colloquial)
Oka Yōchien	fictitious name of the kindergarten where Japanese field-work took place
ryōsai kenbo	good wife/wise mother construct
seishin kyōiku	spiritual education
sensei	teacher
shiritsu yōchien	private kindergarten
shūdan seikatsu	literally 'life in the group', a socialisation technique
skinship	term used to describe intimacy, or physical closeness
soto	outside group or world
suki-kirai	likes and dislikes
sunao	cooperative, compliant
uchi	inside group or world
unchi	excrement (colloquial)
undōkai	sports day, athletics meeting

yōchien	kindergarten
Yuri	fictitious name of city where Japanese fieldwork took place
yutori-kyōiku	relaxed style of education

Reference

Martin, S. (1997). *Martin's Concise Japanese dictionary: English-Japanese, Japanese-English, fully Romanized with complete kanji & kana*. Tokyo, Japan: Charles E. Tuttle.

Terms from the New Zealand Context

early childhood care and education	umbrella term for the early childhood sector
Kaimai Kindergarten	fictitious name of centre where New Zealand fieldwork took place
karanga	Māori call traditionally used to welcome visitors
kindergarten	centres that are owned and operated by community-based kindergarten associations, clustered in geographical areas
kōhanga reo	total immersion Māori language family programme for children
Māori	the indigenous people of New Zealand
Pākehā:	Māori word for non-Māori people
Playcentre	a parent-led early childhood education and care service
Rata	fictitious name of city where New Zealand fieldwork took place
Te Whāriki	the New Zealand early childhood curriculum
waiata	Māori word for song(s)
whakatoi	Māori word for spiritedness
whānau (tangata)	Māori word for extended family and community

Theoretical or Methodological Terms

bio-power	term coined by Foucault, a way of managing people as a group through the subjugation of bodies
body politic	term which implies that power and control are embodied
body techniques	term coined by Mauss, actions that are effective and traditional
docile bodies	term coined by Foucault, bodies that have been rendered docile through a regiment of disciplinary acts
ethnography	both a qualitative research process conducted by anthropologists, and a product (the outcome of this process in the form of a book or thesis)
fieldwork	living among a group of people, or spending an extended period of time with them, for the purpose of learning about their culture

habitus	a set of dispositions and internalised possibilities which enable a person to socially function
normalisation	term used by Foucault, social processes through which ideas and actions come to be seen as 'natural' or 'normal' in everyday life
participant observation	key research method for anthropologists, involving becoming part of a community while observing people's behaviour and activities within it
panopticon	Jeremy Bentham's circular prison, constructed so that an unseen observer could watch prisoners at all times
PS3C	Preschool in Three Cultures (Tobin et al., 1989, 2009)
social body	natural symbol with which to think about social relationships, culture and nature
three bodies	Scheper-Hughes and Lock's framework, combining the individual (lived) body, the social body and the body politic

SERIES EDITOR INTRODUCTION

The books in Routledge's Changing Images of Early Childhood series reflect a reconceptualization of the field from scholars whose work challenges us all to reflect, and be critical of, assumptions that we may take for granted. They offer an opportunity to critique traditional practices and approaches and also introduce us to cutting edge research on topics and ideas that we might not be aware play a significant part in our everyday lives and our interactions with young children and their families. The books are designed to link theory and practice in new and dynamic ways. Some theoretical perspectives can be complex, yet they remain salient and relevant to our interrogation of educational and cultural practices. This is essential if we are to understand and strive towards an equitable and socially just system for our children's future. The books in this series interrogate contemporary early childhood educational ideas and link theory and practice by providing examples that are grounded in empirical studies. In this way, they make the theoretical frameworks more accessible and relevant to a new generation of educators who are able then to create contexts for learning that reflect a respect for the diversity of cultures and contexts that exist across the globe.

Bodies as Sites of Cultural Reflection in Early Childhood Education by Burke and Duncan interrogates the *body*; its location, regulation, and the ways in which children's lives and bodies are mediated and shaped by rituals, by the natural world, and by design in early childhood settings. The authors argue 'that implicit cultural practices not only shape most of the interactions taking place in early childhood curricula and pedagogy but that many of these practices often go unnoticed or unrecognised as being pedagogy.' In the book, they explore the ways in which children's bodies are represented as a central focus in teachers' pedagogical discussions and how they embody children's experiences in the early years.

The discussion of bodies is underpinned by the theoretical constructs postulated by Mauss, Douglas, and Foucault. Mauss was a pioneer in his advocacy of viewing the body as a form of cultural practice, while Douglas considered the body as symbolic and a reflection of societal and cultural practices. Foucault was concerned with the 'body politic' and how this impacted the ways in which individuals are controlled, constantly under surveillance and manipulated in time and space. These theoretical framings allow for an interrogation of ethnographies of early childhood settings in Japan and New Zealand, which form the context for understanding the central role of the body in social, cultural, and political contexts.

Burke and Duncan state that their research was inspired by the seminal works of Tobin and his colleagues in their *Preschools in Three Cultures* research. Tobin et al's video-cued multi-vocal methodology is incorporated into this work so that reflections on video recorded practices can be obtained from both viewing in the country and by participants in the other country. This allows for a rich discussion of the salient issues from different perspectives and cultural milieus and gives us fascinating insights into the lives of children and their teachers in each locale.

Each chapter in the book takes a different angle on the various notions inherent to the theories and provides the reader with a framework for extending their understanding of early childhood practices and the meaning making processes in a careful consideration of the issues.

The chapters begin by thinking about the body as a contested site that causes anxiety and fear in adults, who seem to be in a constant state of alarm about protecting children's bodies from harm. In Japan, at least, it also would seem that the body is an integral part of the educative process, and there is a highlighted awareness of its role, function, and the rituals associated with its placement in everyday actions and organised events. The authors then discuss risky bodies, disciplining bodies, dirty bodies, and pollution before summarizing their thoughts in the final chapter. This is a bold work that takes a new perspective on linking theory and practice around the issues associated with the body.

Nicola Yelland
Professor of Education
College of Education
Victoria University
Melbourne
Australia

1

INTRODUCTION

Introduction

This book focuses on the body in order to explore the ways in which early childhood education (ECE) settings incorporate implicit cultural practices into pedagogy and practice. We argue that implicit cultural practices not only shape many of interactions taking place in the early childhood context, but many of these practices often go unnoticed or unrecognised as culturally informed. In this book we share our analysis from ethnographic fieldwork conducted in New Zealand and Japan, to demonstrate ways in which children's bodies are viewed, manipulated, protected, ordered, and challenged, and that this provides a useful lens through which to examine unseen cultural ECE practices. The theories of Mauss (1936/1973) position the body as a crucible of bodily techniques. Mauss argues that such techniques cannot be viewed as 'natural', but rather classified as cultural practices. In the chapters which follow, the ideas of Mauss still resonate, but they are complemented by the theories of Douglas (1970/1996) and Foucault (1975/1995). Douglas expands on Mauss' theories and introduces the idea of the body as a natural symbol. Her focus is on the exchange of symbolic meanings between the individual body and the social body. The theories of Foucault centre on the body as political, as a site for discipline, domestication, and training. Foucault contends that institutionalised structures such as the early childhood centre work to produce docile bodies that can be used for state purposes. Weaving the work of these three theorists through ethnographic data provides the framework for an examination of Scheper-Hughes and Lock's (1987) 'three bodies'.

The body has been the subject of anthropological research since the late 1970s and continues to provide a focus for robust discussion by social scientists (Fraser & Greco 2005; Mascia-Lees, 2011). The 'three bodies' approach suggested by Scheper-Hughes and Lock (1987) has been especially useful for unpacking the layers of dialogue that emerged from our research processes. The 'three bodies' express three areas of discrete, yet related, analysis developed by the theorists: Mauss (1936/1973), Douglas (1970/1996), and Foucault (1975/1995). While Mauss was concerned with the experience of the individual, physical body, Douglas looked for symbolic meaning in the social body, and Foucault remained committed to unpacking the body politic. These foundation theorists informed the analysis of our study and shape the chapters in this book.

For the ethnographic study, we used the research methodology developed by Tobin, Wu, and Davidson (1989) and Tobin, Hsueh, and Karasawa (2009) *Preschool in Three Cultures* (PS3C) to stimulate a multi-vocal text to reveal hidden cultural assumptions in culturally different early years contexts. Using video to reflect on comparative material proved to be a powerful way to expose these hidden assumptions. What this method revealed is the central role that children's bodies play in the early childhood experience.

Through this book, we will argue that the ways in which children's bodies are viewed, manipulated, protected, ordered, and challenged provide a useful lens through which to examine unseen and taken-for-granted cultural practices in early years education.

Personal Connections

This book has its roots in a long association with the two countries in the study—New Zealand and Japan—an academic quest that has paralleled our journeys as mothers, teachers, researchers, and scholars.

Rachael spent almost six years living and teaching in small towns in rural Hokkaido, Japan. For three of these years, she was based at Oka Kindergarten, and it was to this centre that Rachael returned to conduct fieldwork. While Rachael and her husband had left New Zealand as newly graduated university students, they came home as parents to three young boys who had already negotiated many aspects of early childhood education in Japan. The family's return to New Zealand meant the boys had to readjust to schooling and kindergarten in their 'homeland'. Rather than being a seamless transition, Rachael was confronted with the reality of early childhood education that bore little resemblance to her own childhood memories of it. She found she was confounded by unspoken assumptions, echoing what she had experienced while her children attended kindergarten in Japan. These implicit practices expected of mother and child provided the impetus for this book, and for an earlier period of research conducted in Hokkaido centres.

Judith's involvement with early childhood education in New Zealand spans more than thirty years, and her connections with early childhood in Japan over the last decade. Working with Japanese academic colleagues and Japanese postgraduate students has enabled Judith to engage in cultural conversations and experiences in both New Zealand and Japan, collectively comparing theoretical ideas and cultural experiences—challenging assumptions and expectations in both countries. Over several visits to Japan, Judith has spent rich time in early childhood centres in Hiroshima, Osaka, Kobe, and Imabari, discussing ideas and pedagogical decisions with teachers and principals. These embedded experiences have enabled Judith to reframe her thinking about early childhood education and her own assumptions about early childhood, and set the scene for supporting Rachael's investigative research, reported in this book.

Theoretical Underpinnings

The body, the focus of this book, has been the subject of anthropological interest for several decades. In the late 1970s, the body first emerged as the focus of ontological and epistemological research by social scientists. By the 1980s, the body had become such a significant object of study that "the anthropology of the body" was recognised as a subfield of the discipline (Mascia-Lees, 2011, p. 1). In the case of other disciplines, such as sociology, studies placing the body at the centre of research exploded during the 1990s when the paradigm of 'embodiment' was developed. This paradigm takes the actual, lived experience of the body, or 'being-in-the-world', as a starting point. Csordas (1999) distinguishes this from the anthropology of the body, which considers the body as an external object of analysis through a focus on bodily metaphors. Space limitations do not allow for a comprehensive review of the vast literature devoted to the body, but readers are directed to Lock (1993), Csordas (1999), and Fraser and Greco (2005), who provide clear overviews and a starting point for further understanding.

Marcel Mauss and the Emergence of the Body in Anthropological Theory

Although there is a diverse range of scholars from various academic disciplines now concerned with the corporeality of the self, it is claimed that the body emerged for the first time in anthropological theory as a central object of research through the work of British anthropologist Mary Douglas (Synnott & Howes, 1992). Yet, in her book *Natural Symbols* (1970/1996), Douglas draws on the work of Marcel Mauss who initially outlined a systemic anthropology of the body. In his pioneering essay, *Techniques of the Body* (1936/1973), Mauss identifies ordinary bodily actions as 'techniques'. By techniques he means the varying ways people in different societies know how to use their bodies. Rather than viewing these techniques as natural and outside the remit of culture, Mauss argues that these actions can be classified as cultural practices. Therefore, the naked body can be repositioned as "man's first and most natural instrument" (Mauss 1936/1973, p. 70).

The Work of Mary Douglas

Douglas (1970/1996) builds on Mauss' assertion that the human body be treated "as an image of society and that there can be no natural way of considering the body that does not involve at the same time a social dimension" (p. 74). In other words, every natural symbol originating from the body contains and conveys a social meaning, and every culture selects its own meaning from the myriad of potential body symbolisms. Douglas argues that Mauss' view of bodily actions as techniques prioritised cultural variation to the point of discounting any behaviour as natural. This approach contrasts with Lévi-Strauss (1964), who focused on symbolic universals, which he felt informed the way human bodies were socially constructed.

Douglas's work addresses the space between these two contrasting theoretical approaches. Douglas argues that the 'natural' body, in the sense that it is universally apparent across cultures, is not the physico-biological body, but the exchange of meanings between *two* bodies, the individual body and the social body.

> The social body constrains the way the physical body is perceived. The physical experience of the body, always modified by the social categories through which it is known, sustains a particular view of society. There is a continual exchange of meanings between the two kinds of bodily experiences so that each reinforces the categories of the other.
>
> *(Douglas, 1970/1996, p. 69)*

These two bodies, the 'individual' and the 'social', are sometimes "so near as to be almost merged; sometimes they are far apart. The tension between them allows the elaboration of meanings" (Douglas, 1970/1996, p. 87). Critics such as Van Wolputte (2004) have argued that Douglas's distinction between the two bodies only serves to reaffirm the dualism of mind and body, and privilege the former. In contrast, the theory of embodiment does not imply "the neglect of 'mind', but it does situate mind in 'practice'" (Strathern & Stewart, 2011, p. 397).

Michel Foucault and the Body

While Douglas (1970/1996) viewed the individual, physical body and the social body as reciprocally symbolic, Michel Foucault (1975/1995) saw the body as a site of discipline, domestication, training, and punishment by the state. Through these measures, the body is rendered 'docile' for economic or military purposes: "The body becomes a useful force only if it is both a productive body and a subjected body" (Foucault, 1975/1995, p. 26). The creation of these 'docile bodies' is accomplished through the micro-physics of bio-power, which is the power exercised on the body through to the minutest physical actions. Foucault's theories contend that the state produces docile bodies through institutionalised structures such as the prison, the hospital, and the school. But Foucault (1975/1995) goes further than that, arguing that, through constant surveillance and inspection, society itself becomes a prison:

> [The political technology of the body] cannot be localized in a particular type of institution or state apparatus. For they have recourse to it; they use,

select or impose certain of its methods. But, in its mechanisms and its effects, it is situated at a quite different level. What the apparatuses and institutions operate is, in a sense, a micro-physics of power, whose field of validity is situated in a sense between these great functionings and the bodies themselves with their materiality and their forces.

(p. 26)

Through this process of assessment, coordination, and ultimately, surveillance, emerges the "disciplinary individual" who has been created by these new techniques of power (Foucault, 1975/1995, p. 227). Foucault's theories have been criticised as overly pessimistic through his neglect to consider agency, and his inability to provide a means of overcoming the current forms of power (Erickson & Murphy, 2008). Despite this, Foucault is regarded as making a significant contribution to anthropology through the way he repositioned the body at the centre of scholarly consideration (Synnott & Howes, 1992).

The Three Bodies

While Foucault was concerned with the body as political, and Douglas the body as symbolic, in the mid-1980s, medical anthropologists Nancy Scheper-Hughes and Margaret Lock (1987) called for anthropologists to problematise the body another way. Taking a view of the body as "simultaneously a physical and symbolic artifact, as both naturally and culturally produced, and as securely anchored in a particular historical moment", Scheper-Hughes and Lock (1987, p. 7) proposed 'three bodies' and three anthropological approaches. At the first level of analysis is the 'individual body' in the phenomenological sense of embodied experiences people have of their bodies. With reference to Mauss (1936/1973), Scheper-Hughes and Lock assume that all people share a sense of the embodied self as separate to other individual bodies. At the second level of analysis is the 'social body', which functions as a natural symbol with which to think about social relationships, culture, and nature (Douglas, 1970/1996). At the third level is the 'body politic', which asserts that power and control are also embodied. Here the work of Foucault (1973a, 1973b, 1980, 1975/1995) is evident through the ways in which the body is subjected to surveillance, regulation, and control. The stability of the body politic depends on its ability to regulate the social body and to discipline individual bodies. In outlining their theoretical approach, Scheper-Hughes and Lock (1987) state that

[t]he 'three bodies' represent, then, not only three separate and overlapping units of analysis, but also three different theoretical approaches and epistemologies: phenomenology (individual body, the lived self), structuralism and symbolism (the social body), and poststructualism (the body politic).

(p. 8)

Scheper-Hughes and Lock (1987) argue that what mediates between these three bodies are emotions. Whether public or private, individual or collective, emotions are imbued with cultural meaning, providing an important missing link between the mind and body, the individual, social, and body politic.

Inspired by Scheper-Hughes and Lock (1987), this book will move back and forth between a discussion of the three bodies as a means of illuminating and understanding the place of the body in the New Zealand and Japanese early childhood contexts. The search for an applicable theory had already led to the work of Mauss, Douglas, and Foucault. The ideas of Scheper-Hughes and Lock (1987) lent validity to using these three theorists to explore different aspects of the data. However, rather than expanding on the theories of Scheper-Hughes and Lock, this book looks back to the original theorists to examine the individual, social, and political body.

This means that the work of Mauss (1936/1973), Douglas (1970/1996), and Foucault (1975/1995) provide a framework for analysis, and while these theories are classic rather than contemporary, we propose that they remain a valuable means of unpacking the ethnographic data. We acknowledge that while Scheper-Hughes and Lock (1987) see emotions as binding the three bodies together, this study stops short of exploring this aspect of the data. The study of emotions reflects the postmodern turn towards the paradigm of embodiment. As a result, this study does not take 'being-in-the-world' (Csordas, 1999) as its starting point, but follows the lead of Mauss, Douglas, and Foucault in approaching the body as an object of study.

Methodology behind the Scenes

This book draws on participant observation methodology to generate data and a theoretical framework. Bernard (2006) defines participant observation as "immersing yourself in a culture and learning to remove yourself every day from that immersion so you can intellectualize what you've seen and heard, put it into perspective, and write about it convincingly" (p. 344). Participant observation is regarded as the defining research method of social anthropologists (DeWalt & DeWalt, 2002). Through first-hand observation of real-life situations, known as fieldwork, the researcher becomes the "instrument for data collection and analysis" (Bernard, 2006, p. 359). Rather than commencing with a theory to prove, social anthropologists draw on their experiences in the field to shape their analysis, then look to theory to explain or clarify the associations.

In the case studies we discuss in this book, the empirical data has been generated from the many hours of video, discussions, analysis, and feedback from the participants in the two field sites and during the focus group sessions. The data was very rich in terms of the breadth of experiences and issues raised through this process. But, working through it carefully, overlapping, concentric circles of commonality began to emerge. At the very centre of these circles was the body. Over and over, the prevalence of children's (and teachers') bodies permeated the discussions, and therefore, the data. The body became the primary locus for analysis.

Introduced to Tobin et al.'s (1989) book *Preschool in Three Cultures,* Rachael was struck by how much of Tobin's writing resonated with her own experience of preschool Japan, and how a seemingly simple methodology had revealed complex social and cultural patterns. The films and ethnographies, *Preschool in Three Cultures* (Tobin et al., 1989) and *Preschool in Three Cultures Revisited* (Tobin et al., 2009) present comparative views of Japanese, Chinese, and American preschools through the eyes of teachers empowered to speak as anthropologists. Members of each culture were (re)filmed as they critically analysed both their own country's early childhood practice and made judgements about the other two centres in the study. This method views film less as data but as a way of encouraging dialogue, which in turn illuminates culturally informed philosophies and practices of early childhood education within wider social patterns. In describing the *Preschool in Three Cultures* (PS3C) method, Tobin and Hsueh (2007) have written that "the videos function primarily neither as data nor as description but instead as rich nonverbal cues designed to stimulate critical reflection" (p. 77). Such an approach also removes the anthropologist from the powerful role of 'all seeing narrator' common in early ethnographic film, yet recognises the subjective nature of edited videotapes.

The video-cued PS3C method "collapses and accelerates" the traditional ethnographic fieldwork process in which the anthropologist observes and participates in a specific cultural context (Tobin et al., 2009, p. 6). Instead of spending the traditional year in the field, this method provides a focus for interviews and discussions with participants in the form of the videotapes. This approach not only quickly identifies major themes and issues, but it helps to reduce the kind of ambiguity that can occur when interviewing across cultural contexts. For example, if early childhood teachers are asked about their views on how children learn, the question may be too large or too vague to elicit a meaningful response. But by using the video as a prompt, teachers can be asked how they would act in specific situations, such as when a Japanese boy refuses to draw a picture, or children wander away from a baking activity at the New Zealand centre. Teachers' reactions to scenes such as these not only highlight the implicit cultural expectations underlying practice at their own centres, but they reveal the way the issue is viewed in the 'outsider' culture.

The Field

This book draws on case study fieldwork conducted at Oka Kindergarten,[1] a private kindergarten in Hokkaido, Japan, and Kaimai Kindergarten, an education and care centre in Rata,[2] New Zealand.

Oka Kindergarten is situated in the city of Yuri on Hokkaido's Eastern coast. The island's sub-arctic climate and geographical isolation mark it as distinct from mainland Japan, and it retains a utopian image in the minds of the Japanese public. In reality, life for the prefecture's residents is increasingly difficult as economic decline and depopulation take their toll (Ministry of Internal Affairs and Communications, 2011). The city of Yuri is the commercial hub for the local agricultural industry.

Oka is one of the largest kindergartens (*yōchien*) in Yuri. It is identifiable by its bright, spacious facilities and an enormous, animated clock. Children arrive at the kindergarten each morning aboard a fleet of brightly painted buses. The one-storey block of classrooms is set on expansive grounds bordered by large trees in the middle of a middle-class neighbourhood. Over the past decade, the kindergarten has retained its position as a popular choice for middle-class parents who approve of the energetic, well-qualified teaching staff and the extensive curriculum.

As a private institution, the kindergarten earns revenue by charging fees to parents, although it also receives limited funding from the local city and prefecture. In contrast to many of the surrounding kindergartens and childcare centres, which have seen their rolls decrease in line with the dropping birth rate, Oka has managed to keep its roll stable by regularly introducing a number of new services to satisfy parents.

Like staff at the vast majority of Japanese kindergartens, all of the teachers at Oka are graduates of two-year junior colleges and one or two have degrees from universities. Ben-Ari (2008) suggests that the high numbers of qualified teachers means that the educational level of Japanese early childhood staff is amongst the best in the world.

In contrast to the economic decline facing the residents of Yuri, the New Zealand city of Rata has been experiencing a population boom. While the local economy has been challenged during the global economic crisis, it has not been enough to deter people wishing to move to the area in search of a laidback coastal lifestyle. Kaimai Kindergarten is a community owned not-for-profit early childhood education and care centre situated on a peninsula in a middle-class suburb. The physical structure of the centre consists of a one-level wooden prefabricated building, which is predominantly open plan but contains a few separate areas for the centre's kitchen, the office, and the bathrooms.

The teachers are all fully qualified, which is seen as a mark of both pride and quality within the centre. Like most New Zealand centres, children attending Kaimai come from culturally diverse backgrounds. This diversity is a source of pride, and the early childhood curriculum of New Zealand, *Te Whāriki,* stresses how important it is for the links between family, home, and the centre to be valued and affirmed (Ministry of Education, 1996).

As Ben-Ari (1997, p. 26) has pointed out, the terms "typicality" and "representation" are disputed terms within the social sciences. Despite the contested nature of individual situations, recurring rhythms and patterns form the foundation of social research. The majority of Oka Kindergarten routines were easily recognisable and familiar to Japanese viewers if somewhat traditional in terms of pedagogy and practice. New Zealand teachers found common ground in the freedom children enjoyed at Kaimai Kindergarten, as well as the emphasis on unstructured, outdoor play and minimal routines. As Sato (2004) has pointed out however, although teachers may work within a shared set of ideas and practices, they are themselves individuals and their classrooms reflect both their personalities and their own diverse pedagogical approaches.

Field Site Structure and Daily Routines

In each centre, the day was structured in ways that reflected the ideology of both the nation and the institution. In New Zealand, while the day technically commenced at 8:45AM, children arrived sporadically with their parents throughout the early morning. After choosing a cubbyhole in which to stow their bag, the children would then wander off to join in play with friends, or sit down at one of the activity tables set up by the teacher. This might involve them in creating something with dough and paint or digging in the sandpit. With the exception of a break for morning tea and a ten-minute 'mat time' at the end of the day, children were free to create their own play and learning opportunities. This approach is supported by the New Zealand early childhood curriculum, *Te Whāriki* (Ministry of Education, 1996), which views children as competent, capable learners enmeshed in community.

Most of the children would be collected by their parents at lunchtime, except for a small group of children who tucked into sandwiches, fruit, and yoghurt outside under the supervision of one teacher while the other staff retreated to the staffroom for their lunch break. The afternoon marked the commencement of a new session and the arrival of different, younger children. The four teachers 'on the floor'[3] moved between individuals and groups of children, assisting, chatting, and interacting where required. The day finished around 3 PM with a short communal gathering before leaving.

At the Japanese centre, the majority of the children arrived together on one of the three kindergarten buses that conducted pick-up routes around the city. As each group arrived, they would be met by the principal and expected to give a hearty morning greeting. The children would then go and locate their labelled cubby hole containing their inside shoes, change shoes, and proceed to their classroom to put away their bag, take off their outside uniform smock and hat, before enjoying some free play time before morning assembly. Following assembly, children would return to their classrooms for some kind of group activity, which had usually been decided prior by the teachers. Sometimes the morning session would be dedicated to special or seasonal events, such as the communal birthday party, making rice cakes, planting vegetables, celebrating festivals, or training for concerts or the sports day.

Lunch was a ritualised affair with children carefully laying out their lunchboxes, chopsticks, and cups, then waiting for the appropriate greeting (*itadakimasu*) to commence eating as a class group. The end of the meal was similarly accompanied by ritualised greetings and songs, performed to music played on the piano by the classroom teacher. Ritualised chanting and greetings mark transition points in the Japanese kindergarten classroom and are used for beginning, finishing, eating, and the arrival of visitors, among other things. The afternoon session was dedicated to free play, and children would spread out throughout the classrooms, hall, staffroom, and grounds tossing balls, constructing with large wooden blocks, drawing, and making swords or fairy wands. By 2PM, the clean-up music could be heard across the kindergarten, and the farewell rituals completed by 2:30PM.

Fieldwork Methods

The fieldwork consisted of one month spent observing, participating, and filming children and staff in each of the centres. In New Zealand, a maximum of thirty children attended the centre during each session with four teachers present. In Japan, children are separated into classes, and this study focussed on the four-year-old class with one teacher in charge of thirty-three children. In both countries, the intention was to film a 'typical' day in line with Tobin's stated aim.[4]

Hours of footage were edited down to a sixty-minute video, which was screened to the classroom teacher and then again at a focus group meeting with other teachers of the 'insider' culture. The videos functioned less as data or description "but instead as rich nonverbal cues designed to stimulate critical reflection" (Tobin & Hsueh, 2007, p. 77). The purpose of screening the videos to each case study centre was to confirm that the video was a good representation of the centre, and to give teachers the opportunity to analyse their own practice (the first layer of voice in Tobin's multi-vocal methodology). While teachers were interested in viewing their own centres, they generally didn't feel the need to analyse their own practice in depth. Teachers in both New Zealand and Japan agreed that the video showed a typical day at each centre and that the children's behaviour appeared 'natural' with little in need of explanation. However, as scholars have pointed out, "comparative material can lead us to reinterpret behaviour as cultural that we have assumed to be natural" (Schieffelin & Ochs, 1998, p. 50).

Following language subtitling (English↔Japanese), the film was then ready for screening to teachers of the 'outsider' culture. This meant that the New Zealand teachers not only critically analysed their own kindergarten's video, but also that of the Japanese kindergarten, and vice versa. This marks a second layer of voice. Finally, the videos were shown to early childhood academics, students, and staff at other centres in both countries, marking a third layer of dialogue. While one centre cannot claim to represent the diversity of a whole nation, neither can five nor fifty. The purpose of this step was to open a space for discussion around what practices and ideology made the video familiar and identifiable, or not, to their audiences.

In order to uncover this third layer of dialogue, focus group sessions were conducted in both countries. This part of the research consisted of seven focus group sessions in New Zealand (two in Christchurch, one each in Dunedin, Nelson, Wellington, Napier, and New Plymouth) and nine sessions with members of the Japanese early childhood sector (a group from Hiroshima and Nara held in Christchurch, and sessions in Tokyo, Saitama, Osaka, Eniwa and three in Kutchan in Japan). The size of the focus groups varied between four (the smallest) and twenty-six participants (the largest). Two individual interviews were also conducted with a Bay of Plenty early childhood teacher and a former Tokyo kindergarten teacher in Rata. In total, seventy-four participants took part in the New Zealand focus group sessions. In Japan, the number was practically the same with seventy-five participants involved in discussing the videos. All of these discussions were filmed, and these form the basis for the textual analysis.

The Development of Early Childhood Services in New Zealand and Japan

New Zealand

The roots of New Zealand early childhood education sprung from social concerns about abandoned and impoverished children (May, 2002; Munro, 1996; Prochner, 2009) with the first kindergarten opening in Dunedin in 1889 (Davison, 1997). By the late nineteenth century, the government had begun to embrace the idea of a free kindergarten as part of a moral agenda to stem political concerns over social problems (May, 1997). By the first half of the twentieth century, the state had increasingly turned its attention to the health of the nation's children and kindergartens were quick to stress their role as supporting the efforts of the well-regarded Plunket[5] programme (Powell, 2003). In 1947, the Bailey Report[6] called for total state control over all early childhood services. Despite assuming greater responsibility for funding and regulations, this aim was never realised, and to this day, services remain in the community-private sector. State policy for early childhood services was formalised in 1948 when kindergartens and their staff came under government control (Dalli & Te One, 2002).

From the 1950s to the early 1980s, kindergartens grew in popularity and benefited from generous state support (Davison & Mitchell, 2008). However, other forms of early childhood services had been forced to compete for state funding resulting in a plethora of differing services and fee structures by the end of the 1980s. Publication of the Meade Report[7] in 1988 drew attention to the inequalities in early childhood services in terms of access, funding, and quality (Dalli & Te One, 2002). In 1986, New Zealand transitioned from administering separate education and care departments to an integrated approach for preschoolers under the auspices of the Ministry of Education (Moss, 2000). This meant that the same funding structures would be applied for kindergartens, education and care centres,

Playcentres, and *kōhanga reo*. This funding has supported a growth of ECE provision in New Zealand, and over 96% of children in 2013 have attended an ECE service in the six months prior to starting school at five years old (Ministry of Education, 2013).

The adoption of *Te Whāriki* (Ministry of Education, 1996) as the national early childhood curriculum in 1996 also served towards resolving the historical dichotomy between education and care (Cullen, 1996). Following consultation with the many diverse stakeholders in the early childhood education arena, a bicultural curriculum framework was developed using the metaphor of a *whāriki* (woven mat) for all to stand on. Both developmental and social/cultural ideologies were included in the curriculum through the key theme of empowering children to learn and grow. *Te Whāriki* also emphasised the importance of children's reciprocal relationships and included family, *whānau*,[8] and community within its structure (May & Carr, 2000). It is this context-specific fluidity and departure from previous developmentally driven goals that marks *Te Whāriki* as a unique document (May, 2004).

Japan

Early childhood education occupies a powerful place in Japanese society, with over 90% of preschool aged Japanese children attending sessions or classes at an early childhood institution (Ellington, 2009). Studies of Japanese early childhood settings have tended to either emphasise the uniformity or the diversity of the system (Imoto, 2007). In reality, both perspectives are represented within the myriad of early childhood settings spread throughout Japan, but the vast majority of these centres can be categorised as either a kindergarten (*yōchien*) or a childcare centre (*hoikuen*). Within these categories, there are public and private institutions, licensed, and unlicensed centres, those that are linked to churches, corporations or educational institutes, and even those that operate from rural homes (Holloway, 2000).

Japan's first private kindergarten was founded in 1875 and attached to a primary school in Kyoto (Imoto, 2007). The curriculum has evolved over the decades from life oriented, to subject focused, and then in favour of practice that focussed on children's individual abilities and personalities (Oda & Mori, 2006). Despite Western perceptions (Cummings, 1989), the aims of Japanese early childhood education have never promoted academic ability, but have developed to reflect the prevailing social conditions.[9] The roots of the modern Japanese childcare facility can be seen in the *takujisho* (day nurseries) founded in Kyoto in 1875 to serve the needs of working women (Shwalb, Shwalb, Sukemune, & Tatsumoto, 1992). Unlike the educational emphasis of the kindergarten curriculum, the childcare centre (*hoikuen*) concentrated on improving children's eating habits, personal hygiene, and morals (Boocock, 1989; Imoto, 2007).

In 1947, the Japanese government passed the *School Education Law*, which placed kindergarten *(yōchien)* under the control of the Ministry of Education *(Mombusho)*,[10] and the *Child Welfare Law*, which made childcare centres *(hoikuen)* part of the Ministry of Health and Welfare *(Kōseisho)* (Boocock 1989, p. 45). For many scholars, this remains the fundamental difference between the two forms of early childhood education in Japan, with the *yōchien* seen as preparing children for school, while the *hoikuen* serves the needs of the poor and working women (Boocock, 1989; Hendry, 1986; Shwalb et al., 1992; Smith, 1995).

In 2006, the Japanese government introduced the accredited children's centre *(nintei-kodomoen)*. Combining characteristics of both the kindergarten and the childcare centre, the impetus for developing the *nintei-kodomoen* focussed on relieving the stress of working parents, reducing waiting lists for institutions, and to balance the inconsistencies between demand and supply of places at kindergarten and childcare centres (Imoto, 2007). The government believes the solution to these issues is the creation of a new ministry to deal with childcare issues, introducing a merged facility to be known as the *kodomo-en* (children's facility or children's garden). The integration process began in 2013 and is scheduled to be completed within ten years. This move marks a radical departure from governmental policy that had always emphasised the separation of the *yōchien* (kindergarten) and *hoikuen* (childcare centre) in both administrative and ideological terms. This period promises to be one of provocation and transition in the Japanese early childhood sector as the government seeks to address these changes (Takahara, 2010).

These developments have the potential to fundamentally affect how Japanese children's bodies are socialised in early childhood settings, because as Mauss (1936/1973) notes, "the child's education is full of so-called details which are really essential" (p. 78). Mauss (1936/1973) writes that

> the constant adaptation to a physical, mechanical or chemical aim (e.g. when we drink) is pursued in a series of assembled actions, and assembled for the individual not by himself alone but by all his education, by the whole society to which he belongs, in the place he occupies in it.
>
> *(p. 76)*

Bodily Practices

In New Zealand, child-rearing practices, the education system, and the wider community, all work to reinforce ideas about appropriate bodily practices. This notion is equally relevant to the Japanese context, where the body techniques internalised by Japanese children are specific to their society.

In both the New Zealand and Japanese contexts, the acts of children, teachers, and parents reflect implicit expectations surrounding appropriate practice in the home, in the early childhood setting, and beyond, in wider society. Mauss

(1936/1973) observed how each society imposes a rigidly defined use of the individual body through the training of a child's bodily needs and actions. Through an examination of child-rearing practices it becomes clear how 'natural' bodily practices such as sleeping, toileting, and feeding are, in fact, reflections of social and cultural contexts.

Within the context of child-rearing, the spectre of the body is never far away. In New Zealand, the body of the colonial child was considered insignificant, but around the turn of the century, children's bodies were repositioned as a form of social capital (McDonald, 1978). This ideology is reflected in the way mothers' and children's bodies were medicalised and regulated through the regimes of the Plunket Society in the 1950s. Through the work of the Plunket Society, a pattern of child-rearing developed that emphasised routine and limited physical contact between mother and baby (Olssen & Levesque, 1978). This approach contrasted with traditional Māori society, which encouraged co-sleeping and limited mother-child separation (Ritchie & Ritchie, 1997). In order to discipline children, punishment was administered directly to the body in the form of smacking, and continues to occur today despite parents' reservations.[11] In post-millennium New Zealand, families are increasingly diverse, in terms of both structure and ethnicity, resulting in a wider variety of child-rearing practices (Morton et al., 2010). In order to facilitate a smooth transition between home and the early childhood setting, links between the family and the wider community are acknowledged and extended to create a shared sense of belonging (Ministry of Education, 1996).

New Zealand child-rearing approaches contrast with Japan, where the ideology of *skinship* prevails (Caudill, 1972). The bodies of mother and child are seen as linked through embodied practices such co-sleeping, massage, and prolonged physical contact (Schooler, 1996). Rather than taking a disciplinarian approach, Japanese mothers indulge their children in order to foster *amae* or dependency (Doi, 1973). Japanese mothers also carefully monitor everything that enters and leaves her child's body, to the extent that even minor illness in a child is attributed to a mother's lack of care (Lock, 1980; Picone, 1989). This attention to the body continues in the early childhood context, where children spend a great time of learning to control their bodily activities and develop orderly habits (Hendry, 1986). In fact, transition from home to kindergarten is marked by the separation of the bodies of mother and child. While an indulgent home life provides children with a strong emotional base, in the early childhood setting children's bodies are ordered and regulated to assist them in realising that their own desires are now secondary to that of the group (Peak, 2001).

Mauss argued that the impact of society on the individual can be seen most clearly in the domain of child-rearing (Fournier, 2006). Within this framework, familiar child-rearing practices, such as the sleeping, feeding, and disciplinary practices described above, can be reassessed as culturally constructed body techniques. The way a mother responds to her child's cries, carries him or her, or teaches table manners, all reflect learned body techniques. For example, while New Zealand child-rearing practices encourage children's bodies towards gradually gaining independence from that of their mothers, Japanese practices work to foster interdependence between the two bodies. Even an act as simple as walking is, therefore, reflective of training that has been imposed on the child's body (Mauss, 1936/1973). The way in which early childhood services are developed in each society also reflect and reinforce this training of one generation by another.

In drawing on Tobin et al.'s (2009) PS3C methodology, we focus on the body as a locus of anthropological meaning. The next chapter marks the beginning of this analysis, through an examination of the early childhood experience as mediated through the lens of the body. The body is 'problematised' according to Scheper-Hughes and Lock's (1987) "three bodies" framework, which situates the body as a product of specific social, cultural and historical contexts (Lock, 1993, p. 134; Scheper-Hughes & Lock, 1987, p. 7).

Outline of the Book

The book consists of six chapters, which seek to place children's bodies in context. This framework arose as a result of the video-cued multi-vocal methodology (PS3C). Like that of Joseph Tobin, whose work and methods inspired this project, the aim of this study was to produce a multi-vocal text and it is throughout this section that the voices of the teachers can be heard most clearly. The issues that are presented here are those which resonated most strongly during the many hours of observations, video, discussion, and analysis by all those who participated in this study.

Chapter two discusses the discourses surrounding children's bodies in early childhood education which suggest that the body is in danger of vanishing in Western contexts yet retains a central place in Japanese settings. In New Zealand, as in other Western contexts, children's bodies have increasingly become the focus of surveillance and regulation (Foucault, 1975/1995). In contrast, Japanese children's bodies are viewed through a lens of nostalgia and innocence (Creighton, 1997; Robertson, 1988) despite challenges to this ideology. With reference to Douglas (1970/1966), this chapter also considers the extent to which bodily products may be classified as polluting in each culture.

Chapter three examines how the body both engages in and reflects the curricula of each nation through a closer view of sensory play, embodied techniques, and physicality. This chapter draws on the ideas of Mauss (1936/1973) who argues that children's play should always be seen as culturally constructed, rather than dismissed merely as 'natural' acts.

Chapter four asks how a global discourse of risk has influenced practice and policy in the New Zealand and Japanese early childhood sector, albeit through contrasting means. Children's bodies are increasingly becoming the focus of these risk discourses, but in order to identify how different practices are labelled risky, the cultural biases of each context need to be laid bare (Douglas, 1992). This chapter argues that the New Zealand context is marked by health and safety discourses which seek to control and minimise bodily risk (Foucault, 1975/1995), while at the Japanese centre, the management of children's bodies takes a more fatalistic approach.

Chapter five considers how New Zealand and Japanese early childhood teachers seek to discipline and order children's bodies through an exploration of three themes: noise, conflict, and finally, concepts of time and space. Foucault (1981, 1975/1995) has shown how the body is rendered docile through the civilising power of modern institutions such as the school. This chapter argues that the regulation of children's bodies, as articulated by Foucault, is a culturally mediated operation.

Chapter six asks how intangible cultural concepts such as pollution and impurity collide with the reality of hygiene and dirt in the early childhood environment. It questions how teachers and children embody these beliefs in a practical and ritual sense. Calling on Douglas's (1966, p. 35) definition of dirt as "a matter out of place" this chapter discusses the body as a site of pollution, polluted spaces, and rituals around food labelled in or out of place. The book concludes with a final chapter, which revises the main argument and presents the findings of the research in a condensed format.

While the thematic chapters have been arranged so that the reader can progress through the ideas in a logical, linked manner, each chapter may also be read on its own as an introductory essay on a particular implicit cultural practice. As this is a small study, it is by no means exhaustive and cannot possibly represent the myriad of early childhood experiences throughout New Zealand and Japan. Rather, it can be seen as a first step towards a framework for more extensive research. We hope this work will provide an impetus for robust discussion about the cultural meaning behind practice, policy, and pedagogy in early childhood centres and give cause for practitioners, academics, parents, and children to question the 'naturalness' of their everyday interactions.

Notes

1 Fictitious names have been given for the two centres where fieldwork took place in Japan and New Zealand, as well as pseudonyms for all children and teachers' names.
2 Fictitious names have been given for the two cities where fieldwork took place in Japan and New Zealand.
3 This term refers to the times when teachers are assigned to be with the children: playing, supervising, and scaffolding learning experiences. When not 'on the floor', teachers may complete administration tasks, or attend meetings and professional development seminars.
4 The word 'typical' is problematic, but we agree with Tobin, Hsueh, and Karasawa (2009) who argue that it is the most appropriate word in this case (p. 8). Like Tobin et al., we do not claim that the centres or the events captured on video were representative of all early childhood settings in New Zealand and Japan. Rather, video analysis by the

staff at each centre combined with comments from teachers around the country lead us to believe they were not particularly unusual or atypical. To try and deal with this semantic dilemma, early childhood researcher Daniel Walsh (2002) does not claim that his five primary research sites were *typical,* but that "all sites were *identifiable* examples of Japanese early schooling" (p. 215).

5   Otherwise known as the Royal New Zealand Society for the Health of Women and Children, Plunket works with families to support the development and well-being of children under five.

6   The full title of the Bailey Report is the "Report of the Consultative Committee on Preschool Education Services" (1947).

7   Commonly referred to as the Meade Report, after its author Anne Meade, the correct title of the document is actually "Report of the Early Childhood Care and Education Working Group" (1988).

8   *Whānau* is a Māori word for extended family.

9   For a comprehensive history of early childhood pedagogic concepts in Japanese pre-schools, see the excellent article by Ishigaki (1991), which discusses prominent theorists and how their views influenced Japanese educational trends.

10   *Mombusho* has since been renamed *Mombukagakushō* (Ministry of Education, Culture, Sports, Science and Technology).

11   In 2009, the Section 59 Crimes Act Repeal Bill was passed in New Zealand. Popularly known as the 'anti-smacking' law, the Bill was the focus of sustained and polarising public debate prior to its introduction. However, a 2012 poll shows that many parents ignore the law, and continue to smack their children despite the threat of prosecution ("Parents ignore anti-smacking law, poll shows", 2012).

References

Ben-Ari, E. (1997). *Body projects in Japanese childcare: Culture, organization and emotions in a preschool.* Richmond, UK: Curzon Press.

Ben-Ari, E. (2008). Formal caring alternatives: Kindergartens and day-care centers. In J. Robertson (Ed.), *A companion to the anthropology of Japan* (pp. 247–260). Malden, MA: Blackwell.

Bernard, H. R. (2006). *Research methods in anthropology: Qualitative and quantitative approaches.* Lanham, MD: AltaMira Press.

Boocock, S. S. (1989). Controlled diversity: An overview of the Japanese preschool. *Journal of Japanese Studies, 15*(1), 41–65.

Caudill, W. (1972). Tiny dramas: Vocal communication between mother and infant in Japanese and American families. In W. Lebra (Ed.), *Transcultural research in mental health: Volume II of mental health research in Asia and the Pacific* (pp. 25–48). Honolulu: University Press of Hawaii.

Creighton, M. (1997). Consuming rural Japan: The marketing of tradition and nostalgia in the Japanese travel industry. *Ethnology, 36*(3), 239–254.

Csordas, T. J. (1999). The body's career in anthropology. In H. L. Moore (Ed.), *Anthropological theory today* (pp. 172–205). Cambridge, UK: Polity Press.

Cullen, J. (1996). The challenge of Te Whāriki for future developments in early childhood education. *Delta, 48*(1), 113–126.

Cummings, W. K. (1989). The American perception of Japanese education. *Comparative Education, 25*(3), 293–302.

Dalli, C., & Te One, S. (2002). Early childhood education in 2002: Pathways to the future. *New Zealand Annual Review of Education, 12,* 177–202.

Davison, C. (1997). *The sinking of the early childhood education flagship?: Government's plan to privatise kindergartens: The bulk-funding story.* Wellington, New Zealand: Institute for Early Childhood Studies, Victoria University of Wellington, New Zealand.

Davison, C., & Mitchell, L. (2008). The role of the state in early childhood care and education: Kindergartens as a case study of changing relationships. *New Zealand Annual Review of Education, 18,* 123–141.

DeWalt, K. M., & DeWalt, B. R. (2002). *Participant observation: A guide for fieldworkers.* Walnut Creek, CA: AltaMira Press.

Doi, T. (1973). *The anatomy of dependence.* Tokyo, Japan: Kodansha.

Douglas, M. (1966). *Purity and danger: An analysis of concepts of pollution and taboo.* Harmondsworth, UK: Penguin Books.

Douglas, M. (1970/1996). *Natural symbols: Explorations in cosmology.* London, UK: Routledge.

Douglas, M. (1992). *Risk and blame: Essays in cultural theory.* London, UK: Routledge.

Ellington, L. (2009). *Japan: A global studies handbook.* Santa Barbara, CA: ABC-CLIO.

Erickson, P. A., & Murphy, L. D. (2008). *A history of anthropological theory* (3rd ed.). Toronto, Canada: Higher Education University of Toronto Press.

Foucault, M. (1973a). *The birth of the clinic.* New York, NY: Pantheon Books.

Foucault, M. (1973b). *Madness and civilization: A history of insanity in the age of reason.* New York, NY: Vintage Books.

Foucault, M. (1975/1995). *Discipline and punish: The birth of the prison* (A. Sheridan, Trans.). New York, NY: Vintage Books.

Foucault, M. (1980). The eye of power. In C. Gordon (Ed.), *Power/knowledge: Selected interviews and other writings, 1972–1977: Michel Foucault* (pp. 146–165). Hemel Hempstead, UK: The Harvester Press.

Foucault, M. (1981). *The history of sexuality, Volume 1: An introduction.* Harmondsworth, UK: Penguin.

Fournier, M. (2006). *Marcel Mauss: A biography* (J. M. Todd, Trans.). Princeton, NJ: Princeton University Press.

Fraser, M., & Greco, M. (Eds.). (2005). *The body: A reader.* London, NY: Routledge.

Hendry, J. (1986). *Becoming Japanese: The world of the pre-school child.* Honolulu: University of Hawaii Press.

Holloway, S. D. (2000). Accentuating the negative: Views of preschool staff about mothers in Japan. *Early Education and Development, 11*(5), 617–632.

Imoto, Y. (2007). The Japanese preschool system in transition. *Research in Comparative and International Education, 2*(2), 88–101.

Ishigaki, E. H. (1991). The historical stream of early childhood pedagogic concepts in Japan. *Early Child Development and Care, 75,* 121–159.

Lévi-Strauss, C. (1964). *Mythologiques I: Le cru et le cuit.* Paris, France: Plon.

Lock, M. (1980). *East Asian medicine in urban Japan.* Berkeley: University of California Press.

Lock, M. (1993). Cultivating the body: Anthropology and epistemologies of bodily practice and knowledge. *Annual Review of Anthropology, 22,* 133–155.

Mascia-Lees, F. E. (2011). Introduction. In F. E. Mascia-Lees (Ed.), *A companion to the anthropology of the body and embodiment* (pp. 1–2). Chichester, UK: Wiley-Blackwell.

Mauss, M. (1936/1973). Techniques of the body. *Economy and Society, 2,* 70–88.

May, H. (1997). *Discovery of early childhood.* Auckland, New Zealand: Auckland University Press/Bridget Williams Books & the New Zealand Council for Educational Research Press.

May, H. (2002). "Blue skies" talk in the "playground". *Delta, 54*(1/2), 9–28.

May, H. (2004). Te Whāriki: A woven mat for all to stand on. In J. Bennett (Ed.), *Starting strong: Curricula and pedagogy in early childhood care and education: Five curriculum* (pp. 14–20). Paris, France: OECD.

May, H., & Carr, M. (2000). Empowering children to learn and grow—Te Whāriki: The New Zealand early childhood curriculum. In J. Hayden (Ed.), *Landscapes in early childhood education: Cross-national perspectives on empowerment—A guide for the new millennium* (pp. 153–169). New York, NY: Peter Lang Publishing.

McDonald, D. J. (1978). Children and young persons in New Zealand society. In P. G. Koopman-Boyden (Ed.), *Families in New Zealand society* (pp. 45–51). Wellington, New Zealand: Methuen.

Ministry of Education. (1996). *Te Whāriki: He Whāriki Mātauranga mō ngā Mokopuna o Aotearoa. New Zealand early childhood curriculum*. Wellington, New Zealand: Learning Media.

Ministry of Education. (2013). *Annual ECE Census Summary Report 2013*. Retrieved from www.educationcounts.govt.nz/statistics/ece2/annual-ece-summary-reports

Ministry of Internal Affairs and Communications. (2011, February). Population and households—Japan, all shi, all gun and prefectures. *Portal site of official statistics of Japan.* Retrieved from www.e-stat.go.jp/SG1/estat/ListE.do?bid=000001029548ecycode=0

Morton, S. M. B., Atatoa Carr, P. E., Bandara, D. K., Grant, C. C., Ivory, V. C., Kingi, T. R., . . . Waldie, K. E. (2010). *Growing Up in New Zealand: A longitudinal study of New Zealand children and their families. Report 1: Before we are born.* Auckland, New Zealand: Growing Up in New Zealand.

Moss, P. (2000). *Training and education of early childhood education and care staff: Report prepared for the OECD:* Thomas Coram Research Unit, Institute of Education, University of London.

Munro, J. (1996). *The story of Suzanne Aubert.* Auckland, New Zealand: Auckland University Press.

Oda, Y., & Mori, M. (2006). Current challenges of kindergarten (yochien) education in Japan: Toward balancing children's autonomy and teachers' intention. *Childhood Education, 82*(6), 369–373.

Olssen, E., & Levesque, A. (1978). Towards a history of the European family in New Zealand. In P. G. Koopman-Boyden (Ed.), *Families in New Zealand society* (pp. 1–26). Wellington, New Zealand: Methuen.

Parents ignore 'anti-smacking law', poll shows. (2012, 2 April). *TVNZ.* Retrieved from tvnz.co.nz/national-news/parents-ignore-anti-smacking-law-poll-shows-4810633

Peak, L. (2001). Learning to become part of the group: The Japanese child's transition to preschool life. In H. Shimizu & R. LeVine (Eds.), *Japanese frames of mind: Cultural perspectives on human development* (pp. 143–169). Cambridge, UK: Cambridge University Press.

Picone, M. (1989). The ghost in the machine: Religious healing and representations of the body in Japan. In M. Feher (Ed.), *Fragments for a history of the human body: Part two* (pp. 466–489). New York, NY: Zone.

Powell, J. (2003). *Plunket pioneers: Recollections of Plunket nurses from 1940 to 2000.* Auckland, New Zealand: Heritage Press Ltd.

Prochner, L. (2009). *A history of early childhood education in Canada, Australia and New Zealand.* Vancouver, Canada: University of British Columbia Press.

Ritchie, J., & Ritchie, J. (1997). *The next generation: Child-rearing in New Zealand.* Auckland, New Zealand: Penguin.

Robertson, J. (1988). Furusato Japan: The culture and politics of nostalgia. *Politics, Culture and Society, 1,* 494–518.

Sato, N. E. (2004). *Inside Japanese classrooms: The heart of education.* New York, NY: Routledge Falmer.

Scheper-Hughes, N., & Lock, M. (1987). The mindful body: A prolegomenon to future work in medical anthropology. *Medical Anthropology Quarterly, 1*(1), 6–41.

Schieffelin, B., & Ochs, E. (1998). A cultural perspective on the transition from prelinguistic to linguistic communication. In M. Woodhead, D. Faulkner, & K. Littleton (Eds.), *Cultural worlds of early childhood* (pp. 48–63). London, UK: Routledge.

Schooler, C. (1996). William Caudill and the reproduction of culture: Infant, child and maternal behavior in Japan and the United States. In D. W. Shwalb & B. J. Shwalb (Eds.), *Japanese child-rearing: Two generations of scholarship* (pp. 139–163). New York, NY: Guildford Press.

Shwalb, D. W., Shwalb, B. J., Sukemune, S., & Tatsumoto, S. (1992). Japanese nonmaternal child care: Past, present, and future. In M. E. Lamb, K. J. Sternberg, C. Hwang, & A. G. Broberg (Eds.), *Child care in context: Cross-cultural perspectives* (pp. 331–354). Hillsdale, NJ: Lawrence Erlbaum.

Smith, H. W. (1995). *The myth of Japanese homogeneity: Social-ecological diversity in education and socialization.* Commack, NY: Nova Science.

Strathern, A., & Stewart, P. J. (2011). Personhood: Embodiment and personhood. In F. E. Mascia-Lees (Ed.), *A companion to the anthropology of the body and embodiment* (pp. 388–402). Chichester, UK: Wiley-Blackwell.

Synnott, A., & Howes, D. (1992). From measurement to meaning: Anthropologies of the body. *Anthropos, 87*(1/3), 147–166.

Takahara, K. (2010, 17 November). Kindergartens, day care centers may merge. *The Japan Times.* Retrieved from www.japantimes.co.jp/news/2010/11/17/reference/kindergartens-day-care-centers-may-merge/#.U-1ux-OSx8E

Tobin, J., & Hsueh, Y. (2007). The poetics and pleasures of video ethnography of education. In R. Goldman (Ed.), *Video research in the learning sciences* (pp. 77–92). New York, NY: Lawrence Erlbaum.

Tobin, J., Hsueh, Y., & Karasawa, M. (2009). *Preschool in three cultures revisited: China, Japan and the United States.* Chicago, IL: University of Chicago Press.

Tobin, J. J., Wu, D. Y. H., & Davidson, D. H. (1989). *Preschool in three cultures: Japan, China and the United States.* New Haven, CT: Yale University Press.

Van Wolputte, S. (2004). Hang on to yourself: Of bodies, embodiment, and selves. *Annual Review of Anthropology, 33,* 251–269.

Walsh, D. J. (2002). The development of self in Japanese preschools: Negotiating space. In L. Bresler & A. Ardichvili (Eds.), *Research in international education: Experience, theory and practice* (pp. 213–245). New York, NY: Peter Lang Publishing.

2

CHILDREN'S BODIES AS CONTESTED SITES

The body both encodes cultural values and creates personal meanings.

(Gottlieb, 2004, p. 4)

Introduction

Children's bodies are increasingly absent from anthropological discussion (Mascia-Lees, 2011; Van Wolputte, 2004). In 2004, Tobin asserted that

> [t]he body is disappearing in early childhood education. Once a protected site within the larger world of education in which the body could flourish, preschools are now a battle-zone in the war against the body, sites where the bodies of children and the adults who care for them fall under increasing scrutiny and discipline.
>
> *(p. 111)*

The discourses surrounding children's bodies in early childhood education appear to support Tobin's statement that the body is in grave danger of vanishing in Western contexts (Bresler, 2004; Johnson, 1997; Shapiro & Shapiro, 2002; Surtees, 2008).

As Gottlieb (2004) has pointed out, the body reflects both cultural and personal meanings. This chapter argues that in New Zealand early childhood education, like other Western contexts, the child's body has become the focus of civilising routines, which limit physical touch between adults and children, and minimise attention to the body and its products. The chapter will discuss how the New Zealand early childhood centre has become a site of constant surveillance, turning teachers into "disciplinary individuals" (Foucault, 1975/1995, p. 227) who are internally controlled by their own behaviour.

In Japan, the body is also subject to routine and management, but this chapter focuses on perceptions of the naked child and approaches to bodily functions. In contrast to New Zealand, where children's bodies conjure up feelings of anxiety, Japanese children's bodies are still viewed through a lens of nostalgia and innocence (Creighton, 1997; Robertson, 1988). The strength of this ideology, known as *furusato* in Japanese, persists despite a growing trend towards personal privacy and changing notions of child safety. While orifices and 'leaking bodies' (Turner, 2003) may be metaphors for disorder in the New Zealand early childhood setting, the Japanese centre reflects a pragmatic, relaxed approach to bodily functions. Here, we draw on the theories of Douglas (1966) to show how the margins of the body hold different meanings in these different cultural contexts.

Children's bodies have increasingly become the focus of surveillance and regulation (Foucault, 1975/1995). This increased regulation is in Western contexts, where the child's body is viewed as a site for anxiety and fear in the face of rising debate over appropriate policy and practice (Phelan, 1997; Piper & Stronach, 2008). Children's bodies have been repositioned as embodying a moral panic, resulting in previously insignificant early childhood routines to be viewed with suspicion (Farquhar, 1997; Jones, 2001; Robinson, 2008; Tobin, 1997). This has not only impacted on pedagogical practice, but on the quality and type of research able to be conducted around the issue of children's bodies as well. Montgomery (2009) has noted that children's sexualities have rarely been examined through an anthropological lens. She attributes this to Western sensitivities surrounding child sexual abuse. She argues these concerns have not only made it extremely difficult for adult researchers to speak to children about their sexual experiences, but also that sensitivity surrounding the issue has discouraged most people from focusing on the subject.

This literature (Farquhar, 1997; Jones, 2001; Montgomery, 2009, Robinson, 2008), however, contrasts with research carried out in Japan, which still places children's bodies at the very centre of the early childhood experience. Ben-Ari (1997) argues that preschool experiences such as co-sleeping, eating, and bathing together serve to embody certain traits and qualities identified as Japanese. Walsh (2004) suggests that the Japanese child is viewed essentially as a physical self whose body is pivotal to intellectual development. Hendry (1986) and Lebra (1976) have stressed the importance of intimate physical contact both within families and in the context of early childhood education. This bodily contact is seen as a natural and necessary part of a child's development. In Japanese early childhood centres, it is common to see teachers lying down to sleep with a child who is having trouble nodding off at naptime, bawdy jokes between teachers and children about bodily functions and body parts, or a lone teacher assisting a child with toileting.

The (Un)clothed Body

The first clue that New Zealand and Japanese perceptions of children's bodies differ came during the screening of each video to the 'outsider' culture. The Japanese video was shot in mid-summer when the temperature regularly rises above 30 degrees Celsius. The Hokkaido summer is relatively short, so the warm days represent a welcome opportunity for children to indulge in water play. The video depicts the teacher first explaining in detail how to get changed into underwear and singlets for this activity. She draws a chubby, androgynous figure on a piece of cardboard pinned to the display board before using a marker pen to outline a singlet over the chest and then a pair of underpants. While drawing, she jokes with the children about the breasts (*oppai*) and penis (*chinchin*) disappearing under each layer of clothing.

The teacher tells the children that between taking off their regular clothing and donning the underwear, they will all be "completely naked" (*zuponpon*), just like when one enters the bath. The children shriek but not as loudly as when she explains the class will be barefoot during the water play. Several calls of "no way" (*iya da*) are heard from around the room, but the children begin pulling off their socks and searching for the bags which contain their change of clothes. The camera pans across the classroom as children run about in various states of undress. Some have already changed, others are struggling with pieces of clothing and a few are standing naked watching while a group of boys clad only in singlets chase each other around. Eventually, all thirty-three children have changed and they are led outside by the teacher who has spread outdoor tatami matting and prepared the water play equipment.

Following an exuberant period of splashing, pouring, and squirting water, the children are instructed to line up according to gender. Once again, they are given instructions, this time about the correct procedure for undressing and washing the dirt off their bare feet. In their two lines, the children remove their wet clothing then wait naked as each one has their feet cleaned by the teacher using a hose (see Figure 2.1). As there are a large number of children, this procedure takes over twenty minutes during which time the children remain lined up naked in full view of the adjacent road and park. The teacher carefully sprays the hose over each young body and kneels down to wash away any offending grains of sand from the children's feet. The children are helped to locate their towels and dry off on the tatami mat. Gradually, each one moves back inside the classroom to conduct the undressing routine in reverse.

This scene provoked no response from the Oka Kindergarten teachers when they viewed their own video, but as Rachael had felt ethically conflicted during the filming, she specifically asked them to comment on the footage. The teachers were puzzled by what she was asking them to address. Rachael was reluctant to frame the matter within her own cultural context for fear of influencing their responses, but sensing their confusion, she asked if they could see any issues around the children's nudity in a semi-public place. Their response was illuminating: not only was the scene of little consequence to them, they were intrigued as to why she was enquiring. In brief, Rachael explained how New Zealand early childhood institutions had changed their policies and practices in recent years in order to

FIGURE 2.1 Children wait to be washed down by their teacher at Oka Kindergarten

stem public concerns relating to potential sexual abuse of children. As a result, it was less likely children would be naked for any length of time in a New Zealand early childhood setting. Rachael was also concerned about the ethical implications of filming the children and unsure whether it would be appropriate to show the footage to viewers outside Japan.

The teachers responded swiftly and simply. Children were beautiful and innocent, not objects of adult sexual desire. Seeing the video merely reminded them of how cute (*kawaii*) young naked bodies can be. One teacher commented, "They all just look so cute running around like that, so free and playful. I especially liked the little, round bottoms (*oshiri*) poking out from the classroom door when the boys were heading inside to get changed". Another teacher questioned what kind of country New Zealand could be if teachers were afraid to let children enjoy the freedom, which comes with a naked state. When Rachael explained that the scene was potentially more contentious because of the men playing in the park across the road, one of the teachers burst out laughing and asked, "Are there perverts lurking behind all the bushes in New Zealand then?" The teachers agreed that they could not see any problems with screening the footage to an outside audience.

This response is interesting on two counts: the first because their views resonated with many (but not all) Japanese reactions Rachael encountered around Japan and second, because their comments strongly contrasted to those of the

New Zealand viewers. What could this mean? In the following section, we discuss Japanese cultural contexts in reference to the body in early childhood settings before moving on to frame the New Zealand responses within the current political and social climate.

The Naked Child in Japanese Educational Settings

Unlike their New Zealand counterparts, none of the Japanese kindergarten teachers viewing the scene of naked children expressed shock at the images. At a childcare centre on the opposite coast of Hokkaido to where the video was shot, the video scene even appeared a bit tame in contrast to their usual approach. For these Hokkaido teachers, the most startling contrast to their own centre was the reserved manner in which children conducted both their play and the orderly way in which cleaning of the body was carried out. At another Hokkaido kindergarten located in the grounds of a Buddhist temple, the staff were perplexed by children's resistant shrieks when instructed by the teacher to remove their shoes and socks. The issue of children's clothing was even less pertinent for this group of viewers who advocate 'naked education' within their kindergarten grounds. These teachers explained that forsaking clothing was encouraged: "For the sake of the body. So that fingers and toes can be refreshed, so that the body can experience some different sensations".

Teachers in Osaka echoed the belief that child nudity was nothing unusual in the early childhood environment and linked it directly to cultural influences: "Japanese people have a bathing culture so they are comfortable being naked. Children understand that their unclothed bodies are different but when they are kindergarten age it's no big deal being naked". The majority of teachers in the focus group sessions gave similar explanations for the water play scene and several groups did not feel the need to address the issue at all until questioned directly about it. In contrast, teachers in a Japanese Catholic kindergarten expressed some surprise that older children in the senior classes would be comfortable totally naked for any length of time. They made a clear distinction on the basis of children's age and areas of the body which might be appropriately left unclothed: "I think it's quite usual for children to be naked from the waist up together but from the waist down I think it might be a bit embarrassing".

For some of the Japanese urban centres where Rachael conducted focus group sessions, there were elements of surprise in the comments made. A teacher in Saitama commented that:

> Perhaps there were some regional differences. For example, they played outside in their swimsuits, right? At that time, were they completely stark naked? It was for a very long time, wasn't it? Seeing that, I thought we're really in the middle of a big city here. If we did that here at our kindergarten we would have a problem. We are conscious of the amount of time children

are naked. Once play has finished and children are getting changed from swimsuits into their clothes, we are also aware of the time it takes. If possible, we find a way to avoid being stark naked for everyone to see.

At that kindergarten, children wear swimsuits when using the pool on the grounds. At the end of the swimming session, children are washed down with water, and just before entering the classroom, their swimsuits are removed and a towel is wrapped around them. At Oka Kindergarten in Hokkaido, both boys and girls changed in the same classroom but teachers in Saitama identified a clear difference in the way the procedure was carried out:

> The children [here] get changed together but they don't do it in such a relaxed, slow manner as in the video. I wonder if that's a regional thing?
> Yes, it would be nice if we could be more open-minded like they are up there.

Some scholars have concluded that regional differences between early childhood centres across Japan do not exist, insisting that experiences of both parent and child are relatively homogeneous (Ben-Ari, 2002; Kotloff, 1998; Peak, 1989). However, Hendry (1993) notes that most anthropological studies of Japanese mothers and small children have been carried out in the Kanto region. This suggests there may be differences in other prefectures throughout the country.[1] Contrasting responses to the water play scenes certainly seemed to support a view of rural centres as less prone to urban pressures and demands. During viewing many of the teachers sighed wistfully and remarked how lucky the children were to be growing up in Hokkaido where life was still so free and surrounded by nature. There appeared to be a nostalgic tinge to their cries of "*ii na . . .*" (that's great, isn't it?). When Rachael asked them if they thought the relaxed attitude could be due to the rural location of the kindergarten, teachers replied that:

> Well, it's true that in a rural area like that you can enjoy a leisurely, relaxed way of life.
> That's right! The road was right there. It was just like Japan in the old days!
> In the past it was also like that in this area. About thirty years ago, the children would just take off their underwear and run around the kindergarten naked. Everyone was completely relaxed about it. These days the teachers have to put a stop to it.

As the next section will explore, these comments serve as a reminder that views on children's bodies can vary across Japan according to ideological axes.

The Japanese Child's Body as a Symbol of Nostalgia

The island of Hokkaido retains a utopian image for the Japanese public, especially by those in crowded, urban areas. Many of the Japanese teachers who viewed the video had never visited Hokkaido. This seemed to add to the illusion that the area was somewhat mystical and detached from the rest of the country in terms of cultural practices. In metropolitan areas, Rachael's participants nostalgically linked rural communities to a romanticised, less threatening era for children and parents. Clark (1994) has discussed the phenomenon of Japanese describing aspects of culture that they believe are more faithfully replicated or preserved in other parts of the country. In urban areas, Clark was advised to visit the countryside where he would find the real (*hontō no*) Japan and witness traditional practices. Conversely, his trips to rural regions resulted in the advice that such practices no longer continued in that particular area but could be found elsewhere where customs were "more backward or more traditional, depending on the informant's perspective" (Clark, 1994, p. 70).

Nostalgia for a more 'authentic' lifestyle has become personified in the ideology and symbolism of *furusato* (home village or native place) that has become increasingly ubiquitous throughout post-war Japan. In the minds of the Japanese public, the notion of *furusato* is strongly linked to a rural landscape, an agrarian existence, and a community-based social life that shaped a shared sense of belonging (Creighton, 1997). *Furusato* imagery has been used extensively in the travel industry for promotional purposes, with some villages even reviving once defunct festivals and crafts to satisfy the demands of tourists (Love, 2007; Martinez, 1990; Moon, 2002). Robertson (1988, p. 495) has linked the growing cultural significance of *furusato* ideology to a feeling of "nostalgia *for* nostalgia, a state of being provoked by a dissatisfaction with the present on the grounds of a remembered, or imagined, past plenitude".

Viewed through the lens of *furusato* ideology the unclothed child's body takes not a menacing form, as it might in a New Zealand context, but a nostalgic, benign objectification. Many Japanese teachers around the country made implicit reference to the desire to return a less constrained existence, both professionally and personally. Others had taken more concrete action to recreate experiences for children from a Japan many see as disappearing (Kerr, 1996).

Skinship as Cultural Ideology

The origin of the term *skinship* is linked to research by Caudill (1972), who identified a difference in the way Japanese mothers interact with their children. Caudill concluded that the Japanese mother views the baby as an extension of herself, therefore unnecessary verbal communication is limited in favour of more vitally important physical contact (cited in Schooler, 1996). Picone (1989, p. 485) suggests that within this cultural ideology, the bodies of mother and child become irrevocably linked, to the extent that mothers are understood as "constantly recreating or preserving her children" well beyond the months of pregnancy. Ben-Ari (1997) has noted *skinship* is an integral part of many daily activities carried out within the home such as co-sleeping, breast-feeding, nonverbal communication, and bathing together. In the early childhood setting too this close physical contact is seen as a valuable means of embodying the group experience. Here the emphasis is firmly on intimacy rather than sexuality. This kind of interaction is not limited to kindergarten children and their teachers, it is a feature of many Japanese organisations. Ben-Ari (1997), Clark (1994), Hendry (1999), Kondo (1992), and Rohlen (1974) have discussed trips and overnight stays with friends, work colleagues, classmates, and club members which have culminated in shared bathing and sleeping experiences.

The recollections of these writers echo Rachael's experiences while working at a kindergarten in Hokkaido. Once or twice a year, a teachers' trip would be organised to a hot spring resort (*onsen*) at a nearby lake where the entire staff would end a day spent sightseeing with an evening meal and a bath together before heading back to relax on *futons* in the communal sleeping spaces. While almost all of these *onsen* enforce separate areas for men and women, during Rachael's first experience of an office trip in an isolated, rural part of Hokkaido all members of the organisation bathed together naked in a natural spring in the middle of the forest. This recollection has been met with surprise by Japanese in other regions who insist this is very unusual in modern times although it was apparently quite common in the past (Clark, 1994).

The Collective Unclothed Body

However, there are signs that Japanese attitudes to the collective unclothed body are changing amid rising perceptions of personal privacy. Clark (1994) associates sensitivity to cross-sexual nudity with the decreasing custom of visiting public bathhouses (*sentō*). Guichard-Anguis (2009) writes that Japanese inns or *ryokan* serve as important producers of Japanese identity, adding that conceptions of privacy are beginning to creep into the bathing rituals which play such a major role during a visit to these establishments. In both these spaces, it was once common for the attendant (*bandai-san*) to position themselves in an area where they could view both the men's and women's dressing and bathing areas. This position allowed the attendant to supervise children moving back and forth between their mother and father in the baths, monitor bathers' possessions, and enjoy conversations with customers as they dressed and undressed. To address issues of privacy, attendants in some newer facilities have been relocated to a space where they cannot see either gender.

Tobin, Hsueh, and Karasawa (2009) have addressed changing notions of the communal body as seen in rising levels of privacy in public spheres and a more conservative approach to sexually provocative dialogue. They identify this shift as "a form of embourgeoisement, the spread of middle-class Western styles, values, and notions of the self to other classes and cultural contexts" (p. 119). They argue that like the public bath (*sentō*) and hot springs, early childhood centres are one of the few sites in which contemporary Japanese can embody pleasure in a public context. They also see these opportunities as diminishing, therefore early childhood settings are significant for maintaining or reviving cultural values and practices that are either threatened or need to be restored.

Japanese early childhood teachers and academics in the focus group sessions appeared to support Tobin et al.'s (2009) suggestion that early childhood centres can play a large part in forming cultural constructions of the body. While Oka Kindergarten's practice of structurally organising children in a naked state was not common and some of the respondents found it surprising, the overwhelming response was one of approval due to the implicitly understood and shared ideals of skinship and bodily freedom. There were also positive links made between the state of the child's unclothed body and traditional cultural values which teachers saw as eroding under multiple pressures: urbanisation, parental demands, environmental risk, and the shrinking family unit. While the practice of allowing children to interact naked in a Japanese early childhood setting may not be common, the "cultural logic" is (Tobin et al., 2009, p. 9).

Although New Zealand may be regarded as a liberal environment as far as nudity is concerned (Carr-Gomm, 2010), communal nakedness is not a part of New Zealand cultural identity due to Christian influences, which discouraged this practice (Barcan, 2004; Morris, 1992). However, New Zealand teachers indicated that allowing children to play naked was once relatively common in their centres as well, but in recent years, not only has the unclothed child become much rarer, but he or she has the potential to incite danger and suspicion within the early childhood environment (Jones, 2001). The following section draws on the work of Foucault (1975/1995, 1980, 1981) to explore these fears and the state policies that have become ingrained in the cultural fabric of the modern early childhood setting.

The Protected Body in New Zealand Early Childhood Education

For the Japanese teachers and children at the centre of the water play scene, the fact that members of their kindergarten were unclothed for a relatively lengthy period of time in direct view of the passing public was unremarkable. For Japanese viewers of the scene, the reactions ranged from surprise to total indifference but most expressed their support of the ideals associated with nakedness which they linked to skinship and nostalgic images of a rural past lost to urban dwellers (Robertson, 1988). This represents a contrast to the New Zealand teachers who were immediately perturbed by the scene, yet reluctant or unable to initially verbalise what the offending issue appeared to be. However, a Foucauldian analysis of these responses would suggest that the teachers are internally regulating their gaze and reproducing safe behaviour. Through a process of assessment, coordination, and ultimately, surveillance, the teachers emerge as "disciplinary individuals" who have been created by these techniques of power (Foucault, 1975/1995, p. 227).

The following discussion, between Kaimai Kindergarten teachers viewing the footage, reveals their ambivalence about the unclothed child. There are distinctions made about the appropriateness of children who are 'necessarily' naked for brief periods of time in order to change clothes and those who are clearly seeking pleasure from their naked state.

I don't have a problem with it.

No, if you'd come outside this morning we had water slides outside today and we had nudey children walking round, but not while they're sliding. I mean just while they're getting changed, not while they're playing. They can do that, it's fine while they're getting dressed, but I wouldn't want them running around naked.

As the discussion progresses, it becomes obvious that, according to the group, a myriad of potential dangers exist for naked children in the early childhood environment: damage from the sun, potentially conflicting messages regarding behaviour at home and centre, a lack of dignity.

I don't know, it's respecting dignity for us . . .

And also we don't know, in their own homes [parents] might be not quite comfortable with it either, so when we've got their children running around naked, they could be quite uncomfortable.

And it's not necessary to run around naked at kindergarten. You know it's not a feature that you set up.

Well, what does it do for you? Can you learn from it?

[There's a risk of] sunburn, and at kindergarten we wear clothes.

You don't say that to the child. You say at kindergarten we wear clothes. It's probably a cultural thing altogether. If you wear no clothes at home, that's fine but at kindergarten you do. Plus, it's like, you don't jump on the couch at kindergarten. You might jump on the couch at home, you don't eat your food nicely . . .

Yes, these are the rules we have here.

However, as some scholars have pointed out, the real message seems to be that naked children are a danger not to themselves but to the staff who may feel afraid of being accused of inappropriate behaviour (Duncan, 1998). Kaimai Kindergarten teachers made a distinction between parent-led centres and their own teacher-led centres where they felt the need to be particularly vigilant about being responsible for the physical state of the child.

It's also a lot to do with respect. Like at Playcentre[2] it might be completely different because you've got the mothers there, whereas you haven't got family members here.

And you sort of have to be a stand-in for them really. So we have to be conservative and even if they don't mind their children running around naked we still need to be aware of that.

It's also a staff safety issue now. That has changed with those cases more than anything. That you have someone to back you up, that you're not on your lonesome.

The teachers were not only mindful of respecting parents' wishes and values, they were anxious about the impressions unclothed children might create in the wider public sphere. This lead to links with possible pedophilia, accusation of inappropriate staff behaviour, right through to the unauthorised exchange of children's images over the internet.

For all the New Zealand teachers interviewed in both the field site and the focus groups, there was a very real sense that the levels of nudity seen in the Japanese video were no longer either appropriate or comfortable in New Zealand early childhood settings. In contrast, Japanese viewers overwhelmingly linked the images of children's naked bodies to expressions of approval, pleasure, and a sense of nostalgia. Scholars writing about the issue of touch in the New Zealand early childhood context suggest that the difference lies in the changing perception of the space "between the bodies of the teacher and the child" (Jones, 2001, p. 9).

Bodies under Surveillance

The rising anxiety and regulation associated with children's bodies has been labelled a moral panic by New Zealand researchers (Jones, 2001; Farquhar, 2001), but it is a phenomenon common to other Western nations as well. In Australia, McWilliam (2003, p. 35) has repositioned the child as a new pedagogical subject with the "fleshy body" being replaced by an object of "risk minimisation". In the United Kingdom, Piper and Stronach (2008) have discussed educational settings where all, or part of, children's bodies are designated dangerous, and viewing or touching them can result in the prosecution of teachers. And in an American context, Phelan (1997) has suggested it is not only the children who have experienced the erasure of pleasure derived from the bodily, but teachers who must repress their own desires in the classroom.

Duncan (1999) has pointed out that the concerns of most New Zealand kindergarten teachers do not centre on fears about child abuse occurring, or the trustworthiness of their colleagues, but rather the threat of an allegation of child sexual abuse. Duncan draws on Foucault's notions of surveillance to examine the changing nature of policies designed to prevent child abuse in early childhood settings. She suggests that much of the current climate of fear and anxiety stems from the 1993 trial of Peter Ellis, a Christchurch childcare centre worker convicted of sixteen charges of sexual abuse against children (McLoughlin, 1996, cited in Duncan, 1999).

After the trial, many regular practices carried out at early childhood centres, such as a lone adult changing a nappy or supervising children on a walk, came to be viewed with suspicion. The early childhood sector swiftly developed policies to allay public fears, and after a period of consultation, a code of ethics was also released.[3] From these documents four key recommendations emerged: increased visibility; adults could not be alone with a child; tasks requiring physical contact such as toileting and bathing must be carried out by at least two centre staff visible at all times; and parents must be kept informed. Comments from the teachers Duncan interviewed revealed this has meant a huge change in practice. They cited staff members being required to supervise other teachers showering a child, referring to toileting contracts listing which staff have permission to remove children's clothing (for example, in the case of a toileting accident), and needing to fill in a detailed form every time this occurred.

Drawing on Bentham's Panopticon, Foucault (1980) describes a state of constant visual attention by which "people turn themselves into self-observing subjects who are controlled inwardly by their own constraints and actions" (Duncan 1999, p. 245). In this way, the early childhood setting becomes a site of constant surveillance, both in structural terms as buildings are redesigned to open viewing and in terms of policy which sees staff, parents, and members of the community entering in, out and around the centre each day. The teachers are also policing themselves, reproducing safe and controlled behaviour as expressed in child protection documents yet all the while mindful of powerful public opinion expressed through media and community outlets (Piper & Stronach, 2008).

Jones (2003) has pointed out that policies relating to the sexual abuse of children were based on dubious research at a time when social anxiety about the issue was particularly high. She rejects the notion that the risks were carefully considered, instead linking the change in New Zealand early childhood policy to a combination of a focus on child protectionism, sensationalist American research into abuse, and the high profile allegations against Peter Ellis in 1992. Jones argues that the 'abusing teacher' was not in fact a new risk, but one created by media attention with the perception that this individual was potentially lurking undiscovered in every centre across the country. In reality, it was often difficult to ascertain if sexual abuse had occurred, and prosecutions against childcare workers for such a crime were rare. As Duncan (1999) has shown, the result of this intense public scrutiny resulted in teachers becoming the object of surveillance and the accusing children turning into the risk. Jones (2003, p. 24) sums up this new risk nicely:

> For staff, the 'risky business' in which early childhood workers find themselves is not the risky environment where child abuse can occur, but the

risky environment where they are open to unfounded accusations. Staff willingly co-operate in the new 'safe' practices not so much because these practices protect children, but primarily because 'safe' practices are insurance for themselves.

Normalising the Clothed Body

For the New Zealand teachers involved in this project, the feelings of being under constant surveillance were clearly omnipresent, even when the children, their parents, or members of the wider community were not present. As articulated by Foucault (1975/1995, 1981), they had come to internalise and enforce the belief that viewing images of naked children's bodies was not only inappropriate, it was quite possibly dangerous. During a screening of the Japanese video at Kaimai Kindergarten one evening, the tape was paused so the group of staff could hear the comments being made. It is important to note that there were no children or parents at the centre during this screening. By chance, the video froze on the image of a naked boy's bottom framed by a classroom door. The group quickly pointed out that maybe the tape needed to be moved on to a more appropriate point.

> Well, that's an awesome place to stop!
> Oh, that's a bit sensitive . . . quick, fast forward, fast forward!

However, they swiftly engaged in some critical cross-cultural consciousness and began to examine their own reaction to the completely unplanned result. One of the teachers noted that "Yeah, that's interesting they [the Japanese] wouldn't comment!" but the group reasoned that it was necessary to be more careful in a New Zealand context considering the current climate. Douglas (1970/1996) argues that a community under threat responds by expanding the number of social controls relating to the body. In contemporary New Zealand, the threat of child sexual abuse allegations is the omnipresent threat, which serves to both reproduce disciplined individuals (Foucault, 1980) and regulate the adult gaze. The child's body is also subject to these diffuse forms of power rendering the naked body as a menace to order (Foucault, 1975/1995). In contrast, the clothed body has become normalised under arbitrary criteria, such as those given by the New Zealand teachers earlier in this chapter.

Like the nostalgic Japanese teachers however, some of the more experienced educators could remember a time when New Zealand children also spent long periods of time outside naked, and they expressed their regret at how the early childhood environment had changed. At a focus group session in Wellington, one teacher drew on her own childhood memories of naked play to argue for educators today to be more relaxed about nudity. The teacher made a positive, if tenuous, link between her own memories of unrepressed embodied play and the eradication of violence and child sexual abuse.

This approach brought her into conflict with the dominant discourse expressed by others around her. The majority of New Zealand teachers interviewed associated the unclothed child with negative outcomes, and they were cautious about the potential of images of Japanese children to end up on illicit websites. The most frequently asked question was: "Is there no child sexual abuse or pornography in Japan?" It is an interesting question.

Keeping the Japanese Child's Body Safe

Douglas (1970/1996) sees the physical body as a "microcosm of society, facing the centre of power, contracting and expanding its claims in direct accordance with the increase and relaxation of social pressures" (p. 76). Examining the Japanese child's body under this rubric, it becomes clear why early childhood teachers in Japan do not work in constant fear of abuse allegations. While measures concerning Japanese children's physical safety have certainly become more stringent in the past two decades following a sharp increase in reported child abuse (Al-Badari, 2006; "Record 44,210 Child Abuse Cases Logged in '09", 2010), the same attention to child sexual abuse has not been evident.

Historically, this issue has received less scrutiny in Japan than in other countries such as the United Kingdom and the United States where sexual abuse has almost become synonymous with child abuse as a whole (Hacking, 1991). The first government survey, in 1973, to address issues of child abuse in Japan did not include a category for sexual abuse but concentrated on murder, violence, and abandonment. In 1988, a major survey was conducted which included sexual assault under the umbrella of child abuse, yet the numbers affected by this crime were said to be less than 5% (Fujimoto, 1994). More recent statistics show that these figures have changed very little in the two decades since that survey was released, with a paper by the Ministry of Health, Labour, and Welfare (2008) reporting that sexual abuse still only accounted for just over 3% of the total number of child abuse cases in 2007.[4]

Kingston (2004) suggests that Japan's massive sex industry is generally tolerated by both the wider public and the authorities. This attitude contributed to Japan's tardiness in legally banning child pornography and child prostitution in 1999. According to Kingston, this ban was not realised out of moral concern but in order to protect Japan's image at a time when the country was internationally being viewed as a leading producer of internet child porn. In his discussion of child pornography on the internet, Jenkins (2001) also accepts that Japan is a prolific source of soft-core images of naked children in utopian settings. Prior to the 1999 legislation, the volume of images was considered so high that Interpol suggested up to 80% of internet pornography originated from Japanese sources.

Jenkins (2001) disputes this claim but concedes that Japan remains legally permissive of pedophile boards, which "advertise illicit materials posted on temporary and transient pages on otherwise innocuous servers" (p. 199).

Goodman (2002) agrees that external pressure propelled the Japanese government towards legislating against sexual offences, but cautions that tacit acceptance of certain sexual practices and a reluctance to investigate cases in order to avoid embarrassment has hampered progress. He uses the example of incest that is still not recognised as a crime, making it difficult for victims to press charges unless rape has taken place. As a result, most of the sexual abuse cases involve girls over the age of ten who are willing to take on the difficult task of proving the assault has occurred. Goodman (2002) points out "the idea that young boys and girls can be sexually abused has proved to be the most difficult perception to change" (p. 142). More than a decade after the anti-child porn legislation was passed, it seems to be having little effect due to permissive attitudes to pornography, sexual exploitation, and a huge, thriving sex industry.

This issue has not gone unnoticed within the early childhood community or the wider public. An editorial in *The Japan Times* called for readers to pressure the government for change to halt the sexual exploitation of children, musing that "child prostitution and pornography are not just a matter of unsavoury international reputation; they reflect the values of our own society" (Kingston, 2004, p. 273). There are indications that these values are indeed changing, and during focus group sessions, several Japanese early childhood teachers expressed concerns similar to New Zealand teachers over the possibility of children's images falling into the wrong hands.

Unlike the New Zealand context where the perceived threat to children often appears to be from *inside* the institution (in the form of the teacher as potentially abusive), the Japanese teachers, however, were specific about dangerous elements penetrating the kindergarten environment from the *outside*. In areas that were highly populated, the risk seemed to them to be heightened.

As a response to perceptions of rising risk in educational environments, kindergartens and schools are adopting more stringent safety measures designed to assuage the fears of anxious parents and children. For example, Ikeda Elementary School in Osaka (which was the site of a massacre of eight children in 2001) became the first primary school in Japan to be designated an international safe school in 2010. To be awarded this status, the school employed a number of measures such as posting security guards at the entrance, instigating patrols by parents around the school grounds, and conducting safety classes in which students are taught to defend themselves ("Ikeda Elementary School designated international safe school", 2010).

In Saitama, the teachers contextualised their concerns in the light of increasingly violent and random attacks on children by strangers. They explained that while children were free to roam around, even to remove their clothing and play naked in the past: "These days, ideas about those kinds of things have very much changed". When questioned as to why the change had occurred, the Saitama teachers revealed concerns on multiple levels:

> Well, as you know, it's about threats to security from the outside. The mothers have asked us to take precautions as they are worried.
>
> It is because of the emergence of suspicious characters (*fushinsha*), isn't it? Since then it has changed. Here, there, all around the country, there were various cases of questionable circumstances and after that it all changed.
>
> We had an incident in which children were involved. Not exactly a case of a peeping tom but involving an adult who had an interest in looking at and videotaping children. Mothers at this kindergarten became very anxious about it all. We had to reassure them that everything was fine and that we were doing everything possible to avoid that kind of incident here.

At Oka Kindergarten, teachers were certainly also aware of the sensationalist media coverage given to gruesome events involving young children or staff of early childhood settings (Lewis, 2006; Sims, 2001; Masters, 2008; "Woman knifes teacher at school", 2001; "Boar attacks 5 in Osaka then barges into kindergarten", 2008). Not long after a mentally disturbed man wandered into a childcare centre in Tokyo, the Oka principal made the incident the topic for his weekly assembly talk. The children were told to remain vigilant for the presence of strangers in the playground and to alert a teacher immediately if they saw something strange. The teachers also discussed the appropriate response to this kind of threat during their daily staff meeting. As a large part of the grounds are unfenced and there are no security systems or locked doors at the entrance this gesture seemed to be more of a token than indicative of concrete action. Within two or three weeks, the behaviour of the children and the teachers returned to normal. The perception seemed to be that it was unlikely the same kind of trauma would occur in a small Hokkaido town on the periphery of Japanese society.

Framing the Child's Body

How do these contrasting views of children's bodies, both clothed and unclothed, seen as in need of protection, yet often given great freedom, objectified at once as sexualised and non-sexualised, fit into the early childhood setting? And what do they reflect about the cultural processes within and around them? The major difference seems to lie in the way the body is perceived and re-produced by others. Viewed through a Japanese lens a child's naked body can be seen as a gateway to a nostalgic, remembered, or re-created past. In this case, sexuality is not explicitly linked to the child's body, which instead represents a form of purity, innocence, and beauty (Chen, 1996). For teachers working within the Japanese early childhood setting, looking at the physical form neither implicates nor condemns. However, there is a cultural shift taking place within these arenas. While *furusato* ideology may support the nostalgic notion that a child can run free and unclothed without fear of prying eyes or danger, this attitude is being challenged in the light of rising awareness of child abuse issues (Goodman, 2002), international media attention, and changing notions of privacy. There is a growing realisation of the need to protect children from external threats, most often identified by the teachers Rachael spoke to as the internet and strangers entering the early childhood centre.

In a New Zealand context, the child's naked body has become a site for danger and surveillance for those who come into contact with it. This issue is not restricted to a New Zealand context, nor is it just the children's teachers who are under surveillance. For example, in the United States, Furedi (2002) describes a society that suspects almost every home hides a potential abuser. In these communities, children are taught to mistrust adults, parents wonder anxiously about a hug their child received from a teacher, and neighbours watch for signs of abuse. Furedi argues that the changing view of the naked child, from symbol of innocence to provocation of immorality, is linked to society's negative perception of itself and its members.

Sexuality, through its overt repression, becomes a more salient part of embodied interactions. The teachers recreate these powerful dominant cultural discourses through their actions and language (Foucault, 1980). While the New Zealand teachers expressed their fears of being "on your lonesome" and the need for "someone to back you up", the Japanese teachers were not operating in a comparable environment of constant observation and anxiety. Many New Zealand teachers could also remember a time when they practised in a similar political and social climate, but that style of education was longer an option for most. In a moment of reflection, several of the New Zealand group surmised that the real key to the relaxed Japanese attitudes to nudity and comfort with the body lies in Asian bathing and toileting practices which they contrasted with prudish Anglo-Saxon upbringings. As one would expect, toileting takes place at the Japanese early childhood setting but bathing practices have also been incorporated. Likewise, in New Zealand, toileting and washing are a necessary part of daily procedures. Both the Japanese curriculum (Ministry of Education, Science, Sports, and Culture, 2001) and *Te Whāriki* (Ministry of Education, 1996) make explicit reference to this use of the body as a tool for learning, but as this next section will explore, they are carried out in quite different ways in the two contexts.

Notions of Privacy

Clark (1994) has pointed out that the seemingly mundane activity of bathing is not only a cultural act, but it may be deconstructed as a means of understanding deeper values and beliefs. Bathing is "embedded functionally, symbolically, and behaviourally" (Clark, 1994, p. 8) in the Japanese cultural system through its practices and ideas which reflect wider social patterns. The same could be said of a study of such practices in New Zealand. Washing, bathing, and toileting routines in early childhood settings mirror the systems of the dominant cultural group which dictate the 'correct' manner in which to deal with such necessary bodily functions (Elias, 2000; Foucault, 1973).

In contemporary Japanese society, technological and economic developments mean that most households now have a bathroom of their own, but the culture of public bathing remains strong. Many of Japan's public bathing facilities were destroyed during World War II (Clark, 1994). This resulted in difficulties in bathing, which lead to the domestic bath becoming a symbol of both recovery and social status in the post-war period. While less than 66% of Japanese houses had baths in 1968, only fifteen years later, this number had risen to just over 88% (Clark, 1994). The decline in the number of public bathhouses has been similarly dramatic.

Participants interviewed by Clark (1994) spoke sadly of this decline as the public bathhouse represents a space for young children's introduction to sex education. To be naked with one's peers allows an opportunity to learn the differences between the sexes, the functions of the genitals, and not to be ashamed of the body. Media reports link more Japanese families bathing at home to children who are embarrassed to bathe naked with their classmates during school trips. While it would be considered inappropriate in a New Zealand context to even consider that twelve- or thirteen-year-old children would bathe naked together, in Japan, children, who insist on wearing swimsuits, are treated with derision by teachers and other students.

These differing attitudes are also prevalent in the early childhood arena where showering, toileting, and often the changing of clothes associated with these activities takes place. Showering or bathing is not common in the New Zealand centre but may be necessary after a child has soiled through illness or a toileting accident. This is usually an individual affair for the child who will be assisted or supervised by at least two staff members as per state policy. In Japan, there are more opportunities for children at a centre to share a communal bathing experience, either through water play, at the pool, at a summer camp, or during a kindergarten sleepover night. In the case of visiting hot springs, staff may also enter the water as well as get changed alongside the children. This issue arose while viewing the Japanese video with the Kaimai Kindergarten teachers, bringing into sharp relief the contrasting views on professionalism, the body, and bathing practices.

> It happened to me once [getting changed in the same room] and I waited until that child had finished.
> I would have to go into a side room or something because I wouldn't be changing in front of children or parents.
> I'd be turning around and going away!

For these New Zealand teachers, keeping the body covered was linked to multiple issues: a need to maintain professionalism, feelings of embarrassment, and a desire to protect the children, even as they acknowledged this did not seem to be working in practice. But yet for this group, allowing the body of both child and teacher to be viewed during washing represented a conflict with their aims of safety and protection. Paradoxically, in the very same interests of safety, children's bodies have become more exposed. Following policy changes to increase visibility in New Zealand early childhood settings, many toilet spaces have become more open by removing doors or installing mirrors. At Kaimai Kindergarten, each toilet was divided by a partition but open at the front, which meant anyone washing their hands at the sink or passing by the area could see children urinating or defecating. This was in contrast to the Japanese field site where the toilets all had doors which were brightly decorated with anthropomorphised animals such as elephants or hippos. Ironically, this means that New Zealand children are in many ways far more exposed than Japanese children while carrying out toileting rituals.

Duncan (1998) has reported that this kind of structural change to New Zealand kindergarten and childcare centres has resulted in 'constant surveillance'. It seems ironic that teachers at Kaimai Kindergarten mentioned privacy (in the earlier section on the unclothed child) as one reason why nakedness was inappropriate considering the lack of toilet doors, which means children are now in full view of other children and adults passing by the bathroom area. As Duncan (1998) has asked,

> What messages do children get about their own bodies, and how they feel about being watched by adults, or other children when they are being changed? Are they learning that adults cannot be trusted? That it is okay for adults to watch you dress and undress? To toilet? To shower?
>
> *(p. 12)*

Under the rubric of child protection and safety, New Zealand children have become the subject of "permanent visibility" concealed within the apparatus of supervision and building structures (Foucault, 1975/1995, p. 201).

In the United Kingdom, Piper and Stronach (2008) have also touched on the irony of new policies designed to protect children from potential abuse. As in New Zealand, privacy has been sacrificed for safety leading to children being dressed, toileted, and changed in public areas or within sight of more than one adult. Piper and Stronach perceive this scenario as part of an ever-expanding set of circles of observing researchers, teachers, managers, parents, and the media, each contributing a level of surveillance. They note that while these "circles of concern" (Piper & Stronach, 2008, p. 71) are intertwined, practice in early childhood is dominated by the need to protect the adults from accusation rather than the children from abuse.

A good example of these circles of concern became apparent to Rachael when she took part in a Kaimai Kindergarten trip to a local garden centre. At the time, Rachael's son was attending the kindergarten, and she was assisting on the trip as a parent helper in charge of her child and another little boy. All the parent help-ers were instructed by the teachers that if any of the children needed to go to the toilet, they were to come and find a staff member to accompany the child. In reality, when the little boy suddenly felt an urgent need to urinate, there was no teacher in the vicinity. The three of them were, however, right next to the toilet, which the child begged to be allowed to enter. Realising that he was about to wet his pants, Rachael pushed him into the toilet and called through the door asking if he was alright, all the time feeling like a potential criminal in the midst of watch-ful shoppers. Afterwards, Rachael dutifully reported the incident to the teacher in charge, while later reflecting on the foreignness of the panic she had experienced.

Rachael's reaction very much replicates the feelings of guilt and panic experi-enced by Tobin when a mother arrived to pick up her daughter from childcare. At the time, the child was sitting in Tobin's lap, but he quickly pushed the child off and explained himself to the mother, only later reflecting on why he had reacted in such a way or how it may have affected the young girl (Tobin 1997, p. 120). Changing notions of privacy can be seen as an attempt to regulate behaviour within a disciplinary society (Foucault, 1975/1995, 1981). Elias (2000) suggests that an inhibited attitude towards the body emerged as Europe became civilised around the sixteenth century. At the same time, natural bodily functions came to be seen as shameful and dirty. These ideas persist today, as the following section explores.

The Body as a Site of Excretion

Douglas (1966) claims that the extent to which bodily fluids and excretions are regarded as polluting varies from culture to culture. This section argues that while bodily processes and functions may be seen as metaphors of disorder (Douglas, 1966; Turner, 2003) in the New Zealand early childhood context, the Japanese construct these secretions as functional, organic matter. New Zealand concepts of bodily processes and secretions are embedded in European constructs of the civilised body (Elias, 2000). Holliday and Hassard (2001) argue that the disciplined and regimented docile body, as expressed by Foucault, is accorded high status in Western culture. In contrast, Bakhtin's (1984) grotesque body is linked to loss of control, and therefore reviled and denigrated. In a reflection of the Cartesian mind/body dichotomy, said to be characteristic of Western philosophy (Lock, 1993), the mind is privileged. While the disciplined body is connected with the mind in order to overcome bodily excesses, the grotesque body is associated with a weak mind whose inferior status has (historically) justified its exploitation.

In contrast to the Cartesian mind/body dualism, Japanese concepts of the body have been described as holistic. Picone (1989) suggests "all aspects or parts of a person's body are thought to be interrelated, and the body in turn is itself only one element in a universe of interrelated entities" (p. 469). Within this framework, bodily processes and fluids are not positioned as metaphors of disorder (Douglas,

1966; Turner, 2003) as they may be in the West, but reconstructed as legitimate, organic functions, and products.

While greater surveillance has become a feature of ablution routines in New Zealand, quite the opposite has occurred in Japan with toileting having become a private matter in contrast to the past when open, communal toilet spaces were a feature of early childhood settings (see Figure 2.2). Tobin et al. (2009) recount the story of a Japanese preschool director, who insisted on having his photo taken while squatting over a Chinese communal toilet trough, which he viewed nostalgically as a "disappearing cultural artefact" (p. 51). In both the Japanese and Chinese contexts, Tobin et al. view newly partitioned public toilets as a symbol of modernity expressed through modified concepts of privacy, space, modesty, and the body.

Despite these rising levels of privacy however, there remains in Japanese early childhood settings a level of comfort with the body not replicated in the New Zealand centres. Tobin et al. (2009) have noted how relaxed Japanese children and adults are about discussing bodily functions. They describe at length a "pee lesson" given by a five-year-old boy to a two-year-old child learning how to use the urinal (p. 114). Acting without the presence of adults, the children are

FIGURE 2.2 Partitioned toilets with lockable doors are a feature of this modern Hokkaido kindergarten

comfortable with discussing the functions and apparatus of their bodies, which makes the lesson a relaxed, enjoyable experience. As Tobin et al. point out, this vignette takes on a different cast in an American setting when viewed through lens of sexual abuse fears.

By the same token, cartoons and television programmes that deal with these themes are a regular feature of daytime television. When living in Japan, one of Rachael's children's favourite television programmes featured an animated character, called *Unchi kun* (Mr Poo), who would carry out all manner of adventures sliding around in the toilet bowl. When the children's grandfather visited from New Zealand, he was both surprised and mildly disgusted by the content of this series. Although Rachael's children were very young at time, they sensed there was some kind of cultural misfit occurring and delighted in turning up the volume every time *Unchi kun* appeared for the benefit of Granddad.

More recently, during the March 2011 earthquake and tsunami, which devastated northern Japan, the *unchi* metaphor was used to explain the unfolding Fukushima nuclear crisis to children ("Nuclear Boy", 2011). In the animated clip, which was posted on YouTube and widely viewed both throughout Japan and the rest of the world, the nuclear power plant is depicted as 'Nuclear Boy'. In the clip, Nuclear Boy is suffering from a sore stomach and declares he can't hold his poo in any longer. At this point, he releases a powerful fart (*onara*), which is deemed to be particularly smelly. The fart represents the potentially lethal gases coming from the plant, which the clip assures viewers may be smelly to those nearby but are hardly discernible to those further away. The narrator declares that it would be disastrous if Nuclear Boy could not contain his poo as the smell is truly awful, therefore 'doctors' are sent to administer 'medicine' in the form of seawater and boron which will cool him down. Other previous nuclear accidents are also personified, with 'Chernobyl Boy' described as having contracted diarrhea and making a huge mess everywhere.

The Body as Teacher in Japanese Early Childhood Education

The discussion of body parts and of bodily wastes is as implicitly accepted as normal in Japanese early childhood circles as it is considered unfit for conversation in New Zealand circles. In discussing this topic in New Zealand it was pointed out to Rachael many times that it was not something that should be talked about at the same time as eating, or it was embarrassing, or it was just not worthy of discussion. The casting off of waste products is seen by Douglas (1970/1996) as the most unwanted, irrelevant of social events. Acts such as defecation, urination, and vomiting, and their products, "carry a pejorative sign for formal discourse" and therefore need to be screened out of regular social intercourse (Douglas, 1970/1996, p. 76).

However, Japanese concepts of the body locate it within a complex feedback system, where the relationships of the body parts, orifices, and organs are linked to

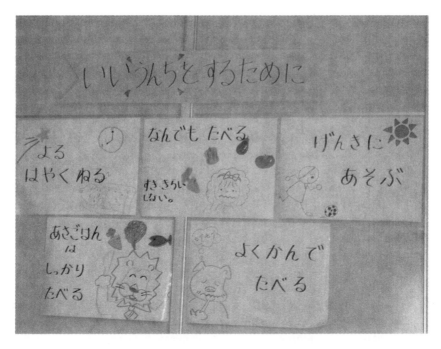

FIGURE 2.3 Display in a Japanese childcare centre explaining how various actions are related to producing a good bowel motion

one another, and to other phenomena both inside and outside of the body (Lock, 1980, Picone, 1989). This notion is nicely illustrated by a display on the wall of a childcare centre in Hokkaido (Figure 2.3). The display shows how the acts of eating, sleeping, and playing are linked directly to defecation. Prepared by one of the teachers, the title (*ii unchi o suru tame ni*) could be translated formally as "in order to pass a good bowel motion" or less formally as "how to have a good poo". Accompanied by diagrams to make it easier for younger children to understand, each segment of the poster stresses a particular action, which will contribute to the desired result. The first segment advises children to "go to bed early", while the next box notes one should "eat everything on the plate and not be fussy" (*suki-kirai*). The following segment links vigorous outdoor play with the functions of the digestive system, asking children to "play energetically" followed by "eat a good breakfast". The final segment admonishes children to "chew your food thoroughly". The links between consumption of food, movement of the body, periods of physical exertion and rest, and the correct means of consuming food are made eminently clear even at this simple level of expression.

Ohnuki-Tierney (1984) uses the notion of 'good' bowel movements to illustrate how Japanese mothers employ more indirect modes of communication than parents in the West. She points out that "a mother uses a statement about her infant's bowel movement as a way of expressing her feelings toward him or her" (Ohnuki-Tierney, 1984, p. 52). It is also common to see Japanese mothers using a clean towel to wipe sweat off their young children's back or forehead, as it is believed that perspiration left on the body will lead to a cold. Ohnuki-Tierney explains that it is expected that children will report both the condition of their body and bodily functions to their mothers as they traverse from childhood to adulthood.

As Tobin et al. (2009) have pointed out, joy, openness, and pride in the body is not seen as limited to the individual but something to be shared with the group:

> The comfort with touch and with the body characteristic of Japanese pre-school is the kind of pleasure in the body . . . to be found not in the body of the individual, but in the collective body of the people, in bodies in contact in large gatherings, and in the gleeful acknowledgement of the fact that everyone has a body and these bodies have orifices.
>
> *(p. 117)*

At Oka Kindergarten, where the Japanese video was filmed, this shared implicit cultural knowledge of bodily process and practices was brought home to Rachael one day at the regular morning assembly. On stage with the other teachers during a lecture on healthy habits as the winter loomed, the principal suddenly turned to Rachael with the microphone in his hand. He had been extolling the virtues of eating nutritious food, but his question to her came as a surprise: "Rachael *sensei*, what shape was your bowel motion (*unchi*) this morning?"

With over one hundred and sixty small pairs of eyes trained on her, Rachael was completely stumped. She had no idea what she was supposed to reply, but she gathered by the way the other teachers were looking expectantly at her that there was indeed a correct response. Unfortunately Rachael was culturally igno-rant of just what that response should be. After a long, pregnant pause, one of the more sensitive teachers piped up and said, "What was that? Did I hear you say, a banana shaped poo?" Everyone looked very relieved and the principal pro-ceeded to launch into a detailed explanation about the merits of banana shaped bowel motions, which indicated a healthy, varied diet. He went on to contrast the banana with other shapes, which revealed nutritional or lifestyle deficiencies. Bowel motions, which resembled a bunch of grapes, indicated constipation due to a lack of vegetables and fruit. A round shape like a peach indicated the reverse (diarrhea) and so on. Back in the staffroom, the other teachers were very amused that Rachael was more ignorant than kindergarteners about the metaphorical links between fruit and bowel motions.

In international circles, this relaxed attitude towards scatological issues has been viewed as inappropriate and been the subject of ridicule on websites. Toys such as poo hats, 'pee and poo' soft toys, children's interactive board games focussed on toilet training, and golden poo chains, have been labelled 'downright weird' and 'baffling' by viewers from outside Japan (Bucholz, 2007). The issue of excrement (*unchi*) crops up regularly not only within Japanese society but in icons of popular culture such as animated comic books (*manga*), which have become globally popular. This has presented difficulties for translators in cultures who are unused to being so open about the issue and struggle to find the correct nuance in translation (Lee & Shaw, 2006).

Reflecting on Children's Bodies as Culturally Contested

This chapter has discussed the culturally contested space that children's bodies occupy in the early childhood arena. In Western contexts, the child's body has become a site for anxiety and fear in the face of rising debate over appropriate policy and practice. This construction is reflected in the New Zealand early childhood setting, where children's bodies are increasingly subject to surveillance and regulation (Foucault, 1975/1995). As Tobin (1997) writes,

> the pervert lurking in the cracks and on the fringes of the world of early childhood education is a spectre that haunts our thinking and practice, distorting the way we see ourselves and each other and the decisions we make about practice.
>
> *(p. 143)*

In terms of this project, Tobin's statement has an eerie truth about it when one considers that Japanese teachers literally asked if New Zealand was "full of perverts" during discussion over policy relating to children's bodies. A group of naked children outside on a hot summer's day after water play looked to be an innocent, even beautiful, scene to the majority of Japanese viewers. During many of the focus groups these images on the screen created links to a nostalgic, remembered, or (re)imagined past (Robertson, 1988). However, concepts of privacy combined with changing notions of child safety have become a reality especially in urban centres. Japanese teachers are increasingly aware of both the possibility of external threats to children's bodies and the need to balance traditional pedagogies with the anxieties of modern mothers.

For the New Zealand viewers, the 'pervert lurking in the cracks' is an omnipresent phantom which prevents the kind of sensory and physical interactions between teacher and child that were common in early childhood settings twenty or thirty years earlier. Under the rubric of greater visibility and safety, the bodies of children have become more exposed through measures such as removing doors and installing mirrors. Working within a political environment of constant surveillance, teachers in New Zealand early childhood settings expressed their desire to enjoy the same kinds of scenes that they saw at the Japanese centre, but they were mindful of the need to be careful in the midst of a watchful community.

This chapter demonstrates Douglas's (1970/1996) assertion that the extent to which bodily fluids and excretions are regarded as polluting varies from culture to culture. In the New Zealand early childhood setting, European notions of bodily functions can be seen. Elias (2000) contends that the European body emerged as a new canon in the sixteenth century, leading to new standards of refinement and conversely, of disgust. The body became the focus of civilising processes through the polite management of bodily processes. In contrast, the Japanese early childhood setting frames the body and its products as useful metaphors for educating children.

While the teachers at the New Zealand centre may be working in a space of "constant surveillance" and the children the focus of "permanent visibility" (Foucault, 1975/1995, p. 201), bodily contact between these two groups has not been completely subjugated. During the focus group sessions, Kaimai Kindergarten was praised by other teachers around the country as displaying an admirable level of personal interaction. For example, Napier kindergarten teachers noted the "shared affection between the teachers and the children which was really nice to see. The kids were climbing over the teachers and sitting [in their laps] and the teachers seemed quite welcome and open to that". For the Japanese viewers, however, these interactions seemed rather limited and somewhat distant compared to their own approach. They politely suggested that New Zealand teachers appeared to be less engaged with both children's play and their physical bodies. To illustrate their point, teachers in Osaka showed Rachael photographs of themselves huddled together with children, all of them covered in body paint. In Kutchan, the principal described the experience of nodding off to sleep surrounded by seventy of his pupils in the kindergarten hall.

The next chapter examines how children and teachers in both settings embody the curriculum in ways that are specific to their centres and their cultural contexts.

Notes

1 Most ethnographic studies of early childhood settings have been conducted on Japan's main island of Honshu: Ben-Ari, (1997 [Kyoto]); Boocock, (1989 [Kyoto]); De Coker, (1990 [Kyoto]); Hendry, (1986 [Chiba]); Holloway, (2000 [Osaka, Kobe]); Kotloff, (1998 [Kanazawa]); Lewis, (1995 [Nagoya, Tokyo]); Peak, (1991 [Nagano]); Tobin, Wu, & Davidson, (1989 [Kyoto]); Walsh, (2004 [Yashiro, north of Osaka]), and most of them have examined institutions in urban areas. An exception to this is the study by Hendry (1986), which is based in part on fieldwork in kindergartens in rural Kyushu.
2 Playcentre is a New Zealand parent-led service, that involves parents as the teachers of their own children.
3 See Combined Early Childhood Union of Aotearoa (1993) and Early Childhood Education Code of Ethics National Working Group (1995).
4 The survey of child abuse reported that out of a total of 40,639 abuse cases report in 2007, there were 1,293 sexual abuse cases (3%) compared with 7,621 cases of psychological abuse (19%), 15,429 cases of neglect (38%), and 16,296 physical abuse cases (40%).

References

Al-Badari, D. (2006, June 27). Japan hit by huge rise in child abuse. *The Guardian*. Retrieved from www.guardian.co.uk/world/2006/jun/27/japan

Bakhtin, M. (1984). *Rabelais and his world*. Bloomington: Indiana University Press.

Barcan, R. (2004). *Nudity: A cultural anatomy*. Oxford, UK: Berg.

Ben-Ari, E. (1997). *Body projects in Japanese childcare: Culture, organization and emotions in a preschool*. Richmond, UK: Curzon Press.

Ben-Ari, E. (2002). State standardisation and 'normal' children: An anthropological study of a preschool. In R. Goodman (Ed.), *Family and social policy in Japan: Anthropological approaches* (pp. 111–130). Cambridge, UK: Cambridge University Press.

Boar attacks 5 in Osaka then barges into kindergarten. (2008, April 9). *Japan Today*. Retrieved from www.japantoday.com/category/national/view/boar-attacks-5-in-Osaka-then-barges-into-kindergarten

Boocock, S. S. (1989). Controlled diversity: An overview of the Japanese preschool. *Journal of Japanese Studies, 15*(1), 41–65.

Bresler, L. (2004). Dancing the curriculum: Exploring the body and movement in elementary schools. In L. Bresler (Ed.), *Knowing bodies, knowing minds: Towards embodied teaching and learning* (pp. 127–151). Dordrecht, The Netherlands: Kluwer Academic.

Bucholz, C. (2007, November 13). *The 25 most baffling toys from around the world*. Retrieved from www.cracked.com/article-15670-the-25-most-baffling-toys-from-around-the-world_p2.html

Carr-Gomm, P. (2010). *A brief history of nakedness*. London, UK: Reaktion Books.

Caudill, W. (1972). Tiny dramas: Vocal communication between mother and infant in Japanese and American families. In W. Lebra (Ed.), *Transcultural research in mental health: Volume II of mental health research in Asia and the Pacific* (pp. 25–48). Honolulu: University Press of Hawaii.

Chen, S.-J. (1996). Positive childishness: Images of childhood in Japan. In C. P. Hwang, M. E. Lamb, & I. E. Sigel (Eds.), *Images of childhood* (pp. 113–128). London, UK: Routledge.

Clark, S. (1994). *Japan: A view from the bath*. Honolulu: University of Hawaii Press.

Combined Early Childhood Union of Aotearoa. (1993). *Preventing the sexual abuse of children within early childhood services*. Wellington, New Zealand: Author.

Creighton, M. (1997). Consuming rural Japan: The marketing of tradition and nostalgia in the Japanese travel industry. *Ethnology, 36*(3), 239–254.

De Coker, G. (1990). Japanese preschools: Academic or nonacademic? In J. J. Shields (Ed.), *Japanese schooling: Patterns of socialization, equality and political control* (pp. 45–58). University Park: The Pennsylvania State University Press.

Douglas, M. (1966). *Purity and danger: An analysis of concepts of pollution and taboo*. Harmondsworth, UK: Penguin Books.

Douglas, M. (1970/1996). *Natural symbols: Explorations in cosmology*. London, UK: Routledge.

Duncan, J. (1998). *I spy: Sexual abuse prevention polices: Protection or harm?* Wellington, New Zealand: Institute for Early Childhood Studies, Victoria University of Wellington.

Duncan, J. (1999). New Zealand kindergarten teachers and sexual abuse protection policies. *Teaching and Teacher Education, 15*(1), 243–252.

Early Childhood Education Code of Ethics National Working Group. (1995). *Early childhood education code of ethics for Aotearoa/New Zealand*. Wellington, New Zealand: Author.

Elias, N. (2000). *The civilizing process: Sociogenetic and psychogentic investigations*. Oxford, UK: Blackwell.

Farquhar, S. E. (1997). *A few good men or a few too many?* Palmerston North, New Zealand: Department of Educational Psychology, Massey University, New Zealand.

Farquhar, S. E. (2001). Moral panic in New Zealand: Teachers touching children. In A. James (Ed.), *Touchy subject: Teachers touching children* (pp. 87–98). Dunedin, New Zealand: University of Otago Press.

Foucault, M. (1973). *The birth of the clinic*. New York, NY: Pantheon Books.

Foucault, M. (1975/1995). *Discipline and punish: The birth of the prison* (A. Sheridan, Trans.). New York, NY: Vintage Books.

Foucault, M. (1980). The eye of power. In C. Gordon (Ed.), *Power/knowledge: Selected interviews and other writings, 1972–1977: Michel Foucault* (pp. 146–165). Hemel Hempstead, UK: The Harvester Press.

Foucault, M. (1981). *The history of sexuality, Volume 1: An introduction*. Harmondsworth, UK: Penguin.

Fujimoto, T. (1994). *Crime problems in Japan*. Tokyo, Japan: Chuo University Press.

Furedi, F. (2002). *Culture of fear: Risk-taking and the morality of low expectation*. London, UK: Continuum.

Goodman, R. (2002). Child abuse in Japan: 'Discovery' and the development of policy. In R. Goodman (Ed.), *Family and social policy in Japan* (pp. 131–155). Cambridge, UK: Cambridge University Press.

Gottlieb, A. (2004). Foreword: Falling into trust. In L. Bresler (Ed.), *Knowing bodies, moving minds: Towards embodied teaching and learning* (pp. 1–5). Dordrecht, The Netherlands: Kluwer Academic.

Guichard-Anguis, S. (2009). Japanese inns (ryokan) as producers of Japanese identity. In S. Guichard-Anguis & O. Moon (Eds.), *Japanese tourism and travel culture* (pp. 76–101). London, UK: Routledge.

Hacking, I. (1991, Winter). The making and molding of child abuse. *Critical Inquiry, 17,* 243–248.

Hendry, J. (1986). *Becoming Japanese: The world of the pre-school child*. Honolulu: University of Hawaii Press.

Hendry, J. (1993). *Wrapping culture: Politeness, presentation, and power in Japan and other societies*. Oxford, UK: Oxford University Press.

Hendry, J. (1999). *An anthropologist in Japan: Glimpses of life in the field*. London, UK: Routledge.

Holliday, R., & Hassard, J. (2001). *Contested bodies*. New York, NY: Routledge.

Holloway, S. D. (2000). Accentuating the negative: Views of preschool staff about mothers in Japan. *Early Education and Development, 11*(5), 617–632.

Ikeda Elementary School designated "international safe school". (2010, March 5). *Japan Today*. Retrieved from www.japantimes.co.jp/news/2010/03/06/national/who-designates-ikeda-elementary-safe-school/#.U_E5R8WSx8E

Jenkins, P. (2001). *Beyond tolerance: Child pornography on the internet*. New York: New York University Press.

Johnson, R. (1997). The "no touch" policy. In J. Tobin (Ed.), *Making a place for pleasure in early childhood education* (pp. 101–118). New Haven, CT: Yale University Press.

Jones, A. (2001). Introduction. In A. Jones (Ed.), *Touchy subject: Teachers touching children* (pp. 9–13). Dunedin, New Zealand: University of Otago Press.

Jones, A. (2003). A short history of anxiety about touch in early childhood education. *The First Years: Ngā Tau Tuatahi: New Zealand Journal of Infant and Toddler Education, 5*(1), 22–24.

Kerr, A. (1996). *Lost Japan*. Melbourne, Australia: Lonely Planet.

Kingston, J. (2004). *Japan's quiet transformation: Social change and civil society in the twenty-first century*. London, UK: RoutledgeCurzon.

Kondo, D. (1992). Multiple selves: The aesthetics and politics of artisanal identities. In N. R. Rosenberger (Ed.), *Japanese sense of self* (pp. 40–66). Cambridge, UK: Cambridge University Press.

Kotloff, L. J. (1998). ". . . And Tomoko wrote this song for us". In T. Rohlen & G. LeTendre (Eds.), *Teaching and learning in Japan* (pp. 98–118). Cambridge, UK: Cambridge University Press.

Lebra, T. S. (1976). *Japanese patterns of behaviour*. Honolulu: University of Hawaii Press.

Lee, W., & Shaw, Y. (2006, Fall). A textual comparison of Japanese and Chinese editions of manga: Translation as cultural hybridization. *International Journal of Comic Art*, 34–55.

Lewis, C. C. (1995). *Educating hearts and minds: Reflections of Japanese preschool and elementary education*. Cambridge: University of Cambridge.

Lewis, L. (2006, February 18). Children stabbed by mother on school run. *Times Online*. Retrieved from ww.thetimes.co.uk/tto/news/world/asia/article2612200.ece

Lock, M. (1980). *East Asian medicine in urban Japan*. Berkeley: University of California Press.

Lock, M. (1993). Cultivating the body: Anthropology and epistemologies of bodily practice and knowledge. *Annual Review of Anthropology, 22*, 133–155.

Love, B. (2007). Fraught field sites: Studying community decline and heritage food revival in rural Japan. *Critical Asian Studies, 39*(4), 541–559.

Martinez, D. P. (1990). Tourism and the ama: The search for a real Japan. In E. Ben-Ari, B. Moeran, & J. Valentine (Eds.), *Unwrapping Japan: Society and culture in anthropological perspective* (pp. 97–116). Honolulu: University of Hawaii.

Mascia-Lees, F. E. (2011). Introduction. In F. E. Mascia-Lees (Ed.), *A companion to the anthropology of the body and embodiment* (pp. 1–2). Chichester, UK: Wiley-Blackwell.

Masters, Coco. (2008, 9 June). Japan reeling from stabbing spree. *Time*. Retrieved from http://content.time.com/time/world/article/0,8599,1812808,00.html

McWilliam, E. (2003). The vulnerable child as pedogogical subject. *Journal of Curriculum and Theorizing, 19*(2), 35–44.

Ministry of Education. (1996). *Te Whāriki: He Whāriki Mātauranga mō ngā Mokopuna o Aotearoa. New Zealand early childhood curriculum*. Wellington, New Zealand: Learning Media.

Ministry of Education, Science, Sports, and Culture. (2001, April). *National curriculum standards for kindergartens*. Retrieved from www.mext.go.jp/english/news/2001/04/010401.htm

Ministry of Health, Labour, and Welfare. (2008). Annual health, labour and welfare report 2007–2008. *White papers and reports*. Retrieved from www.mhlw.go.jp/english/wp/wp-hw2/

Montgomery, H. (2009). *An introduction to childhood: Anthropological perspectives on children's lives*. Chichester, West Sussex, UK: Wiley-Blackwell.

Moon, O. (2002). The countryside reinvented for urban tourists: Rural transformation in the Japanese muraokoshi movement. In J. Hendry & M. Raveri (Eds.), *Japan at play: The ludic and the logic of power* (pp. 228–244). London, UK: Routledge.

Morris, B. (1992). *Hearing my mother's voice: A study of sisters and mothers*. Wellington, New Zealand: New Zealand Council for Educational Research.

Nuclear boy. (2011, March 15). *Onaradaijobu*. Retrieved from www.youtube.com/user/onaradaijobu

Ohnuki-Tierney, E. (1984). *Illness and culture in contemporary Japan: An anthropological view*. Cambridge, UK: Cambridge University Press.

Peak, L. (1989). Learning to become part of the group: The Japanese child's transition to preschool life. *Journal of Japanese Studies, 15*(1), 93–123.

Peak, L. (1991). *Learning to go to school in Japan: The transition from home to preschool life.* Berkeley: University of California Press.

Phelan, A. M. (1997). Classroom management and the erasure of teacher desire. In J. Tobin (Ed.), *Making a place for pleasure in early childhood education* (pp. 76–100). New Haven, CT: Yale University Press.

Picone, M. (1989). The ghost in the machine: Religious healing and representations of the body in Japan. In M. Feher (Ed.), *Fragments for a history of the human body: Part two* (pp. 466–489). New York, NY: Zone.

Piper, H., & Stronach, I. (2008). *Don't touch!: The educational story of a panic.* Abingdon, UK: Routledge.

Record 44,210 child abuse cases logged in '09. (2010, July 29). *The Japan Times.* Retrieved from http://search.japantimes.co.jp/cgi-bin/nn20100729a3.html

Robertson, J. (1988). Furusato Japan: The culture and politics of nostalgia. *Politics, Culture and Society, 1,* 494–518.

Robinson, K. (2008). In the name of 'childhood innocence': A discursive exploration of the moral panic associated with childhood and sexuality. *Cultural Studies Review, 14*(2), 113–129.

Rohlen, T. P. (1974). Seishin kyoiku in a Japanese bank: A description of methods and consideration of some underlying concepts. In G. D. Spindler (Ed.), *Education and cultural process: Toward an anthropology of education* (pp. 219–229). New York, NY: Holt, Rinehart and Winston.

Schooler, C. (1996). William Caudill and the reproduction of culture: Infant, child and maternal behavior in Japan and the United States. In D. W. Shwalb & B. J. Shwalb (Eds.), *Japanese child-rearing: Two generations of scholarship* (pp. 139–163). New York, NY: Guildford Press.

Shapiro, S., & Shapiro, S. (2002). Silent voices, bodies of knowledge: Towards a critical pedagogy of the body. In S. Shapiro & S. Shapiro (Eds.), *Body movements: Pedagogy, politics and social change* (pp. 25–43). Creskill, NJ: Hampton Press.

Sims, C. (2001, June 9). Knife-wielding man kills 8 children at Japanese school. *New York Times.* Retrieved from www.nytimes.com/2001/06/09/world/knife-wielding-man-kills-8-children-at-Japanese-school

Surtees, N. (2008). Teachers following children?: Heteronormative responses within a discourse of child-centredness and the emergent curriculum. *Australian Journal of Early Childhood, 33*(3), 10–17.

Tobin, J. (1997). Playing doctor in two cultures: The United States and Ireland. In J. Tobin (Ed.), *Making a place for pleasure in early childhood education* (pp. 119–158). New Haven, CT: Yale University Press.

Tobin, J. (2004). The disappearance of the body in early childhood education. In L. Bresler (Ed.), *Knowing bodies, knowing minds: Towards embodied teaching and learning* (pp. 111–125). Dordrecht, The Netherlands: Kluwer Academic.

Tobin, J., Hsueh, Y., & Karasawa, M. (2009). *Preschool in three cultures revisited: China, Japan and the United States.* Chicago, IL: University of Chicago Press.

Tobin, J. J., Wu, D. Y. H., & Davidson, D. H. (1989). *Preschool in three cultures: Japan, China and the United States.* New Haven, CT: Yale University Press.

Turner, B. S. (2003). Social fluids: Metaphors and meanings of society. *Body and Society, 9*(1), 1–10.

Van Wolputte, S. (2004). Hang on to your self: Of bodies, embodiment, and selves. *Annual Review of Anthropology, 33,* 251–269.

Walsh, D. J. (2004). Frog boy and the American monkey: The body in Japanese early schooling. In L. Bresler (Ed.), *Knowing bodies, moving minds: Towards embodied teaching and learning* (pp. 97–109). Dordrecht, The Netherlands: Kluwer Academic.

Woman knifes teacher at school. (2001, June 20). *The Japan Times.* Retrieved from www. japantimes.co.jp/news/2001/06/20/national/woman-knifes-teacher-at-school/ #.U_E_e8WSx8E

3

EMBODYING THE
CURRICULUM

The body is, at one and the same time, a malleable material good capable of being fashioned in a certain manner, an entity which represents social relations and notions, and an embodiment of affective attitudes and stances towards the world.

(Ben-Ari, 1997, p. 1)

Introduction

While the previous chapter focused on how children's bodies are culturally constructed in the early childhood settings of New Zealand and Japan, this chapter looks at the ways in which the body both engages in and embodies the curricula of each nation. This chapter draws on the ideas of Mauss, who points out that while seemingly insignificant acts such as walking, digging, or jumping may appear 'natural', children's embodied play is always culturally constructed. He defines techniques as actions that are "effective and traditional" (Mauss, 1936/1975, p. 75).

Curriculum can be viewed as a cultural constructed technique. For example, New Zealand's early childhood document, *Te Whāriki*, reflects this philosophy, defining curriculum as "the sum total" of everything children experience (Ministry of Education, 1996, p. 10). Curricula are, of course, political documents, which reveal agendas of the state, yet they are also cultural documents situated within a community (Mutch, 2003). Despite a written instrument to guide them, teachers invariably implement their own methods to direct and structure children's bodies during play, learning, and periods of orderliness. Using the concepts of sensory play, order, and physicality as framing devices and techniques, this chapter looks at the ways in which the implicit practices of teachers (and sometimes parents) are reflected through pedagogy and policy. Children are also active participants in this process, sometimes resigning their bodies to the kindergarten structure and at other times, subverting the dominant paradigm to suit their own interests and needs.

Engaging the Body in Sensory Play

In discussions with teachers in both New Zealand and Japan, the importance of children using their bodies within the context of play was stressed many times. This view is supported by the literature (Mori, Nezu, Samizo, Naito, & Ishizuka, 2009; White et al., 2009) and the curricula of the two countries. Therefore, it is not surprising that the issue frequently arises. The ways in which the bodies of children and teachers are incorporated into play situations and routines vary according to the cultural context and within centres. When the New Zealand video was first screened to the Japanese teachers, one of the questions they asked was, "Do the teachers also take part in games where they run around in a '*genki*' manner like the children? It looks like they are sitting quietly most of the time." To conduct oneself in a *genki* way means to behave energetically or enthusiastically and there is great emphasis on this in the Japanese early childhood setting (LeVine & White, 2003). The extent to which children are encouraged to display *genki* has been commented on by visiting scholars who have been shocked by the resulting behaviour and the tolerance levels of teachers present (Lewis, 1995; Tobin, Wu, & Davidson, 1989; White, 1987). Early childhood teachers are also expected to be able to keep up with children's high energy levels and to participate whole-heartedly in games and activities.

For the Japanese teachers, watching scenes from Kaimai Kindergarten, it appeared that their New Zealand counterparts were less than enthusiastic about embracing play with their whole selves. They suggested that this might be linked to the age of the teachers in New Zealand, who appeared to be considerably more varied in terms of experience than their Japanese counterparts.

> How old are those teachers? It looks like experience is respected in New Zealand, whereas here the administration wants *genki* young teachers rather than older ones.
>
> If the teachers are too old, they don't have the energy to run around with the children.
>
> Yes, that's why kindergartens prefer younger teachers.
>
> What about in the sandpit? Do the teachers get in there and make things for the children as well, or do the kids have to make it themselves?

In New Zealand, teachers were quick to point out that what may appear as reluctance to engage is often a deliberate strategy to allow children to develop their own working theories. For example, in the case of the New Zealand sandpit scene, teachers sat on the side offering suggestions and resolving conflicts as children built waterways and mounds (see Figure 3.1). But they did not often climb into the sandpit or squat in the muddy puddles with the children. This part of play was left to the children. Teachers explained that sociocultural theory, on which the national early childhood curriculum *Te Whāriki* is based, views

FIGURE 3.1 A New Zealand teacher observes children's play in the sandpit

children's development as occurring through activities framed within a larger social and cultural context (Carr, 2001; Fleer, 1992). Rather than being the recipient of adult's efforts, children are encouraged to actively explore their environment and take charge of their learning with assistance from their teachers when required (Smith & May, 2006).

The Japanese teachers' assessment of their New Zealand peers echoes the findings of Fujita and Sano (1988) who conducted cross-cultural research in early childhood settings in Japan and the United States. Japanese teachers interviewed in the study felt that their American counterparts appeared lazy as they did not get down and play at children's level. For the Japanese teachers, the epitome of internalising a learning experience involves the whole bodies of all members of the group; therefore the teachers will also join in, and energy levels are high. An illustration of this kind of thinking can be seen in the criticism which was leveled at staff of the Japanese kindergarten by focus groups in their own country. Following the images of water play at the Hokkaido kindergarten, a teacher in Osaka commented that:

> The water play was fun but I think the activity could have been made more dynamic. They were playing quite reservedly with that mud but if it had been me I would have piled mud all over their bodies, on their heads. In our kindergarten, the teachers would also join in. We would put mud all over our bodies too and join in the play with the children. We're always doing that, teachers and children together getting all muddy and wet. When you do that children get really excited, their eyes come alive with it all and they call out, "We want to do that too!"

At kindergartens in Yokohama and Osaka, teachers presented photographs of their classes involved in body painting. The images showed children wearing nothing but underpants, their bodies and faces completely smeared with brightly coloured paint. In amongst the groups of children, the teachers could also be seen dressed in t-shirts and shorts and similarly streaked in paint. The teachers explained that the children particularly enjoyed this activity during the summer months when all members of the centre could experience the pleasure of body painting together in the warm sunshine. One photograph depicted two children deep in concentration as they painted yellow flowers on their teacher's shoulders. She in turn was squatting to face the exposed belly of a young boy as she covered him in vivid green. This image contrasts sharply with the American early childhood context where scholars have noted that "children's bodies, especially in their proximity to other bodies pose a menace to order. Proximity is taboo in many childhood classrooms" (Phelan, 1997, p. 82). In Britain, there are strict guidelines on how to deal with children's "dangerous bodies" (Piper & Stronach, 2008, p. 36).

Wrapping and Unwrapping the Body

Messy play has been identified as presenting a challenge to children and parents arriving in New Zealand early childhood settings from diverse cultural backgrounds. Terreni (2003) describes the reactions of mothers from Jordan and India who were initially upset to find their children wet and dirty at the end of a day at kindergarten. This was in direct contrast to their own experiences with centres in their home countries, where it was important to ensure the children were well-presented at all times and that clothing was kept clean. At Kaimai Kindergarten, substances, such as paint, dye, and 'slime' on clothing, are not currently classified by teachers, parents, and children as "matter out of place" (Douglas, 1966, p. 35), yet there are signs that this may be changing. For example, in recent years, some Kaimai parents have suggested that aprons be introduced to protect children's clothing, but this idea was rejected by staff and other parents at the kindergarten, who argue that early childhood settings are a sacred space for children. Here, the constructions of dirt, which might apply in the home, are waived in the name of childhood freedom and creativity. The enquiring parents were therefore reminded that children should be sent to the centre in worn, valueless clothing. In another example, a mother, who had served on the Parents' Committee at Kaimai Kindergarten, told Rachael that staff were eager to build a mud pit in the grounds so that children could freely engage in a more visceral way with nature. However, parents were not so enthusiastic about the new venture and the idea was quietly shelved. The mother indicated that parents of girls were especially unsupportive of the idea. She felt that parents didn't want their daughters rolling around in the mud and getting their clothes filthy.

At Oka Kindergarten, many of girls were dressed in restrictive, fussy outfits, reflecting the Japanese obsession with all things cute (Richie, 2003; Uchino, 2009). Despite this, Oka staff encouraged boys and girls equally to take part in activities involving dirt, water, or mess. However, while reactions from the Japanese focus groups showed the importance of using the body in a dynamic, whole-hearted manner in sensory play opportunities, it remained important to take the appropriate steps beforehand. Smocks are required before art sessions, gloves are donned during work in the garden, and the children change into underwear before taking part in water play (see Figure 3.2). At the centres Rachael visited, it was clear that children and staff were also expected to 'unwrap' the layers surrounding the body before engaging in vigorous play with mud, dirt, or water. The body could then be cleaned and 'rewrapped' before returning to the internal space of the classroom (Hendry, 1993).

In New Zealand, the distinction between clean and dirty bodies was blurred, with teachers happy to allow children to partake in activities that left them soiled. However, the bodies of the teachers generally remained clean throughout the day, as no expectation existed for them to participate at the same level of physicality. Although 'getting dirty' is seen as linked to childhood freedom in New Zealand,

FIGURE 3.2 Children at Oka Kindergarten wear smocks during an arts and crafts session

many of the 'activity tables' set up both inside and outside privileged children's use of fingers and hands over other parts of the body. These activity tables also support the development of gross and fine motor skills, but it is interesting to note that Rachael never saw any children sliding their faces in the slime for example.

This is in stark contrast to scenes from Japanese centres Rachael visited where children would pile mud on top of their heads or strip to their underpants to roll in water-filled sandpits. Sometimes children would engage in this kind of play spontaneously, but more usually, it occurred after being encouraged by their teachers to do so. During the Japanese video, the teacher rolls up her track-pants and tries to engage the children first in squirting each other with water pistols and later in squishing their feet into mud. "Look", she exclaims, "all the water has made the mud into a kind of hot pool. Come and try it, it feels good". The little girls watching around her are reluctant at first to squeeze the mud between their toes but eventually squat down beside their teacher and replicate her actions.

Messy Play

Akin to the joy expressed by Japanese children during bouts of body painting and water play is the pleasure drawn from 'messy play' in the New Zealand early childhood setting. Messy play is seen as an integral part of the New Zealand curriculum by many teachers who see it as an opportunity for children to integrate sensory experiences, express their creativity, develop theories about the material world, and learn new vocabulary (Bradley, 2007). At Kaimai Kindergarten, messy play was represented by a variety of different activities that changed every day. A very popular activity was the 'slime' table where children could enjoy playing with the slippery substance. The slime was a mixture of cornflour, water, and soap flakes, dyed various colours with the addition of food colouring, but most often a livid green or bilious yellow. Other instances of messy play included a table covered in shaving foam, a large shallow bucket full of watery clay, and finger-painting sessions. In most cases, however, the emphasis seemed to be on children engaging tactilely with 'mess' through their fingers and arms rather than their whole bodies.

During the New Zealand focus groups, teachers frequently identified the opportunity for 'messy play' as pedagogically unique and valuable to the country. For example, in response to a question on the purpose of early childhood education, kindergarten teachers in Nelson replied:

> To be a child.
> Yeah, I think that's what it is. You only get one opportunity [to be a child]
> To have fun, get dirty, play outside.
> Sometimes now people live in such perfect homes and there's not the opportunity for them to experience some of things that they get to do during outside play. There can be a lot of structure, especially if the parents are working, and this is a place where they can come and be free.

Just as there is nostalgia in Japan for the days when children could play naked in public spaces (see chapter two), New Zealanders reminisced about times when children were able to run wild with little fear of adults intruding. However, as discussions of 'cotton wool kids' (Jones, 2007; Dungey, 2008) become more common in the media, New Zealand early childhood centres also see their role as providing a space for play that may not occur elsewhere. This can be clearly seen in the provision of 'messy' play activities, which parents may be reluctant to provide at home due to the energy required to clean up and raised expectations for tidy homes. Encouraging children to experiment with messy or wet substances was seen as a defining mark of the early childhood experience by the New Zealand focus groups:

> I couldn't help but look at it with a Kiwi eye and think, 'Ooh, I wonder what other cultures would think of this?' The mess, particularly things like the finger painting, especially there at the end where there is a big mess but also the boy at the beginning who was mixing dye with felts.
> It's like the messy play too. The finger play was very messy and I could imagine that's not necessarily the way some places would do it.

In some places you wouldn't paint your bodies. They would just be horri-fied! The clothes were getting dirty, it wasn't just their hands, their clothes were getting quite dirty so I could imagine it would be horrifying to some people.

Many of the Japanese teachers were openly envious of this scene described ear-lier (see Figure 3.3), in which two little girls liberally daub paint over their canvases then proceed to squeeze and squirt the liquid between their fingers and up their arms. By the end of the activity, the girls have paint all over their hands, arms, on their faces, and smeared across their pale-coloured clothing. While openly admir-ing of the creative freedom on display, the Japanese teachers were concerned about parents' reactions to the girls' spoiled clothing.

Douglas (1966) argues that dirt is never an isolated event, but can only be found where there is a "systematic ordering and classification of matter, in so far as ordering involves rejecting inappropriate elements" (p. 35). For example, food may not be dirty in itself, but becomes dirty when it is splattered on clothing. In other words, pollution occurs when objects or ideas confuse or contradict cher-ished classifications. In the Japanese early childhood setting, paint is not inherently dirty, but becomes so when it is splashed across uniforms, shoes, or clean tabletops. For the Japanese child, interacting with paint means one must first change into an art smock, which has usually been sewn by mother for this very purpose (Allison, 1996). Only once all the children are appropriately dressed and the paint laid-out on the table does the painting activity begin.

FIGURE 3.3 Girls at Kaimai Kindergarten enjoy a finger-painting session

Art sessions are not seen as a time to allow the wild disorder of free play to creep in. Children come to internalise social values by embodying them through their clothing (Turner, 2008). At Oka Kindergarten, neat, unblemished clothing reflects a child's understanding of Japanese constructions of dirt and displays self-management and independence skills. The well-turned out classes at Oka also reflect a collective pride in the aesthetic. The child that fails to put on his or her art smock during a painting session, or pack a change of clothes for water play, has neglected to internalise these ideals. While Japanese teachers may embrace the notion of using the whole body in play, there are clear expectations around the appropriate clothing required for potentially dirty situations.

The Body as a Counterpoint to Modern Lifestyles

Foucault (1973, p. 189) argues that radical changes in medical discourse occurred towards the end of the eighteen century, when "the being of the disease" disappeared. With the development of clinical medicine, bodies were transformed into objects. A concern with body hygiene, longevity, and the rearing of vigorous children emerged (Foucault, 1981), which positioned dirt as dangerous to health (Elias, 2000). Today, these same medical discourses suggest that some exposure to dirt is actually beneficial to children. This is known as the hygiene hypothesis (Czeresnia, 2005). The focus on messy, embodied play can be seen as both a response to new constructions of dirt, and to provide an adult-sanctioned space for resistance to dominant notions of order and cleanliness (Foucault, 1973).

While engaging the body in sensory play experiences is seen as important in both the New Zealand and Japan early childhood contexts, comments about Rachael's edited videos revealed variations in the way in which the body is manipulated, which parts of the body is used, and whose body takes part. Both New Zealand and Japanese teachers expressed the very real need for children to use their bodies as a counterpoint to perceived restricted, (sub)urban lifestyles. The degree to which the teachers' bodies participated in these acts of play was more noticeable in the Japanese context and often contrary to stereotypes that the New Zealand teachers had formed prior to seeing the video. A Wellington teacher tried to explain how the young, playful Japanese teachers did not initially strike her as qualified professionals:

> I made an assumption after seeing some of the teachers playing with the children during the free play. In the beginning, I assumed they were assistants. I'm not sure if it was because of the aprons or because they seemed quite young or perhaps because I had an assumption about what Japanese teachers would be like and they didn't meet it so perhaps that was a role that I put on them because of my [cultural perspective]. I would have expected it to be a lot more rigid and the teachers to be more "teacher-like" and less

like what we consider ECE teachers to be like . . . playing along with the children and that sort of thing. Perhaps I assumed that that was a lesser job that they would hand off to assistants. I don't know why.

It is revealing that this teacher considered that enthusiastic play with children might be assigned a lower value in the Japanese setting than more academic pursuits and therefore likely to be undertaken by untrained staff members. Or does this thinking reveal more about New Zealand attitudes to the early childhood teacher's role? In their study of New Zealand early childhood settings, White et al. (2009, p. 46) describe the adult in play more as a "guardian" of the child rather than an active participant. While teachers might facilitate play through the provision of materials and assist in extending play experiences, children's agency is given priority. However, for the New Zealand viewers, the most striking observation was not the use of the body during play, but the way in which Japanese children's bodies were ordered within the institutional framework.

Body Techniques

Mauss (1936/1973, p. 75) defined techniques as actions that are "effective and traditional" and viewed the body as at the locus of culture. The theories of Mauss were influential in the work of Bourdieu (1977) who developed the notions of habitus and the body hexis. To understand how certain experiences become embodied as distinctly Japanese, it is useful to turn to Bourdieu's (1977) thoughts on the body hexis. Bourdieu suggests that language and emotions are socially structured expressions of the body. Through these body techniques emotions can become embodied without being attributed solely to either natural or social influences. Bourdieu defines body hexis as "a set of body techniques or postures that are learned habits or deeply ingrained dispositions that both reflect and reproduce the social relations that surround and constitute them" (Abu-Lughod & Lutz, 1990, p. 12).

Ben-Ari (1997) suggests that it is in the early childhood setting that Japanese children first learn to embody thoughts and feelings through the practice of attending to the bodies of others. Over time, these practices become natural and the children begin to share a set of bodily dispositions, which Ben-Ari (1997, p. 73) sees as vital for "learning to group". To illustrate this concept, Ben-Ari gives the examples of children's mirrored sitting postures, collective use of voice in greetings and songs, the control of the body needed to quickly incorporate another child into a line, and the universally understood body postures adopted when a child wishes to enter the play of others. As Mauss (1936/1973) points out, "in group life as a whole, there is a kind of education of movements in close order" (p. 86). These body techniques become a 'natural' part of the Japanese early childhood landscape as encapsulated by the comments of a Nara lecturer upon viewing the video of Oka Kindergarten in Hokkaido: "Yes, it looks like a Japanese kindergarten. Everyone is giving greetings, they are doing things at the right time, bowing and doing what they are expected".

Yet for the Kaimai Kindergarten teachers, the way in which the body is arranged and ordered within Oka Kindergarten seemed incomprehensible. Their way of making sense of this scene was to revert to their own interpretations of Japanese culture:

> Looking at the whole thing, it's regimenting, they look like little robots to me. They are doing what they are told. They are one after another in lines and they just remind me of little robots. It's just yes ma'am, no ma'am, three bags full, you know.
>
> But I guess if you saw the adults getting on the subway, they would be the same wouldn't they?
>
> Well, that's right. That's what we see as part of their culture. That's what we see that they are like.

Douglas (1970/1996) argues that the "the physical experience of the body, always modified by the social categories through which it is known, sustains a particular view of society" (p. 69). While New Zealand viewers might see these scenes as symbolic of a controlling regime, both scholars and Japanese teachers argue that these patterns of behaviour reflect maturity and a growing sense of interdependence, which is an important goal for Japanese children in the early childhood environment. An explicitly stated aim for children attending kinder-garten is to socialise them to life in the group (*shūdan*) environment where the building of strong, cooperative groups is vital. In contrast to many Western cul-tures, which view independence as the norm (Garbarino & Abramowitz, 1992; Higgins, 2000), Japanese society promotes appropriate dependence as an essential skill for children to develop (Doi, 1973). Child-rearing practices, parental involve-ment, and the education system advocate appropriate dependency in order to achieve a compliant and cooperative (*sunao*) child. The kind of ordering of the body described above is indicative of a child becoming *sunao,* but it does not mean an abandonment of one's autonomy, as it might in the West. Instead, it demon-strates an understanding of cooperating with others as a means of enhancing the self (LeVine & White, 2003).

In contrast, writing about the New Zealand early childhood context, San-som (2007, p. 14) argues that requiring the body to be kept still or to conform to acceptable group behaviour places it "in a precarious position because it becomes either objectified or null and void". The kind of ordering of the body described above in the Japanese context was viewed negatively by the majority of New Zealand viewers. However, Sansom (2007) suggests that New Zealand early childhood settings equally endeavour to discipline, control, and repress chil-dren's bodies. Examples of these kinds of shaping mechanisms include placing babies in prams or walkers, conducting physical education drills with toddlers, and instructing children to sit quietly and listen. Play equipment and containers provided in the name of safety often work, in reality, to deny a child's body sensory experiences and physical contact with other children or adults. Sansom (2007) has called for a more embodied interpretation of the early childhood curriculum, arguing that children learn to participate and understand relationships primarily through their bodies. Instead, children are invariably subjected to modes of bodily control, which deny sensory pleasure and self-expression. Despite criticism such as Sansom's, New Zealand teachers overwhelmingly viewed their own practice as the antithesis of the ordered 'robots' they saw on the Japanese video. In reality, both centres employ systems to control children's bodies at a time and place staff see as culturally appropriate (Foucault, 1975/1995).

The Cultural Meanings of Touch

As discussed in the previous chapter, the issue of touch remains problematic in a New Zealand context. Farquhar (2001) suggests that in the New Zealand early childhood setting, any form of touch can potentially be seen as abusive regardless of a child's needs. Regrettably, for many of the teachers interviewed for this study, the subjugation of touch in their centres has become an example of the "progressive individualization" of the body and the self—"the walls constructed between our bodies and those of others" (Leavitt & Power, 1997, p. 65).

However, within the cultural discourse of 'skinship' (Matsuda, 1973), touch in a Japanese early childhood centre is not only seen as desirable but necessary for a child's development. The close body-to-body contact, the transfer of body heat, and the intimate nature of caresses exchanged between teacher and child is called *soine* (Ben-Ari, 1997). This term refers to the Chinese *kanji* for river, which depicts three lines representing two parents lying either side of a child. Within the early childhood context, examples of this kind of "embodied knowledge" (Bresler, 2004, p. 127) or "embodied experience" (Abu-Lughod & Lutz, 1990, p. 12) can be seen in the overnight sleepover (*otomarikai*) and naptime (*ohirune*), which are discussed below.

At Oka Kindergarten, an important event for the oldest children (*nen chō san*) is the sleepover night (*otomarikai*), which occurs during their last year. This special event generally takes place on a Friday afternoon, when the younger children have left for the day. Following time for play and games, the teachers and children cooperate together to prepare the evening meal. In contrast to New Zealand policies relating to overnight stays for school students, a ratio of parents are not required to either attend or assist during the event. After washing the dinner dishes, there is free play-time before preparations begin for the communal sleeping arrangements. Towards 9pm, the teachers instruct the children to begin pulling out their *futons*. Everyone works to spread the bedding in the centre of the hall before lying down together and chatting in pyjamas. The atmosphere is one of cosy familiarity as the group gradually drift off to sleep, a replica of the scene that occurs at a lakeside hotel in the spring when the kindergarten staff spend the night together during their annual trip away.

While there is no naptime (*ohirune*) at the kindergarten, it is common for all children to have a sleep after lunch at childcare centres. Even the youngest children learn how to work with their peers to lay out their *futons* and spread their towels over the sleeping space in the classroom. After the *futons* have been pushed together, and the children have changed into their pyjamas and brushed their teeth, a teacher will pull the curtains as the soothing sounds of classical music fill the air. Other teachers move quietly amongst the children, stopping to stroke the hair of those who remain restless. It is common to see teachers lying down between the children's small bodies, gently patting their backs and softly humming a lullaby. Even in large centres where there may be up to seventy children sleeping in the same room, everyone has nodded off within twenty or thirty minutes (see Figure 3.4). Sometimes teachers also take the chance to enjoy a short nap, which helps children to feel safe and relaxed as well as providing staff with a much-needed respite.

Ben-Ari (1997, p. 51) argues that the accumulated spells of co-sleeping with one's peer group as a child leads to the adult Japanese embodying "the experience of grouping in an intimate manner". The related experiences of co-bathing, and as an adult, drinking and eating parties, form 'key scenarios' (Ortner, 1973) which are found in a variety of contexts within the Japanese culture. While it may seem that co-sleeping replicates the home environment, Ben-Ari (1997)

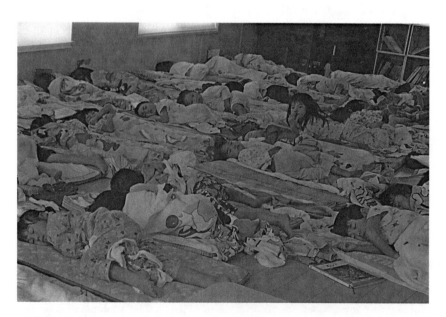

FIGURE 3.4 Children at a Japanese childcare centre settle down for naptime

suggests instead that this shared physical experience helps children to internalise the distinctions between the family and the outside world. Naptime is one way by which the warmth and familiarity of the family dyad is transferred to the wider peer group. Practices such as naptime function to instil particular traits and qualities connected with 'being Japanese'.

The relevance of skinship to regular practices such as naptime and the sleepover, and the part the body plays in these rituals are clear to see. However, other practices involving the bodies of children in the Japanese early childhood setting are less explicit. During a focus group session in Osaka, a mother explained why the principal at her children's kindergarten had chosen to cancel the centre's bus service:

> At my children's kindergarten, which is a public kindergarten, skinship between parents and children is considered very important and for this reason there is no kindergarten bus service. The staff ask that parents walk with their children to kindergarten each morning even if they live far away. Walking in the sun the children can use their legs, their whole bodies while talking with their mothers. They also gain awareness of dangers on the road and traffic safety procedures. The kindergarten staff believe that walking back and forth from home to kindergarten each day provides an opportunity for children to engage in deep conversation with their mothers and for both of them to slow down in their daily life. When my child first entered this kindergarten the principal explained to me how important this is but I wondered how I could manage it as I was very busy with my children and I was always rushing. But I have come to realise how valuable it is to slow down and take this time with my children, to hold their hand and walk with them each day and experience that skinship. It is so important to make that time. Otherwise children will think that mothers are too busy for them, and they will feel lonely instead of enjoying the warmth of skinship.

By taking the approach that he did, the principal at this kindergarten had addressed a number of social and political ideologies by using the child's body as a catalyst. Japanese mothers are under enormous pressure to meet the expectations placed on them by the education system (Allison, 1996; Imamura, 1987). Although this mother stated that she was busy, she eventually embraced the ideology of the good wife/wise mother (*ryōsai kenbō*) construct (Fujita, 1989; Uno, 1993) through the physical experience of walking each day with her child. Other ideologies raised in this monologue are the notions of perseverance (*gambaru*) as children are required to walk long distances if they live far from the kindergarten; the idea of returning to a less hurried life which has shades of the nostalgia (*furusato*) ideology discussed in the previous chapter (Robertson, 1988) and the references to nature as vital to a child's health and well-being. The benefits of children walking to gain an awareness of traffic safety has also been well documented in New Zealand, but in that case, the popularity of 'walking school buses' has been equally driven by a desire to reduce road congestion (Kingham & Ussher, 2007) and childhood obesity. In contrast, the Japanese case described above is based on a desire to promote close bodily contact between parent and child, which is clearly articulated by the mother as skinship.

The Body as a Medium of Communication

While the body can be seen as a medium for developing deeper emotional relationships as described above, it is also used frequently in the Japanese context as a means of communication. The high levels of bodily contact apparent in Japanese child-rearing methods have been described by scholars who contrast this with a preference for verbal communication in Western countries (Hendry, 1986). In the Japanese early childhood setting too, the body can display a number of emotions and directives through subtle movements that are quickly understood by those around. In one of the Japanese scenes, the camera follows the children as they come running from all across the kindergarten to line up outside for morning assembly. Slowly, long lines form in front of the teacher's podium, each one defining not only a class, but the height of the children from shortest to tallest.

One of these children, Kiharu, is reluctant to take his place in line, but he is gently buffeted into position by the others around him. While his classmates all wear the coloured caps, which identify them as members of the same group, Kiharu refuses to put his hat on. As the assembly begins, he fidgets, pokes the children to the front and rear of him and begins to break ranks. The teacher comes across and puts his cap back on his head several times, before using her body to block his movements. As Kiharu continues to try and escape, the teacher squats down beside him and holds his hands close to his sides. Throughout it all, she silently maintains her gaze on the teacher giving the morning speech on the podium at the front (see Figure 3.5).

In Wellington, a New Zealand teacher was surprised by how effective this approach was:

> Kiharu was encouraged quietly by the teacher to hop in line. She physically stayed with him and encouraged him, by being there, to stay in his place. I think in New Zealand there's often not a lot of [physical contact]. I think we can go back to that verbal communication stuff that we talked about in the video. If you are doing mat time, and a child is not conforming, you will actually just stop what you are doing and say, "Liam, can you sit down. Liam, you need to sit down". Another teacher will get involved, and it will be "Liam, sit down", and if he's still not sitting down then physically being there is often the last resort. "Oh well, then I'll just sit with you and then you'll have to sit here!" It's all done quite differently but it was done very peacefully in [the Japanese video], and it was the first step rather than the

FIGURE 3.5 The teacher uses her body to control Kiharu at assembly

nag, nag, nag and then I'll be with you. They recognise that that's the way to do it and she managed to do it. She's still looking after thirty-three children, but the others knew well enough what they needed to do that she could spend that extra time with that one child and focus on him, which I thought was really neat.

Using non-verbal means of communication as the first method of disciplining a child was viewed as rather unusual by the New Zealand teachers, who admitted that their first response would probably be to speak to the child. The teachers' comments are in line with cross-cultural studies which have shown that while Western societies see engaging children in conversation as vital for developing verbal competency, parents in other parts of the world see it as much less important than other skills (Lancy, 2008). Employing the body and non-verbal cues to guide children was seen as an interesting alternative by some New Zealand viewers, although it is important to remember that Japanese children are socialised into understanding these prompts through regular routines and repetition (Peak, 1991):

I don't think [the teacher] said anything throughout that whole time. I couldn't really tell but it wasn't a verbal thing. In New Zealand I don't know why you would have children lined up, maybe in an evacuation or something like that when you would be in a situation outside, you would still have teachers directing orders. You know, "can you sit over there", "you need to stay with the others", "excuse me, you need to go and do this". It wouldn't be so gently done, which I think is interesting, and I really like the way that was done. I think there is something to be learnt from it.

Tobin (2004) has argued that the emphasis on verbal communication in American early childhood education is to some extent a reaction to the anxiety surrounding children's bodies. To illustrate his point, he cites the phrase 'use your words', which is commonly heard in American centres. The phrase is a feature of New Zealand centres too, yet it cannot be translated into Japanese. While Tobin does not contest the aim of early childhood education to promote verbal competency, he suggests that this goal comes at the cost of subjugating the body. Remaining unstated, yet implicitly clear is the clause that follows: 'use your words *and not your body*'. Placing emphasis on children's verbal expression inevitably results in the suppression of children's bodily expression of feeling. Farquhar and Fleer (2007) point out that the New Zealand education system expects children to be competent in communicating when entering early childhood education. In line with American ideology, the dominant mode of communication is verbal, rather than non-verbal, which may contrast with the practices of families from other cultures. As a result, Farquhar and Fleer claim that teachers place little emphasis in seeking out or communicating through non-verbal interactions in New Zealand early childhood centres.

The Physical Self

Both Ben-Ari (1997) and Walsh (2004) have written about the centrality of the body to the Japanese early childhood experience. Walsh draws on the writings of Harada and Saito (1997) who argue that vigorous physical play is the key to intellectual development. With links to risk discourses, which will be discussed in the next chapter, Walsh (2004) was astonished by the daring antics of the Japanese children he observed, such as running across the top of precarious metal swinging frames, perching on the apex of high structures and climbing concrete walls. He also observed his own American-raised children taking more risks and becoming more physically adept during their time in Japanese educational settings. It appears that these activities are not seen as dangerous in a Japanese context as children are given plenty of opportunities to develop 'a physical self' from an early age, in contrast to the 'risk anxiety' thinking that dominates playgrounds in countries like New Zealand, England, and the United States (Freeman & Tranter, 2011).

Mauss (1936/1973) has argued that the human body must be trained to undertake basic activities such as walking, sitting, or dancing. Children learn to master these body techniques in order to function effectively in their own cultural context. In the case of the Japanese early childhood setting, children are given a great deal of freedom and time to practice and perfect complicated body techniques in the playground. While the act of running across the top of climbing frames may become 'natural' for Japanese children, it is not a body technique that is common in New Zealand kindergartens.

Embodying gambaru *in the Japanese Context*

Japanese notions of the child as a physical self not only embrace risk to the body, they support pushing the boundaries in terms of perseverance or *gambaru*. Much has been written about *gambaru* as a key characteristic of the Japanese which is internalised through a series of bodily and behavioural practices (Ben-Ari, 1997; Singleton, 1989; White, 1987). *Gambaru* is the sum of several cultural concepts drawn from the notion of *seishin kyōiku* (spiritual education) including patience (*gaman*), hardship (*kurō*), self-control (*enryo*), and endurance (*shinbō*). Rohlen (1974) has discussed the phenomenon of *seishin kyōiku* in detail, based on his experience as a participant in a company training programme. The programme took three months to complete and consisted of training sessions lasting up to sixteen hours per day, six days per week.

An important feature of the programme was a twenty-five mile endurance walk which was carefully designed to test not only the body but the spiritual strength of the participants. Rohlen (1974) links *seishin kyōiku* with various characteristics associated with Japanese-style education; non-verbal forms of knowledge and behaviour are favoured over oral expression, hardships are considered opportunities to learn rather than barriers and self-reflection is emphasised as the means to social reform. Conformity to the group is viewed as a sign of both self-discipline and unity. The suppression of selfish urges is seen as sophisticated, and competition is structured between groups to ensure cohesion and without losing sight of individuals' internal struggles. Teachers in a *seishin* environment are not necessarily explicit about outcomes or methods but allow their students to learn directly from their experiences.

The influence of *seishin* thinking could be seen at the Japanese kindergarten where Rachael conducted fieldwork, notably in approaches to the body. For example, a coveted annual award was the certificate or prize that was given to the child in each class who had never missed a single day of the academic year. In the frigid mid-winter, this sometimes translated to sick, feverish children arriving at the centre with their mothers who would insist that their child begged to attend kindergarten. The child's temperature would be checked, and if it was above a certain threshold, the mother might be told to take the reluctant child home. In other cases, the illness was relatively mild, and the child would be rewarded by the teacher for making the effort to come to kindergarten despite their discomfort. The child who won the annual prize would inevitably be paraded in front of their classmates as an example of a particularly healthy body and mind.

The kindergarten sports day (*undōkai*) also provides an opportunity for children to show how they have absorbed the lessons of *seishin* through displays of perseverance (*gambaru*). Intensive practice for the Oka Kindergarten sports day begins weeks in advance of the event with children spending hours out in the hot sun to hone marching routines, master ball skills, and jog around the track. On wet days, placards and posters are prepared. There are even cheering practices scheduled for the whole kindergarten to ensure the clapping and calls of *gambatte* (go for it!) are sufficiently jovial. As perseverance is more highly regarded than natural ability (Singleton, 1991), children are urged by teachers and parents to finish their events despite any setbacks such as falling over or getting injured. Children do not compete as individuals, but as part of their class, and events are organised to reflect this structure.

In Japanese early childhood centres that Holloway (2000) visited, physical experiences were deliberately arranged to prove challenging for children. These included marathons, obstacle courses and, in one case, a three-day field trip that required children to climb mountains and cross rivers. Staff were explicit about the goal of such excursions: to expose children to physical hardship (*kurō*). Experiencing hardship, in various forms, is seen as a vital means "of moving from the self-centredness of childhood to the social responsibility of adulthood" (Holloway, 2000, p. 70). Official sports days and overnight trips do not feature on the calendar of most New Zealand early childhood settings, but children at Kaimai Kindergarten did participate in races at the annual school sports day held on the field next door. In contrast to the intensity of the Japanese sports day, these races were of a very relaxed manner and over in a matter of minutes.

In Japan, it is not just the sports day, which showcases the link between perseverance and children's bodies. Ben-Ari (1997) argues that the daily techniques for controlling the body, which can be observed throughout Japanese early childhood settings are a means of internalising the *gambaru* concept. While viewing the Japanese video, the New Zealand teachers remarked both on the length of the morning assembly and the fact that the children were required to stand throughout. One Kaimai teacher commented, "I can't believe the kids are all standing. I can't even stand for fifteen minutes". As Ben-Ari explains, both sitting and standing for long periods of time requires children to learn to control their bodies, to suppress both physical urges and the accompanying discomfort that comes with a static position. In the Hokkaido kindergarten, the *okāsan suwari* (mother sitting) posture was most commonly used for listening to teachers' instructions, taking turns, or waiting in the classroom. In New Zealand, this posture would be referred to as 'sitting on one's knees'. In the playground or during outdoor sports events, children often squat (*shagamu*). For visitors to Japan, both the 'mother sitting' and the squat position are difficult to maintain for any length of time without resorting to constant rearranging of the limbs. For the Japanese child, learning to control one's body is not only crucial for development of the self, but it is also necessary to successfully exist within the group.

Reflections on Embodying the Curriculum

This chapter has discussed some of the ways in which cultural assumptions about the body are represented in the curricula and structures of the two early childhood settings where fieldwork was conducted. In both New Zealand and Japan, the body is viewed by teachers as a key means of exploring sensory play opportunities and developing children's motor skills, confidence, and learning. In New Zealand, children are seen as competent and active learners who are encouraged to engage with their environment and others around them. Teachers take responsibility for providing materials and experiences that will challenge and interest children, but they are less active participants in play than the Japanese teachers who see their role as energetic group members.

Messy play was mentioned by several New Zealand teachers as a uniquely Kiwi feature of the early childhood scene. With links to freedom and creativity, messy play is seen as an enjoyable way for children to use their sense of touch while exploring scientific concepts such as texture, volume, and movement. However, in the early childhood settings Rachael visited, this activity is most often undertaken by children themselves or with a teacher acting in a supervisory role. In spaces such as the sandpit, children were enthusiastic about using their whole body to test their own working theories about things such as sand, water, construction, and gravity. The resulting wet clothing or dirty bodies are dealt with cheerfully by teachers, whose own bodies and clothing remain clean during these sessions.

At the Japanese field site, the teachers have similar aims for children to explore and engage with nature through sensory play opportunities. But whereas this kind of play in the New Zealand centre is often spontaneous and instigated by the children (with support from the teachers), the Japanese children needed to be coaxed into participating in some of the more 'messy' outdoor play activities. Embracing dirt and totally embodied play is seen by teachers as one way of counteracting the limits of modern Japanese society. The Japanese kindergarten teachers not only often model play within this belief in mind, but they commit their whole selves to energetic participation. Appropriate clothing is usually donned beforehand by all members of the group, and changed again after the activity has finished. In Japanese contexts, the concepts of cleanliness and pollution are learnt from an early age (Hendry, 1986) and have a major influence on routines in early childhood settings. Chapter six explores the issue of dirt within the wider context of pollution, both in a tangible and spiritual sense.

Mauss (1936/1973) has shown how different cultures have different body techniques. In order to become a fully functioning member of society, children need to become proficient in these techniques. While scenes of Japanese children simultaneously bowing, chanting, and lining up in an orderly manner were interpreted as disempowering by the New Zealand teachers, Japanese viewers explained that these repetitive body techniques are an essential part of the early childhood experience. Through daily routines, such as the morning greeting, and special events like the sleepover night, children learn to function as a part of a group. This is regarded as an essential skill as they move towards adulthood. In New Zealand, neither regular routines involving the body nor close physical contact are major parts of the early childhood landscape.[1] In discussions concerning the body, teachers interviewed placed more emphasis on promoting health and providing opportunities for children to physically challenge themselves within a supportive, free environment.

The New Zealand curriculum, *Te Whāriki* (Ministry of Education, 1996), makes it clear that early childhood settings should offer children "an environment where they gain confidence in and control of their bodies" (p. 86). The same expectation exists in Japan (Ministry of Education, Science, Sports, and Culture, 2001) where participation in energetic outdoor play is required of all members of the kindergarten, and key concepts such as *gambaru* (perseverance) are taught to children through physical endurance training. However, like scholars before her (Ben-Ari, 1997; Walsh, 2004), Rachael noticed a difference in the levels of children's physicality, which seemed more pronounced at the Japanese kindergarten during periods of free play. Children at the Japanese centre were encouraged to test the limits of their bodies in challenging, risky play, and physical skirmishes were not unusual. In comparison, children at the New Zealand centre engaged in fewer boisterous altercations and were mindful of safety regulations when using play equipment.

Yet New Zealand teachers in focus groups around the country were struck by the rambunctious nature of the New Zealand children in the video. Staff at the centre were described as taking a "very liberal approach" to children's physical behaviour, with some groups labelling it as "aggressive", "very rough", and "too rough and tumble". While the Japanese teachers were intrigued by the high levels of freedom New Zealand children enjoyed, they did not comment on issues of physicality. In line with their own cultural beliefs about the appropriateness of *genki* (energetic) children, the vigorous behaviour of the New Zealand children did not strike them as either unusual or significant. Differing approaches to bodily risk could also be seen in the playground, with children at the Japanese centre free to climb trees and dangle from precariously high equipment, while New Zealand children were banned from scaling heights yet engaged in carpentry with hammers and saws. The following chapter examines these contrasting constructions of risky behaviour.

Note

1 There are, of course, differences according to age as centres which care for toddlers invariably require practices such as naptime and nappy changing, but this study focuses on the experience of four-year-olds at a New Zealand centre. In Māori culture too, ideas about bodily contact differ from the dominant European narrative. However, the pervasive anxiety associated with the risk of touching children has meant that even in some *kōhanga reo* traditional practices such as communal sleeping have been discontinued (Hohepa & Tangaere, 2001).

References

Abu-Lughod, L., & Lutz, C. A. (1990). Introduction: Emotion, discourse, and the politics of everyday life. In C. A. Lutz & L. Abu-Lughod (Eds.), *Language and the power of emotion* (pp. 1–23). Cambridge, UK: Cambridge University Press.

Allison, A. (1996). Producing mothers. In A. E. Imamura (Ed.), *Re-imaging Japanese women* (pp. 135–155). Berkeley: University of California Press.

Ben-Ari, E. (1997). *Body projects in Japanese childcare: Culture, organization and emotions in a preschool.* Richmond, UK: Curzon Press.

Bourdieu, P. (1977). *Outline of a theory of practice.* Cambridge, UK: Cambridge University Press.

Bradley, J. (2007). Messy play: The extraordinariness of ordinary mess. *Playcentre Journal,* (130), 18–19.

Bresler, L. (2004). Dancing the curriculum: Exploring the body and movement in elementary schools. In L. Bresler (Ed.), *Knowing bodies, knowing minds: Towards embodied teaching and learning* (pp. 127–151). Dordrecht, The Netherlands: Kluwer Academic.

Carr, M. (2001). *Assessment in early childhood settings: Learning stories.* London, UK: Paul Chapman.

Czeresnia, D. (2005). The hygiene hypothesis and transformations in etiological knowledge: From causal ontology to ontogenesis of the body. *Cad. Saude Publica, 21*(24), 1168–1176.

Doi, T. (1973). *The anatomy of dependence.* Tokyo, Japan: Kodansha.

Douglas, M. (1966). *Purity and danger: An analysis of concepts of pollution and taboo.* Harmondsworth, UK: Penguin Books.

Douglas, M. (1970/1996). *Natural symbols: Explorations in cosmology.* London, UK: Routledge.

Dungey, K. (2008, September 13). Cotton wool kids. *Otago Daily Times,* pp. 41–44.

Elias, N. (2000). *The civilizing process: Sociogenetic and psychogentic investigations.* Oxford, UK: Blackwell.

Farquhar, S. E. (2001). Moral panic in New Zealand: Teachers touching children. In A. James (Ed.), *Touchy subject: Teachers touching children* (pp. 87–98). Dunedin, New Zealand: University of Otago Press.

Farquhar, S., & Fleer, M. (2007). Developmental colonisation of early childhood education in Aotearoa/New Zealand and Australia. In L. Keesing-Styles & H. Hedges (Eds.), *Theorising early childhood practice: Emerging dialogues* (pp. 27–49). Castle Hill, NSW, Australia: Pademelon Press.

Fleer, M. (1992). From Piaget to Vygotsky: Moving into a new era of early childhood education. In B. Lambert (Ed.), *Changing faces: The early childhood profession in Australia* (pp. 134–149). Canberra, Australia: Australian Early Childhood Association.

Foucault, M. (1973). *The birth of the clinic.* New York, NY: Pantheon Books.

Foucault, M. (1975/1995). *Discipline and punish: The birth of the prison* (A. Sheridan, Trans.). New York, NY: Vintage Books.

Foucault, M. (1981). *The history of sexuality, Volume 1: An introduction.* Harmondsworth, UK: Penguin.

Freeman, C., & Tranter, P. (2011). *Children and their urban environment: Changing worlds.* London, UK: Earthscan.

Fujita, M. (1989). 'It's all mother's fault': Childcare and socialization of working mothers in Japan. *Journal of Japanese Studies, 15*(1), 67–92.

Fujita, M., & Sano, T. (1988). Children in American and Japanese day-care centres: Ethnography and reflective cross-cultural interviewing. In H. T. Trueba & C. Delgado-Gaitan (Eds.), *School and society: Learning content through culture* (pp. 73–97). New York, NY: Praeger.

Garbarino, J., & Abramowitz, R. H. (1992). Sociocultural risk and opportunity. In J. Garbarino (Ed.), *Children and families in the social environment* (2nd ed., pp. 35–70). New York, NY: Aldine de Gruyter.

Harada, S., & Saito, T. (1997). Ashi karano kenkou zukuri: Okaasan to komodo no tameno kenkou zukuri. Tokyo: Chuou Houki.

Hendry, J. (1986). *Becoming Japanese: The world of the pre-school child.* Honolulu: University of Hawaii Press.

Hendry, J. (1993). *Wrapping culture: Politeness, presentation, and power in Japan and other societies*. Oxford, UK: Oxford University Press.

Higgins, J. (2000). Independence as a goal of education. In L. Bird & W. Drewery (Eds.), *Human development in Aotearoa: A journey through life* (pp. 134–135). Sydney, Australia: McGraw Hill.

Hohepa, M., & Tangaere, A. R. (2001). Māori educational settings and touch. In A. Jones (Ed.), *Touchy subject: Teachers touching children* (pp. 50–60). Dunedin, New Zealand: University of Otago Press.

Holloway, S. D. (2000). Accentuating the negative: Views of preschool staff about mothers in Japan. *Early Education and Development, 11*(5), 617–632.

Imamura, A. E. (1987). *Urban Japanese housewives: At home and in the community*. Honolulu: University of Hawaii Press.

Jones, D. (2007). *Cotton wool kids: Releasing the potential for children to take risks and innovate*. Coventry, UK: HTI.

Kingham, S., & Ussher, S. (2007). An assessment of the benefits of the walking school bus in Christchurch, New Zealand. *Transportation Research Part A: Policy and Practice, 41*(7), 502–510.

Lancy, D. F. (2008). *The anthropology of childhood: Cherubs, chattel, changelings*. Cambridge, UK: Cambridge University Press.

Leavitt, R. L., & Power, M. B. (1997). Civilizing bodies: Children in day care. In J. Tobin (Ed.), *Making a place for pleasure in early childhood education* (pp. 39–75). New Haven, CT: Yale University Press.

LeVine, R., & White, M. (2003). Educational mobilization: The case of Japan. In R. LeVine (Ed.), *Childhood socialization: Comparative studies of parenting, learning and educational change* (pp. 159–186). Hong Kong: The University of Hong Kong, Comparative Education Research Centre.

Lewis, C. C. (1995). *Educating hearts and minds: Reflections of Japanese preschool and elementary education*. Cambridge, UK: University of Cambridge.

Matsuda, M. (1973). *Nihonshiki ikujiho [The Japanese way of child-rearing]*. Tokyo, Japan: Kodansha.

Mauss, M. (1936/1973). Techniques of the body. *Economy and Society, 2,* 70–88.

Ministry of Education. (1996). *Te Whāriki: He Whāriki Mātauranga mō ngā Mokopuna o Aotearoa. New Zealand early childhood curriculum*. Wellington, New Zealand: Learning Media.

Ministry of Education, Science, Sports, and Culture. (2001, April). *National curriculum standards for kindergartens*. Retrieved from www.ibe.unesco.org/curricula/japan/ja_ecefw_1998_eng.pdf

Mori, M., Nezu, A., Samizo, C., Naito, T., & Ishizuka, M. (2009). The meaning of play and learning for 0–3-year-old children in Japan. In I. Pramling-Samuelsson & M. Fleer (Eds.), *Play and learning in early childhood settings: International perspectives* (pp. 117–134). New York, NY: Springer.

Mutch, C. (2003). One context, two outcomes: A comparison of Te Whāriki and the New Zealand Curriculum Framework. In J. Nuttall (Ed.), *Weaving Te Whāriki: Aotearoa New Zealand's early childhood curriculum document in theory and practice* (pp. 111–129). Wellington, New Zealand: New Zealand Council for Educational Research.

Ortner, S. B. (1973). On key symbols. *American Anthropologist, 75,* 1338–1346.

Peak, L. (1991). *Learning to go to school in Japan: The transition from home to preschool life*. Berkeley: University of California Press.

Phelan, A. M. (1997). Classroom management and the erasure of teacher desire. In J. Tobin (Ed.), *Making a place for pleasure in early childhood education* (pp. 76–100). New Haven, CT: Yale University Press.

Piper, H., & Stronach, I. (2008). *Don't touch!: The educational story of a panic*. Abingdon, UK: Routledge.

Richie, D. (2003). *The image factory: Fads and fashions in Japan*. London, UK: Reaktion.

Robertson, J. (1988). Furusato Japan: The culture and politics of nostalgia. *Politics, Culture and Society, 1,* 494–518.

Rohlen, T. P. (1974). Seishin kyoiku in a Japanese bank: A description of methods and consideration of some underlying concepts. In G. D. Spindler (Ed.), *Education and cultural process: Toward an anthropology of education* (pp. 219–229). New York, NY: Holt, Rinehart and Winston.

Sansom, A. (2007). Is the body an endangered species? Reconceptualizing the body in early childhood education. *The First Years: Ngā Tau Tuatahi: New Zealand Journal of Infant and Toddler Education, 9*(2), 14–17.

Singleton, J. (1989). Gambaru: A Japanese cultural theory of learning. In J. J. Shields (Ed.), *Japanese schooling* (pp. 8–15). Philadelphia, PA: Penn State University.

Singleton, J. (1991). The spirit of gambaru. In B. Finkelstein, A. E. Imamura & J. J. Tobin (Eds.), *Transcending stereotypes: Discovering Japanese culture and education* (pp. 119–125). Yarmouth, Maine: Intercultural Press.

Smith, A. B., & May, H. (2006). Early childhood care and education in Aotearoa-New Zealand. In E. Melhuish & K. Petrogiannis (Eds.), *Early childhood care and education: International perspectives* (pp. 95–114). London, UK: Routledge.

Terreni, L. (2003). Parents' experiences of different pedagogies. *The First Years Journal. Ngā Tau Tuatahi. New Zealand Journal of Infant and Toddler Education, 5*(1), 28–31.

Tobin, J. (2004). The disappearance of the body in early childhood education. In L. Bresler (Ed.), *Knowing bodies, knowing minds: Towards embodied teaching and learning* (pp. 111–125). Dordrecht, The Netherlands: Kluwer Academic.

Tobin, J. J., Wu, D. Y. H., & Davidson, D. H. (1989). *Preschool in three cultures: Japan, China and the United States.* New Haven, CT: Yale University Press.

Turner, B. S. (2008). *The body and society: Explorations in social theory* (3rd ed.). Los Angeles, CA: Sage.

Uchino, T. (2009). *Crucible bodies: A postwar Japanese performance from Brecht to the new millenium.* London, UK: Seagull Books.

Uno, K. (1993). The death of "good wife, wise mother"? In A. Gordon (Ed.), *Postwar Japan as history* (pp. 293–322). Berkeley: University of California Press.

Walsh, D. J. (2004). Frog boy and the American monkey: The body in Japanese early schooling. In L. Bresler (Ed.), *Knowing bodies, moving minds: Towards embodied teaching and learning* (pp. 97–109). Dordrecht, The Netherlands: Kluwer Academic.

White, M. (1987). *The Japanese educational challenge: A commitment to children.* New York, NY: The Free Press.

White, J., Ellis, F., O'Malley, A., Rockel, J., Stover, S., & Toso, M. (2009). Play and learning in Aotearoa New Zealand early childhood education. In I. Pramling-Samuelsson & M. Fleer (Eds.), *Play and learning in early childhood settings: International perspectives* (pp. 19–49). New York, NY: Springer.

4

RISK AND THE BODY

Risk is the mobilising dynamic of a society bent on change, that wants to determine its own future rather than leaving it to religion, tradition, or the vagaries of nature.

(Giddens, 2003, p. 24)

Introduction

This chapter argues that, in the New Zealand context, risk is used as a political tool to justify certain policies and practices in the early childhood context, and to assign responsibility and blame. Douglas (1992) claims that risk has disputed meanings depending on cultural context. In order to see which risks cause concern in a specific culture, it is necessary to identify the cultural biases of the society under examination. Every culture has a unique set of shared values that are supported by social structures and institutions.

In order to explore these ideas, the chapter focuses on key issues identified as significant by the New Zealand and Japanese participants: the playground, creation of boundaries, teacher supervision, and the use of real tools. Themes in other chapters can also be seen as constituting risky or disruptive practices, but we have chosen to deal with them each in their own right rather than under the umbrella of risk.

Towards a Discourse of Risk

The concept of risk has warranted increasing academic attention over the past two to three decades (Beck, 1992; Caplan, 2000; Douglas, 1992; Douglas & Wildavsky, 1982; Giddens, 1991; Giddens, 1994; Lupton, 1999; Tansey & Rayner, 2009). Risk has also become a frequent word used by parents and teachers alike.

Recent publications in the popular press (Davis & Eppler-Wolff, 2009) are dedicated to teaching the differences between what are considered to be good or bad risks. Others such as Guldberg (2009) reject the argument that the lives of modern children have become riskier and less fulfilling, suggesting instead that our 'safety-obsessed culture' is breeding unnecessary panic within family and education circles.

The fact that this debate is no longer limited to philosophical and theoretical discussion among experts in the field has also been noted (Wynne, 1996). There is a significant body of work that deals specifically with risk located within the arena of education (Adamson, 2005; Bollnow, 1971; Dwyer & Wyn, 2001; Hope, 2005; Monahan, 2009; Oliver, 2005; Severs, Whitlam, & Woodhouse, 2003). Along with the rise of debate and a risk discourse, we have seen new terms enter the world of parent, child, state, and school: for example, terms such as "helicopter parents" (Guldberg, 2009, p. 174; Mercogliano, 2007, p. 5), "cotton wool kids" (Jones, 2007; Dungey, 2008), and "monster parents" ("Pulvers, 2012) were not in common usage even a decade ago.

Beck (1992) states that risk has become such an embedded part of modern life that we are now living in a 'risk society'. Rather than being a rational calculation, perceptions and understandings of risk have led to new forms of social phenomena. But risk was not always constructed this way. Giddens (2003) argues that risk is a relatively recent concept, which originated during the sixteenth and seventeenth centuries as explorers embarked on lengthy ocean voyages. While its original meaning was connected to space, risk became associated with time in the world of banking, and then expanded to various other contexts involving uncertainty. Douglas (1992) acknowledges that risk analysis was prevalent in eighteenth-century marine insurance but claims the concept emerged first in the context of gambling. At that time, risk had a neutral value as it was linked purely to the probability of a positive or negative outcome. Gladwin (2008, p. 68) points out that in modern society "risk" and "hazard" are often used interchangeably, yet they have quite different meanings. Drawing on Adams (1996), Gladwin (2008) defines a hazard as that which can be objectively defined, such as an attribute of the social or physical surroundings that could inflict harm, whereas risk is connected to the probability of a possible outcome occurring.

Douglas (1992) maintains that the concept of risk has not only developed in relatively recent times, but also that its meaning has evolved to reflect contemporary society which has seen a global community replace smaller local centres. Whereas the term was previously neutral, risk is now specific to undesirable outcomes. While risk could therefore previously be seen as either negative or positive, it has come to be viewed as something to be avoided (Furedi, 2002).

Gladwin (2008) traces the journey of risk to its perceived negative position through three historical stages. In the pre-modern stage, the cause of risk is generally unknown; therefore, humans relied on belief systems to avoid it and looked to the supernatural for explanations. In the modern stage, science identified the cause of numerous risks, leading to humans adopting risk management skills. In the post-modern stage, risk is no longer viewed as an objective phenomenon, but as a social construct. The concept of risk therefore varies according to cultural definitions of acceptable and unacceptable practices (Douglas, 1992).

Douglas (1992) argues that a 'blame culture' has developed in modern societies that has led to risk analysis based on concepts of rational individual choice becoming professionalised. Douglas contends that risk must be considered within social context, remaining less an individual choice, but an implicitly political issue located within cultural boundaries. She views the rise of the term 'risk' as a new cultural phase in which every death and accident is seen as chargeable to someone's account or viewed as caused by negligence. Within this cultural schema, death cannot be accepted as a natural part of life, but must be blamed on someone and ideally accompanied by financial compensation for the family of the deceased. This establishes the negative connotations associated with risk in modern societies, which may have been expressed as danger in the past. She claims that in contemporary industrialised cultures, the term 'risk' has become dominant due to its scientific and technical implications which are preferable to the vagaries of the word 'danger' (Douglas, 1992).

The Position of Children in the Risk Society

Giddens (2003) suggests that children occupy a new and somewhat paradoxical position in our increasingly globalised world. Today's children are cherished in part because there are fewer of them, and partly due to the decision process parents go through to commit to having a child. In contrast to traditional societies in which children contributed labour and economic benefits to the family unit, parents in Western countries incur a financial burden. Giddens also points out that modern parents have higher expectations regarding the care and protection of children, which has led to increased anxiety. Guldberg (2009) and Stearns (2003) argue that parenting has become more complicated than ever before in an age ruled by concerns about children's growth, development, academic ability, and exposure to harmful environmental and social factors.

According to several scholars, the drive to reduce risk has not come without sacrifice. Palmer (2007) claims that, in attempt to minimise exposure to danger, today's children are being raised akin to battery chickens, while Mercogliano (2007) suggests that eliminating potential risk from childhood has ironically lead to children being restricted like never before. In the past two to three decades, children's free time has also come under increasing scrutiny and supervision by adults (Elkind, 2007; Freeman & Tranter, 2011). Surprisingly, children in New Zealand and Australia "have less freedom to walk to school alone, to cycle on main roads alone, visit friends alone, use public transport, cross main roads alone and go out after dark than children in countries such as Germany" (Tandy, 1999 cited in Freeman, Quigg, Vass, & Broad, 2007, p. 9).

Research has shown that over one generation the area in which children are able to travel on their own, also called their 'home habitat', has shrunk to one-ninth of its previous size (Gaster, 1991; Hillman, Adams, & Whitelegg, 1990). It has been suggested that this fear of strangers is verging on the paranoid. Gill (2007) points out that in the United Kingdom, less than one child in a million is killed annually by a stranger, while in comparison, ten times as many children are killed by cars, and five times as many at the hands of their own family members (Thomas & Hocking, 2003). In the United States, statistics show that less than one hundred children a year are killed by strangers, but parents remain anxious about the threat of child abduction in the face of rising media coverage of such incidents (Best, 1990; Furedi, 2002).

Likewise, in New Zealand, the national centre for collating and disseminating information about domestic and family violence has stated that child deaths by a stranger are extremely rare events in New Zealand. It concludes that such deaths are much more likely to occur as a result of family violence (New Zealand Family Violence Clearinghouse, 2009). Yet, many parents are not comfortable allowing their offspring to roam around the neighbourhood alone, and the number of children being driven to school has almost doubled in the past two decades (Freeman et al., 2007; Ministry of Transport, 2008).

Comparative studies have shown that this sense of parental fear may not be as prevalent in other countries. In Germany, for example, children experience far fewer restrictions on their independent mobility compared to their British counterparts. Hillman et al. (1990) suggest that German parents anticipate that other adults will both observe and reprimand children if their behaviour is inappropriate. This expectation serves as both a powerful means of surveillance and as a mark of mutual trust between parents. As part of a society that encourages autonomous mobility from a young age, Japanese children also enjoy greater freedom than New Zealand children who are increasingly driven to school (Freeman & Tranter, 2011). From the children's point of view, flirting with danger can offer the chance to learn from risky behaviour. However, much of children's play nowadays is directed and monitored by adults, which reduces these opportunities (Elkind, 2007). This may have implications for the future as Jones (2007) muses:

> The ability to judge risks as adults is not something that we simply acquire at the age of majority. It is a skill that is learnt through exposure to hazards. When as adults, we encounter a new hazard or risk, we apply those skills that we learnt as children to the situation.
>
> *(p. 15)*

Just as society at large has become more conscious of potential dangers facing our children, the early childhood sector has seen the development of stringent safety standards and workplace policies in order to protect its families and staff from harm. But as comparative studies make clear, what constitutes risky practice, behaviour, or equipment is clearly a cultural construct. Douglas and Wildavsky (1982) argue that in order to identify which risks represent concerns for a particular culture, it is essential to identify the cultural bias of that group which is the key to social organisation. They note that

> [o]nce the idea is accepted that people select their awareness of certain dangers to conform with a specific way of life, it follows that people who adhere to different forms of social organization are disposed to take (and avoid) different kinds of risk. To alter risk selection and risk perception, then, would depend on changing the social organization.
>
> *(Douglas & Wildavsky, 1982, p. 9)*

The following sections use Douglas' (1992), Douglas and Wildavsky's (1982), and Foucault's (1975/1995) theories to frame and explore the ways in which risk to the body are articulated by the participants, and approached in practice in the two contexts.

Perilous Play: The Kindergarten Playground as Culturally Contested Space

Foucault's (1975/1995) notion of disciplinary spaces has implications for the way in which kindergarten spaces are constructed to enclose, regulate, and produce docile bodies. He suggests that discipline requires "enclosure, the specification of a place heterogeneous to all others and closed in upon itself" (Foucault, 1975/1995, p. 141). In New Zealand, institutionally imposed structures and regulations are a feature of the early childhood setting. Douglas (1966) offers a further dimension to the interpretation of space, particularly visible in the Japanese context, where internalised cultural values serve to control the ordering of bodies within the playground.

Following the film screening, a significant number of teachers' comments were concerned with the potential risk to the body that the play space of 'the other' represented. For the Kaimai Kindergarten teachers, the lack of impact-absorbing surfacing and the height of the slides in the Japanese kindergarten grounds were instantly apparent and quite disturbing (see Figure 4.1). During these discussions, teachers not only demonstrated detailed knowledge of early childhood regulations, but they were surprised at the risks being taken with children's safety. They acknowledged that the use of such equipment in a New Zealand context could be potentially threatening to staff employment and professional reputations as these comments show:

> The safety surfacing and the height of the slide and the ratios are noticeable. Is there any safety surfacing? What safety regulations are there?
>
> The slide is too high in New Zealand. If a child fell off and it wasn't regulation height, we would be on national TV.

FIGURE 4.1 Children play a class game on the slide at Oka Kindergarten

I actually even wonder what it's made out of it. Even if there was a big mound under it, it wouldn't be ok. You don't see [metal] slides like that in New Zealand.

From a New Zealand perspective, it is not surprising that teachers were shocked by Japanese playground equipment. In the scene being discussed above, the teacher has led her class over to use a slide that towers over a dirt playground strewn with hundreds of tiny, sharp rocks. "That would never be allowed in New Zealand!" the teachers state. They are right. Safety manuals for early childhood centres require that the uppermost part of the slide chute be less than 3.6 metres above the ground.[1] It is also recommended that centres install the slide chutes facing south or south/east or in shaded areas to avoid children getting sunburnt. It is expected that these slides will be erected on impact-absorbing safety surfacing (Standards Association of New Zealand, 1986). In a New Zealand context, the Japanese slide represents a significant safety hazard on all three counts.

Although the video does not linger on other pieces of equipment in the playground, personal observation tells us that Oka Kindergarten's climbing frame breaks New Zealand safety standards with its highest climbing point exceeding 1.5 metres (Jambor, Chalmers, & O'Neill, 1994). In many other centres Rachael visited in Hokkaido, a popular piece of play equipment was a rotating metal roundabout with a grid-like frame. Again, this would not feature in New Zealand centres according to national safety standards which claim these kinds of rotating apparatus present "physical and psychological hazards" due to the fact that children cannot control its movement once in motion (Standards Association of New Zealand, 1986, Part 3: Clause 3.5).

The dirt grounds of the Japanese early childhood centre also represent a counter-image to the expectations of New Zealand teachers. While the grounds of Oka Kindergarten are edged by trees and wildflowers, the majority of the children play on the vast dirt surfacing or in the sandpit. There is no grass covering any of the play space. Children are permitted to wander into the forest area to pick flowers for daisy chains or gather leaves for pressing, but most prefer to roam and wrestle in the dust. The ground is pitted with hundreds of tiny small stones that could inflict a nasty cut if children fell on them. Once or twice a term, the principal would gather all the staff and children outside where he had meticulously divided the ground into a grid pattern using a sharp stick. Children and staff would be organised into groups and challenged to pick up as many stones as they could from their assigned square of the grid. The pile of stones collected at the end would be cast into the wild, wooded area at the end of kindergarten boundary, but by the time the next clearing session rolled around the stones always seemed to have edged their way back into the dust.

For the New Zealand teachers viewing the video, this whole play space represented a risky environment for children's bodies, and the stone retrieving exercise seemed to them to be meaningless and easily avoided by planting grass across the dirt surface. However, the principal of Oka Kindergarten explained that this exercise was not just about removing a potential hazard, but also served to build solidarity and cooperation through children of different ages working towards a common goal. Planting grass would not only be an expensive option in the harsh Hokkaido climate, it would eliminate opportunities such as the stone gathering ritual. The tough surfacing is also a reminder for children to persevere (*gambaru*) in difficult circumstances.

The Japanese teachers were intrigued by the New Zealand playground, which seemed quite organic at first, but on closer inspection was bounded by fences and modified in subtle ways with its safety surfacing barely perceptible under the grass and landscaped paths (see Figure 4.2). These impressions were supported by New Zealand teachers viewing the video of Kaimai Kindergarten. Implicit in their comments was the importance placed on early childhood environments that outwardly appear natural. A kindergarten teacher in Nelson commented that, "They had a lovely outdoor area too which is pretty reflective of New Zealand . . . that range of grass, and trees, and the open sandpit". In reality these spaces had often been carefully altered to eliminate some of the potential hazards to the body that come with a completely untamed area. An early childhood teacher in Christchurch stated, "I liked how it was quite natural, there was grass and that" which was quickly followed by, "That was grass growing through safety surfacing, I'm assuming? I hope it was". Ensuring that there are adequate soft fall surfaces is an important part of reducing risk to children's bodies in New Zealand centres (Education Review Office, 2008).

FIGURE 4.2 The playground at Kaimai Kindergarten

A Pedagogy of Risk

Smith (1998) focuses on the playground as a means of locating a pedagogy of risk. He sees the playground as a valuable space for understanding what is important to children, although it is often overlooked as inconsequential by adults preoccupied with greater concerns. Smith notes that while there have been various theories suggested to explain the creation of the playground, the historical reasons for its development remain contested. Some view the playground as a safe and enjoyable space for children to play, free of physical and social dangers (Zelizer, 1994), while others deride it as a convenient place to confine children and release adults from constant tedious supervision (Wood, 1977). Smith (1998) argues that parents prefer their children to play in places such as school playgrounds or amusement parks than in traditional spaces such as the street or down by the river. Playgrounds that are deemed safe are increasingly characterised as spaces that are in full view of an adult gaze and limited by physical boundaries. According to Smith, contemporary playgrounds are now being designed with the primary aim of protecting children. This design is a reflection of society's view of childhood through the lens of safety.

Jones (2007) agrees that the playground no longer provides a space for children to take risks. In the New Zealand context, slide heights and ground surfacing, spacing between equipment and fencing are just some of the many playground features regulated by national safety guidelines. This kind of legislation is also common in other developed Western countries such as the United States, the United Kingdom, and Australia.[2] Teachers at Kaimai Kindergarten in New Zealand were ambivalent about the impact overseas influenced legislation was having on the risk-taking culture of the kindergarten: "I think it's because of the whole accountability thing. It's gone a little bit too far. Children are not allowed to take risks in New Zealand anymore because they might get hurt."

During Rachael's fieldwork at Kaimai Kindergarten, an expensive new playground was constructed on the school grounds opposite. Despite having shock-absorbent surfacing, smooth tubular framing, and rounded plastic edging, more children broke limbs in the first month of use than over the course of the previous year on the run-down old playground. Teachers and parents put this down to children being complacent about the hazards inherent in the shiny new equipment. The theories of Mauss (1936/1973) would suggest that these accidents are a result of unfamiliar body techniques that the children have not yet mastered in order to negotiate the new play space. While children growing up two or three decades ago may have effortlessly embodied these techniques, many children today have lost this ability as risk discourses have renegotiated the parameters of safe play (Douglas, 1992).

Playgrounds are a response to the increasing desire to protect young bodies, although an element of risk is always incorporated into designs to challenge children. Smith (1998) and Jambor et al. (1994) have focused on the ambiguous position the playground assumes during a child's search for meaningful play. Scholars have pointed out that while a totally safe playground could indeed be constructed, children would have no interest in using it (Wilkinson & Lockhart, 1980).

Dominated by vast dirt surfaces upon which perch metal climbing and swinging structures, the largely unfenced Japanese playground appears to be the antithesis of the ideal New Zealand kindergarten outdoor area (see Figure 4.3). However, in the eyes of many of the Japanese teachers who viewed the video of the Hokkaido kindergarten, the playground was an object of envy rather than a source of danger. This area was transformed into a coveted space that allowed children the opportunity to roam freely, take responsibility for themselves, and enjoy a more natural existence. A Tokyo teacher commented,

> I liked their big, big playground. It's impossible to [have that kind of space] in Tokyo. A big playground and with all those trees around it, that was great. They also did water play, which I thought was good, because some kindergartens never let children do water play or mud play, especially in Tokyo.

In order to create and maintain an environment where children can feel free to safely explore these opportunities for play, boundaries have inevitably been

FIGURE 4.3 The playground at Oka Kindergarten

erected in both the Japanese and New Zealand contexts. What is interesting about these boundaries is the way they are structured in both a tangible and intangible way.

Creating Real and Imagined Boundaries to Minimise Risk

Douglas (1966) argues that the body is symbolic of society, and acts as a model for any bounded system. The boundaries of the body can therefore be interpreted as representing "any boundaries which are threatened or precarious" (Douglas 1966, p. 115). This section argues that the way that the individual physical body is bounded and contained is a reflection of the structural and political discourses shaping the early childhood context. For the New Zealand viewers, a surprising feature of the Japanese kindergarten was the lack of fencing around the outdoor area. While one side of the ground had a loose, strung wire fence running along it, the rest of the area allowed children free access to either the road or a woodland forest. This arrangement also allowed visitors to easily enter the grounds and kindergarten buildings. This contrasts with the New Zealand centre where the whole of the outdoor area was enclosed by a well-maintained wrought iron fence on one side and high wooden fences and hedging on the other. At the entrance to the centre, children, families, and visitors were required to arrive and leave through a self-locking gate.

Very few of the children attending the centre could either reach the release catch or had enough power to pull the knob in order to unlock the gate. As a result, the act of entering and departing the centre was controlled either by parents or teachers. Each day, a teacher was assigned to be on duty at the gate during leaving time. The purpose of this task was primarily to ensure that children did not leave or enter without an approved adult, but it also gave teachers the opportunity to engage in conversation with families. Despite this, focus group participants in Nelson still felt that the farewell procedure could have been managed in a more structured way. One of them explained: "There is a safety aspect to it in terms of knowing where all the children are, where they're going with the parents and that kind of stuff". In contrast to Kaimai Kindergarten, where children were released as a group to their parents following the cessation of 'mat time', this teacher indicated that her Nelson centre preferred to release children one by one after their parent or caregiver had signed them out. In the New Zealand early childhood context, this kind of policy was common and reflected an ideology influenced by notions of health and safety as well as responsibility and accountability. The locking gate and robust fence have become potent symbols of risk minimisation measures as well as tangible boundaries separating children and the potentially dangerous outdoor, unregulated world.

At Oka Kindergarten in Hokkaido, physical boundaries such as fences and gates do not feature as strongly. With most of the outdoor area uncontained, there appears to be nothing preventing children wandering off the kindergarten grounds. This issue, which is of great importance to the New Zealand teachers, was never directly addressed by their Hokkaido counterparts. When questioned about it, however, Oka teachers explained that they relied on children's internalised sense of boundaries and on peer control to preclude any problems. Walsh (2002) points out that Japanese children are given a great deal of responsibility in a necessary step towards realising interdependence. This shared sense of responsibility becomes ingrained over the course of the kindergarten experience. If a new or younger child ever looks like transgressing the invisible safety boundaries of the outdoor area, he or she is quickly retrieved or assisted by older, more experienced members of the kindergarten group.

While all of the centres Rachael visited in Hokkaido had only partial or incomplete fences around the outdoor play area, several of the urban centres in large cities in Honshu had sturdy wrought iron fencing and gates controlled by intercom. When the teachers were questioned about these security measures they explained these were relatively recent changes sparked by a savage attack on children by a deranged man who entered a primary school in Osaka prefecture in 2001. The man's stabbing spree killed eight children and left fifteen others wounded ("Eight Dead in School Stabbing Spree", 2001). This case was not an isolated one, however, as before the events in Osaka, other violent incidents against children had already occurred on Japanese school grounds.[3] Violence at Japanese schools has not been limited to outside attackers with several gruesome killings committed by school children given widespread media attention in both domestic and international circles.[4]

These incidents have contributed to rising anxiety levels about children's safety in educational settings. The 2001 Osaka incident, in particular, provoked changes in the way educational institutions deal with security issues. In response to advice from the Ministry of Education, fences have become more prevalent especially in densely populated urban areas. Urban Japanese teachers interviewed during the focus group sessions explained that fences are now necessary to keep dangerous elements from entering the kindergarten. This is in contrast to New Zealand centres where teachers indicated that the primary reason for physical barriers is to prevent children from wandering off the grounds. In Japan, the barrier is to prevent potential danger from the outside entering the internal and safe world of the kindergarten. In New Zealand, the barrier works to prevent children from entering a potentially dangerous outside world (see Figure 4.4). Both contexts reflect Douglas's (1992) view of society as in the midst of a new cultural phase in which risk is linked to blame and accountability. It has become necessary for someone to take responsibility for children's mobile bodies and to enforce the boundaries which serve to minimise physical risk.

FIGURE 4.4 An unfenced early childhood centre in Hokkaido contrasts with a bounded outdoor area at the New Zealand centre

FIGURE 4.4 (Continued)

Boundaries are not just marked by barriers between the centre and the external world. Walsh (2002) describes the Japanese preschool itself as a separate
space for children marked by boundaries such as the *genkan* which defines the
'outside' and 'parent' world and the 'inside' and 'child' world. Walsh observed
that once morning greeting rituals are over, children are free to roam and be
boisterous, in contrast to American centres where running inside is not permitted and voices must be lowered. Much of the playground equipment available
to Japanese children is considered dangerous to Americans, such as high metal
climbing structures and old cable spools. These reactions were very similar to
those of New Zealand audiences upon seeing the slides and ground surfaces,
yet much of the Japanese equipment was also once common on New Zealand kindergarten playgrounds. Walsh also discovered that correct supervision
of children is culturally defined as the Japanese teachers were comfortable just
knowing where, and what, children were doing, whereas American teachers felt
they needed to watch over activities to be considered doing the job properly. For
the New Zealand teachers viewing the Japanese video, it also appeared that the
children were left to their own devices far too often, which seemed both risky
and rather negligent.

Cultural Definitions of Safe Supervision

Just as the American teachers Walsh (2002) interviewed felt that they needed to be close by to feel they were fulfilling their job responsibilities, the New Zealand teachers indicated that they would not be comfortable with the level of staff supervision in the Japanese kindergarten. At one point in the Japanese video, the teacher runs across the playground with her class of thirty-three children straggling behind in her in a haphazard line. While eventually all of the children catch up, she does not look back to check if they are coming, neither does she cease jogging. She stops at a concrete tunnel submerged under a grass bank, and instructs the leader of the pack to crawl through the tunnel, and once he is out the other side, she moves off in the direction of the slide. One by one, the other children follow suit even though, for those at the back, their teacher and classmates have already moved on to the next piece of equipment. Throughout this exercise, no explanation had been given; the teacher had simply blown her whistle once following the end of assembly and jogged slowly off.

In lieu of direct verbal communication, musical cues such as songs, clapping, or whistles are used extensively in Japanese early childhood settings, to signify both the beginning and end of activities, and to change the pace or mood of the classroom (Tobin, Wu, & Davidson, 1989). Through repetitive socialisation processes (Burke, 2007; Hendry, 1986; Lewis, 1995; Peak, 1991) the children understand that the whistle signifies an instruction to form their class line and follow the teacher. Teachers at Kaimai Kindergarten were surprised at the lack of verbal instruction given to the children about the activity, but also at the apparent disregard for children's whereabouts and safety. They immediately linked the situation to their own circumstances with potentially devastating results:

> If a child ran off into the tunnel, how would the teacher know? How would she get that child back again?
>
> For instance, there was that centre in Wellington that went for a walk and they climbed over the barriers and through the tunnel and it was on national news. People would have lost their jobs for that sort of thing.

Foucault (1975/1995) argues that the perfect disciplinary institution is that in which constant surveillance is possible. In the New Zealand context, it is not only important that the whereabouts of the children is always known, but also that the teachers themselves are objects of the disciplinary gaze. The supervision concerns continue for the Kaimai Kindergarten teachers as the thirty-three Japanese children each take a turn on the slide and are sent back to the classroom. Before leaving, the teacher tells them all to go to the toilet, wash their hands, have a drink of water, and sit down and wait for her to return. The teacher then remains on the playground until the last child has slid down the slide, twenty minutes later. Back in the classroom, the camera follows the four-year-old children chatting, washing their hands, blowing bubbles, and in some cases, fighting. The Kaimai Kindergarten teachers indicated that they felt the directives issued prior to this scene were not only complicated, but superfluous. Many of their concerns were phrased as questions they needed answering from within their own cultural framework. The New Zealanders continued to return to the matter of supervision and the missing teacher, which links back to wider issues of safety and accountability:

> Where's the teacher here? The children are unsupervised.
>
> If someone fell off that slide out there with that one teacher and forty[5] children who would look after that child?

Although constant supervision is accepted as normal, safe practice in New Zealand early childhood contexts, Foucault (1975/1995, p. 201) argues that this kind of constant supervision and surveillance of children and teachers instead works to ensure "the automatic functioning of power".

The Low Profile of Japanese Teachers

The low profile of Japanese teachers has been raised before by researchers conducting cross-cultural fieldwork in early childhood settings. Lewis (1995) was surprised to see just how rarely teachers appeared to exercise authority or supervise children. During spot observations of free play, Lewis noted that only 53% of teachers could see all of their students, while in 13% of the cases, they could not see any of the children. When questioned about this, the teachers reiterated that children were expected to seek an adult if a problem occurred. Lewis observed that teachers often left their classrooms unsupervised, while they attended to other matters. This practice was also common at Oka Kindergarten as teachers might be called away to deal with an administrative matter, a visiting parent, to watch part of another class as part of ongoing training, or to cope with an ill child. To Lewis's "Western eye, the low profile of adult authority occasionally made Japanese preschools look dangerous" (Lewis, 1995, p. 114). She was also uncomfortable with the way resources such as oversized blocks were used to create precarious structures, which could come crashing down on children. She concluded that Americans would prefer children's freedom to be curtailed rather than risk injury or blame.

Douglas (1992) observes that in the Japanese language, there are words for danger, damage, and harm as well as for predicting probability, but there is no word for risk. While the term 'risk' may never arise in a Japanese early childhood setting, or indeed in wider Japanese society, potential hazards and dangers are carefully considered by kindergarten staff and parents.

For the Japanese teachers at the centre of the video, the safety of the children in the scene described earlier was never in doubt. The Oka Kindergarten teachers acknowledge that higher ratios mean that children are often not in close proximity to staff, but insist that their classmates are encouraged to give support and comfort in the case of altercations or minor injuries. Learning to become self-reliant and independent at kindergarten is a fundamental aim, which cannot be achieved if children are over-reliant on the teacher (Peak, 1989). Although classes of forty children are no longer legally allowed, the video of one teacher to thirty-three children was still considered to be critically unbalanced by the Kaimai Kindergarten teachers. In a Japanese context however, Tobin et al. (1989) suggest that large classes specifically serve to prevent the teacher from spending inordinate amounts of time with one child and instead encourage individuals to undertake tasks themselves or consult with their peers for help.

The expectation that children must learn to cooperate and depend on each other represented a challenge for New Zealand teachers' notions about the capability of children, as this Wellington teacher explains:

> Supervision . . . I must admit, I was quite amazed. I put a big 'wow' that the children they weren't supervised, but they did know what they were doing, and I would never expect that here from a group of children. If they had wandered into the toilet, into the bathroom to wash their hands, you have to have someone follow them because they are not expected to know the rules and to know not to splash and not to push. So we make sure we have an adult with them but it sort of seems silly after seeing how capable the children in that video are just with a little bit of coaching initially and some encouragement. It seems silly to follow a group of five children into the bathroom to wash their hands when a big group of thirty has gone in and done it on their own. So I wonder if by doing that if we are just not giving children the opportunity to develop those sorts of social skills and abilities to cope with things on their own.

The Japanese teachers were intrigued by the New Zealanders' concerns over supervision. In their minds, the teacher/child ratios at the Hokkaido kindergarten were not particularly unusual, and the self-monitoring behaviour of the children was to be expected. Walsh (2004) has written about visiting a zoo in Tokyo, where he encountered a single teacher responsible for thirty young children on a class trip. As the teacher led the group, the children followed behind him in a long line, chattering, and jostling. According to Walsh, the teacher never once looked back to check on his students; instead the children were expected to take responsibility for themselves and for any of their peers that might inadvertently wander from the fold.

It appears that implicit in New Zealand teachers understanding of adequate supervision is physical proximity to children's bodies, regular visual and/or verbal checking, and a relatively short time to attend to altercations or minor injuries. The Japanese teachers Rachael spoke with often referred to a 'wait and see' attitude (*mimamoru*) before intervening in children's affairs. This was an approach they had learned informally from more experienced teachers rather than a method that had been explicitly taught during teacher preservice education. They felt comfortable giving children time and space to resolve issues themselves, although they stressed that they would take action if events were becoming dangerous. There is also the reality that in the two centres observed, there are far more teachers in a smaller physical space in New Zealand, compared to larger numbers of children in a vast area in Japan. This naturally impacts on the level of supervision teachers are able to achieve in each setting.

Although cultural constructions of adequate supervision clearly vary between New Zealand and Japan, the 'blame culture' discussed by Douglas (1992) is evident in both countries. In a 'blame culture', risk is contemplated within social context, becoming an implicitly political issue located within cultural frameworks, rather than being an individual act. The next section discusses an example of this, focussing on a scene from Kaimai Kindergarten of two young boys at the carpentry table. This scene elicited great surprise on the part of the Japanese teachers at Oka Kindergarten. Just as images of unsupervised children disappearing in tunnels evoked fears of litigious ramifications for the New Zealanders, the carpentry scene unearthed nervous feelings on the part of the Japanese viewers relating to teacher responsibility and parental pressure.

The Use of Real Tools

At Kaimai Kindergarten, two four-year-old boys are standing at an outdoor wooden carpentry table which has a steel vice attached to one end (see Figure 4.5). Behind them, a selection of saws and hammers hang from pegs on the wall. One of the boys is hammering a nail vigorously into two pieces of wood that he has arranged into a cross shape. The sound echoes across the playground. The other little boy has been thoughtfully studying his wooden construction in the vice and decides to select a saw from the tool wall. As he returns, he and his friend share a smile before they both get down to work. The boy hammering gives one final, loud bang before shouting jubilantly across to the teacher, "Look, I did it!" She asks him if he has nailed the wood to the table like last time, whereupon he quizzically picks up the construction, looks underneath and declares happily, "Nope, I did it". To his left, the other boy continues to saw at his creation despite the tool bending and twisting in his hands.

The Oka Kindergarten teachers were extremely surprised to see that children in New Zealand not only had free access to adults' tools, but that the teacher did not appear to be paying attention to how they were being used. Several of the

FIGURE 4.5 Boys engaged in carpentry at Kaimai Kindergarten

teachers asked if the equipment was real and wondered if the centre had considered replacing the tools with replicas that had unsharpened saw teeth or blunted hammer prongs. Others had more ambivalent feelings:

> Those saws and hammers look really dangerous, but I like the fact the children can use them. It used to be that way in Japan once too.

Tools as Iconic Symbols

Indeed, in the past, foreign researchers carrying out fieldwork in Japanese early childhood settings have reported being equally shocked by similar scenes of Japanese children using hammers and nails or razor knives (Lewis, 1995; Walsh, 2002). However, during a Christchurch focus group session, a young Japanese early childhood teacher, who is now living and working in New Zealand, identified the carpentry corner as a distinctly New Zealand phenomenon. She was also able to trace her changing attitude towards the tools as a metaphor for her assimilation into New Zealand culture and as a means of reassessing culturally based assumptions about risk and the competency of children.

> You can see that you trust children with lots of things which wouldn't be happening in certain other countries. I mean, I'm from an Asian country

and I wouldn't be expecting to see things like the carpentry table. When I first saw it in New Zealand, I was shocked because I couldn't believe children were using that [kind of equipment]. So it's amazing! I can see that now I'm working in a New Zealand setting. The more trust you give the children, the more capable they become. That's something I quite like.

At other focus group sessions around New Zealand, teachers mentioned the carpentry table as one of the long-standing symbols of early childhood education.

I think it was very much the sandpit, the outdoors, the water, you know, the carpentry were all very much traditional New Zealand early childhood things.
  The carpentry, the real tools for the carpentry. I don't think you see that in many other places. It is an iconic [part of New Zealand kindergartens].

Nevertheless, it seems somewhat contradictory that New Zealand early childhood teachers trust children to handle saws, hammers, and vices, all of which could result in a nasty injury if misused, yet they are not comfortable leaving children to discover how to negotiate high climbing equipment or to spend periods alone without adult supervision. What is it about these tools that lead them to be defended as such integral parts of the early childhood experience?

There is very little written about the appearance of the carpentry table in the New Zealand early childhood centre although the benefits of using tools to work with wood has been discussed in terms of improving motor skills, creating problem-solving opportunities, promoting autonomy, increasing understanding of mathematical and scientific concepts, allowing creative expression and exploration, providing chances for dramatic play, and promoting language skills (McLeod, 2005; Sutherden, 1998). A clue to the enduring value of the carpentry area may possibly lie in a comment made by a teacher in Dunedin who noted: "The carpentry does appear to be rather gender specific though". Indeed, while the area was used regularly by the girls at the centre, it was most often dominated by small boys during the time of my fieldwork. It was as one teacher put it, "an incredibly traditional, Kiwi early childhood centre".

Is it possible that the hammers and saws have maintained some kind of cultural value because they seem to link back to New Zealand's pioneering, colonial past, and historical notions of men carving out a living from the untamed bush frontier? In his study of the Pākehā male, Phillips (1996) has discussed how the myth of the physically powerful male wielding a saw or hammer has persisted well into modern times. But, in reality, by the 1950s, this male stereotype was woefully inaccurate as most men were not engaged in this kind of work and no longer even had the capability or knowledge to carry it out. However, when a group of Kaimai children were asked why they thought the carpentry area was important, they replied that "those tools are the kinds of things Dads use every day" and "we need those tools to do our work".

Several kindergarten teachers identified the carpentry area as "iconic" as Napier teacher explains:

> It is important to our kindergarten philosophy because it's the notion of real tools and real work and trusting children to be able to manage it and clearly they did.

Assessing the Risks and Rewards of Real Tools

Under the strand and goal of exploration, the New Zealand early childhood curriculum, *Te Whāriki*, makes the value of real tools explicit. Objects such as hammers, brooms, saucepans, and calculators are seen as providing meaningful learning opportunities in a genuine context of play and work (Ministry of Education, 1996). Considered within the framework of risk to the body, this notion of carrying out 'real work' with 'real tools' is not just unique to New Zealand. Gladwin (2008) gives the example of British early childhood workers visiting an early years setting in Denmark where they were amazed to see four-year-old children using saws and axes to chop wood. The Danish teachers saw nothing unusual at all in this activity. Judith discovered that teachers in Norway included children in food preparation for the lunch-time meal for the centre. When she visited in 2004, the children prepared soup for lunch (standing on stools, stirring bubbling liquid in a metal pot), served the hot soup to the other children (ladles full of soup into bowls from the pot), and cut slices of bread (which they had also made) with a serrated bread knife. Each child received a plate of soup and a slice of bread, prepared and served by other children. The teachers were amused by Judith's incredulity to these activities and her perception of the risks of children handling hot products and sharp knives. Lancy (2008) has pointed out that objects designed solely for the purpose for play, in other words toys, do not feature in traditional societies. Instead, children are free to explore their village and pick up objects, which may possibly be dangerous. As societies became more complex, toys began to be designed specifically for young children and with safety in mind.

In developing societies, children still continue to play with objects that they have found, including real tools. Anthropologists give the examples of young children playing with machetes (Howard, 1970) and bush knives (Lepowsky, 1987; Whiting, 1941). Common also are the observations of children messing with fire (Gorer, 1967) and deadly insects (Marshall, 1972). On a recent trip to Niue[6] Rachael's three young sons, then aged nine, seven, and four, were delighted to be handed machetes by the neighbours and asked to go and trim any low-hanging palm fronds off the trees in the garden. The inference was obviously that they were quite capable of managing this task without causing any injury to themselves, which indeed they did. At the time, Rachael couldn't help but think that this scenario would be highly unlikely in a New Zealand context despite a sup-posedly liberal approach to the use of real tools. Ethnographic accounts of village children running around with knives or burning sticks are in stark contrast to countries, such as New Zealand and Japan, where children are encouraged to collect benign play objects from nature and choose from stores packed full of safety-proofed toys.

Defining Objects in Play as Safe or Risky

In Japan, the need to protect children's bodies from physical harm has been tem-pered with the view that it is important for youngsters to handle objects, such as knives, in order to become self-reliant. But as the teachers viewing the video pointed out, such opportunities are becoming more and more infrequent in the early childhood environment because modern parents are increasingly anxious about exposing their children to any perceived risk.

A good example of this issue is given by Nakano (2005), who discusses the generation gap that became clear during a children's association (*kodomokai*) event. A dispute arose during a curry-making session when a woman, who had missed the preliminary instructional meetings, gave a potato peeler to a child to use. This was in direct contrast to the instructions given by the head of the association who wanted children to have the chance to use knives and prepare the meal with-out interference from adults. The discussion which followed marked the younger mothers as overly protective of their offspring, while the older members lamented the loss of controlled risks for children. The Japanese teachers viewing the New Zealand video had similar lines of thinking to the older volunteers, but were open about the pressures they faced from parents to protect children from danger. They were incredulous that New Zealand parents had not complained to the centre about the carpentry table and that kindergarten management had not put a stop to the practice.

In contrast, the New Zealanders viewers did not see the practice as dangerous at all but rather as a good example of children being given the opportunity to be challenged and then to master a cognitive skill that had value and worth in the 'real' world:

> I just wanted to say something about the carpentry. It was just great to see. You can tell that those boys have been doing carpentry for some time. They had developed a lot of skills and that was really good. They knew someone was keeping an eye out and they just got on with it and they got the ham-mer and they were very confident and that was good to see, although he expected praise for doing well. He sought it and he got it.

Only one New Zealand teacher from a childcare care centre commented that her workplace would insist on having a teacher present at the table if the children were using saws. If the area was not being used, the equipment would be packed up as that particular centre had a policy of constant supervision at the carpentry table. She attributed this to the fact that children were often at the centre all day long as opposed to Kaimai Kindergarten, which has sessions of only three hours each. In contrast to the strict policies of this teacher's childcare centre, Kaimai Kindergarten staff left the equipment out for the entire session and during which time the children were free to access it with or without a teacher being present. The general attitude to the carpentry table was neatly summed up by the teacher, whose centre interestingly insisted on adult supervision throughout: "Kids don't hurt themselves generally and if they do it's a learning process". Douglas (1966) claims that concerns about risk are often projected onto particular social groups that are seen to require control or intervention. Portrayed as completely different from 'self' this dangerous 'other' can confuse boundaries, leading to fear and anxiety. As the above examples illustrate, classification of objects as 'safe' or 'risky' depend largely on the cultural perspective of the person, or society, making the assessment.

Perceptions of Risk and the Body

This chapter has discussed key issues as a means of illuminating differing perceptions of risk in the New Zealand and Japanese early childhood sector: the playground, creation of boundaries, teacher supervision, and the use of real tools. The idea that risk is culturally constructed is not a new one (Douglas & Wildavsky, 1982; Rayner, 1992), but there has been little application of this paradigm to cross-national early childhood settings. In wider terms, studies of risk perception carried out in New Zealand and Japan have found that concerns vary. These perceptions ultimately inform health and safety policy in the nation's early childhood centres.

Studies show that modern Japanese are more likely to be concerned by the kinds of manufactured risks identified by Giddens (2003) than the external natural risks which preoccupied previous generations. A study of risk perceptions in Japan and the United States found that out of thirty activities, substances and technologies, respondents in both countries rated the fear of nuclear waste disposal, nuclear accidents, and nuclear war the highest (Hinman, Rosa, Kleinhesselink, & Lowinger, 1993). In the case of Japan, this is a salient fear which, sadly, has been realised in the wake of the Fukushima nuclear tragedy in 2011. Yet research has also shown that the Japanese appear more fatalistic about risk and the amount of control they might be able to exert (Kitayama, Palm, Masuda, Karasawa, & Carroll, 1996). New Zealanders seem more preoccupied with internal risk over which they believe to have a level of control. A study of New Zealand and German perception of risks found that New Zealanders rated smoking and overeating highest in terms of personal risk exposure, but saw the benefits of taking part in extreme sports as outweighing the dangers (Rohrmann, 1996).

These perceptions of risk are to some extent reflected in the early childhood curriculum as well as the health and safety policies of each country. The Japanese curriculum notes that in order to enhance their understanding of safety, children should acquire the ability to move their bodies in an agile manner through vigorous play, and learn about dangerous places and things. Kindergartens should also develop in children the convention of traffic safety, while conducting drills, which promote appropriate action during catastrophe (Ministry of Education, Science, Sports, Culture, and Technology, 2008).

This emphasis on children experiencing a certain degree of risk themselves, and taking a somewhat fatalistic attitude to the outcome, can be seen in the high slides and metal jungle gyms, as well as the freedom given to explore without structural boundaries or teacher supervision. Peer support and control also work to ensure children's physical and emotional safety (Lewis, 1995). There is also an emphasis on safely negotiating traffic, which is especially relevant to Japan's high-density urban areas and on responses to disasters, which are a legitimate concern in a highly developed, natural disaster-prone nation such as Japan. Early childhood centres across Japan carry out regular drills to familiarise children with the appropriate response to earthquakes and fire.

In the New Zealand context, the emphasis is somewhat different. In a detailed examination of health and safety issues requiring attention at New Zealand kindergartens, ERO[7] "identified inadequate fencing, inadequate fall surfaces, excessive fall distances from some play equipment, lack of appropriate facilities for cleaning and changing soiled or sick children, storage that posed an earthquake hazard, and areas which were difficult to supervise with the number of adults present" (Education Review Office, 2008, p. 37). It is interesting to note that the first three are not addressed at all as safety issues in the Japanese early childhood sector. In fact, Lewis (1995) recalls an anecdote about Japanese friends who rejected a childcare centre precisely on the grounds that it had safety gates, which they saw as confining children like animals. An in-home carer for Rachael's young son in rural Hokkaido refused to use a fire guard for the kerosene stove for similar reasons despite having a house full of toddlers. "Young children will naturally learn to stay away from dangerous things", she told Rachael at the time.

Being free to roam uneven, natural grounds and the experience of dealing with falls from play equipment are normal occurrences in the Japanese early childhood environment. Areas are not designated difficult to supervise as Japanese children are expected to take greater responsibility for their own well-being than New Zealand children who generally play under the watchful eye of a teacher. The earthquake hazard may be the only safety issue, which is common to both countries.

As Douglas and Wildavsky (1982) have pointed out, every culture has a unique set of shared values and social institutions that support and maintain it. These values and institutions are inherently biased towards accentuating particular risks and minimising others. In the case of New Zealand and Japanese attitudes towards risk embodiment, the entanglement of the cultural and the political can be clearly seen in the expression of some of those values in documents issued by the state. In other instances, what constitutes risky or dangerous practice is more implicit. Cross-cultural viewing of the video revealed that Japanese scenes of child nudity and tactile interactions between teachers and children provoked strong reactions in New Zealand, while Japanese viewers were puzzled by New Zealand teachers' reluctance to interact with children in a more physical manner. With links to the risk discourse, but worthy of a discussion in its own right, the following chapter examines the challenges to order posed by children's bodies in the early childhood environment.

Notes

1 The requirement is different for embankment slides which must have a sliding surface less than one metre above the ground (Standards Association of New Zealand, 1986).
2 In the United States, see US Consumer Product Safety Commission (2008) *Public playground safety handbook*, Bethesda, MD: CPSC. In the United Kingdom, see British Standards Institution (2004) *Playground equipment*, London: British Standards Institution. In Australia, refer to Office for Recreation and Sport (1998), *Playground manual*, South Australia: Office for Recreation and Sport.
3 In September 1998, a group of boys wielding swords and sticks injured a junior high school student in Chiba, and in the same year, a man used an axe and a sickle to attack and injure eight students after he broke into a junior high school in Hiratsuka, Kanagawa Prefecture. In December 1999, a pupil was stabbed to death at a primary school in Kyoto after the assailant attacked him in the playground.
4 For example, Seito Sakakibara was the alias of a fourteen-year-old Kobe boy who murdered an eleven-year-old boy and a ten-year-old girl in 1997. Particularly shocking was the fact that Sakakibara left the head of one of his victims at his primary school gate for other students to discover when they arrived in the morning ("Kobe Killer Set Free", 2004). In 2004, an eleven-year-old girl used a stanley knife to slit the throat of her twelve-year-old classmate at a primary school in Sasebo, Nagasaki prefecture ("Sixth Grader Kills Her Classmate, 12", 2004). In 2005, a seventeen-year-old boy returned to his old primary school in Neyagawa, Osaka prefecture, to attack his former teacher leaving one dead and two injured ("Motive key for teen in school rampage", 2005).
5 In fact, there are thirty-three children in the class being discussed, but in previous years, there have been as many as forty children under the supervision of this one teacher.
6 Niue is an island nation in the South Pacific situated approximately 2,400 kilometres northeast of New Zealand.
7 ERO (Education Review Office) reviews schools and early childhood education services and publishes national reports on current education practice. See www.ero.govt.nz for more information.

References

Adams, J. (1996). *Risk*. London, UK: University College London Press.
Adamson, K. (2005). Diversity, risk, excellence and the public good in education. In A. Hope & P. Oliver (Eds.), *Risk, education and culture* (pp. 211–225). Aldershot, Hampshire, UK: Aldershot.
Beck, U. (1992). *Risk society: Towards a new modernity*. London, UK: Sage.

Best, J. (1990). *Threatened children: Rhetoric and concern about child victims*. Chicago, IL: University of Chicago Press.

Bollnow, O. F. (1971). Risk and failure in education. In J. P. Strain (Ed.), *Modern philosophies of education* (pp. 520–530). New York, NY: Random House.

Burke, R. (2007). *Changing times for young minds: Declining class size and shudan seikatsu ideology in Hokkaido preschools*. Unpublished Masters Thesis, Massey University, Auckland, New Zealand.

Caplan, P. (2000). *Risk revisited*. London, UK: Pluto Press.

Davis, S., & Eppler-Wolff, N. (2009). *Raising children who soar: A guide to healthy risk-taking in an uncertain world*. New York, NY: Teachers College Press.

Douglas, M. (1966). *Purity and danger: An analysis of concepts of pollution and taboo*. Harmondsworth, UK: Penguin Books.

Douglas, M. (1992). *Risk and blame: Essays in cultural theory*. London, UK: Routledge.

Douglas, M., & Wildavsky, A. (1982). *Risk and culture: An essay on the selection of technological and environmental dangers*. Berkeley: University of California Press.

Dungey, K. (2008, September 13). Cotton wool kids. *Otago Daily Times*, pp. 41–44.

Dwyer, P., & Wyn, J. (2001). *Youth, education and risk: Facing the future*. London, UK: Routledge/Falmer.

Education Review Office. (2008). *Health, safety and environment. Handbook of contractual obligations and undertakings for early childhood services*. Retrieved from www.ero.govt.nz/Review-Process/For-Early-Childhood-Services-and-Nga-Kohanga-Reo/Handbook

Eight dead in school stabbing spree. (2001, 9 June). *The Japan Times*. Retrieved from www.japantimes.co.jp/text/nn20010609a1.html

Elkind, D. (2007). *The power of play: How imaginative, spontaneous activities lead to healthier and happier children*. Cambridge, UK: Da Capo Lifelong Books.

Foucault, M. (1975/1995). *Discipline and punish: The birth of the prison* (A. Sheridan, Trans.). New York, NY: Vintage Books.

Freeman, C., Quigg, R., Vass, E., & Broad, M. (2007). *The changing geographies of children's lives: A study of how children in Dunedin use their environment*. Dunedin, Department of Geography, University of Otago, New Zealand.

Freeman, C., & Tranter, P. (2011). *Children and their urban environment: Changing worlds*. London, UK: Earthscan.

Furedi, F. (2002). *Culture of fear: Risk-taking and the morality of low expectation*. London, UK: Continuum.

Gaster, S. (1991). Urban children's access to their neighborhoods: Changes over three generations. *Environment and Behavior, 23*(1), 70–85.

Giddens, A. (1991). *Modernity and self-identity*. Cambridge, UK: Polity Press.

Giddens, A. (1994). Living in a post-traditional society. In U. Beck, A. Giddens, & S. Lash (Eds.), *Reflexive modernization: Politics, tradition and aesthetics in the modern social order* (pp. 56–109). Cambridge, UK: Polity Press.

Giddens, A. (2003). *Runaway world: How globalization is reshaping our lives*. New York, NY: Routledge.

Gill, T. (2007). *No fear: Growing up in a risk-averse society*. London, UK: Gulbenkian Foundation.

Gladwin, M. (2008). The concept of risk in play and playwork. In F. Brown & C. Taylor (Eds.), *Foundations of playwork* (pp. 68–71). Maidenhead, Berkshire, UK: Open University Press.

Gorer, G. (1967). *Himalayan village: An account of the Lepchas of Sikkin*. New York, NY: Basic Books.

Guldberg, H. (2009). *Reclaiming childhood: Freedom and play in an age of fear*. Abingdon, Oxon, UK: Routledge.

Hendry, J. (1986). *Becoming Japanese: The world of the pre-school child*. Honolulu: University of Hawaii Press.

Hillman, M., Adams, J., & Whitelegg, J. (1990). *One false move: A study of children's independent mobility*. London, UK: Policy Studies Institute.

Hinman, G. W., Rosa, E. A., Kleinhesselink, R. R., & Lowinger, T. C. (1993). Perceptions of nuclear and other risks in Japan and the United States. *Risk Analysis, 13*(4), 449–455.

Hope, A. (2005). Risk, education and culture: Interpreting danger as a dynamic, culturally situated process. In A. Hope & P. Oliver (Eds.), *Risk, education and culture* (pp. 3–20). Aldershot, Hampshire, UK: Ashgate.

Howard, A. (1970). *Learning to be Rotuman*. New York, NY: Teachers College Press.

Jambor, T., Chalmers, D., & O'Neill, D. (1994). *The New Zealand playground safety manual for early childhood services, primary and intermediate schools, parks and recreation departments*. Wellington, New Zealand: Accident Rehabilitation & Compensation Insurance Corporation (ACC).

Jones, D. (2007). *Cotton wool kids: Releasing the potential for children to take risks and innovate*. Coventry, UK: HTI.

Kitayama, S., Palm, S. I., Masuda, T., Karasawa, M., & Carroll, J. (1996). *Optimism in the United States and pessimism in Japan: Perceptions of earthquake risk* (Unpublished manuscript). Kyoto, Japan: Kyoto University.

Kobe killer set free. (2004, March 11). *The Japan Times*. Retrieved from www.japantimes. co.jp/news/2004/03/11/national/kobe-killer-set-free/#.U_FWm8WSx8E

Lancy, D. F. (2008). *The anthropology of childhood: Cherubs, chattel, changelings*. Cambridge, UK: Cambridge University Press.

Lepowsky, M. A. (1987). Food taboos and child survival: A case study from the Coral Sea. In N. Scheper-Hughes (Ed.), *Child survival: Anthropological perspectives on the treatment and maltreatment of children* (pp. 71–92). Dordrecht, The Netherlands: D. Reidel.

Lewis, C. C. (1995). *Educating hearts and minds: Reflections of Japanese preschool and elementary education*. Cambridge, UK: University of Cambridge.

Lupton, D. (1999). *Risk*. London, UK: Routledge.

Marshall, J. (1972). *Playing with scorpions* [Film]. Watertown, MA: Documentary Educational Resources.

Mauss, M. (1936/1973). Techniques of the body. *Economy and Society, 2*, 70–88.

McLeod, L. (2005). Tool time. *Playcentre Journal*, (123), 28–29.

Mercogliano, C. (2007). *In defense of childhood: Protecting kids' inner wildness*. Boston, MA: Beacon Press.

Ministry of Education. (1996). *Te Whāriki: He Whāriki Mātauranga mō ngā Mokopuna o Aotearoa. New Zealand early childhood curriculum*. Wellington, New Zealand: Learning Media.

Ministry of Education, Science, Sports, Culture, and Technology. (2008, July). *Basic plan for the promotion of education*. Retrieved from www.mext.go.jp/english/lawand-plan/1303463.htm

Ministry of Transport. (2008, December). *1997/98 Travel survey highlights: School children*. Retrieved from www.transport.govt.nz/research/travelsurvey/1997-98travelsurvey highlights-contents/199798travelsurveyhighlights-schoolchildren/

Monahan, T. (2009). The surveillance curriculum: Risk management and social control in the neoliberal school. In A. Dardner, M. P. Baltodano, & R. D. Torres (Eds.), *The critical pedagogy reader* (pp. 123–134). New York, NY: Routledge.

Nakano, L. Y. (2005). *Community volunteers in Japan: Everyday stories of social change.* Abingdon, Oxon, UK: RoutledgeCurzon.

New Zealand Family Violence Clearinghouse. (2009, December). *Family violence statistics fact sheet.* Retrieved from www.nzfvc.org.nz

Oliver, P. (2005). Risk, education and postmodernity. In A. Hope & P. Oliver (Eds.), *Risk, education and culture* (pp. 46–59). Aldershot, Hampshire, UK: Ashgate.

Palmer, F. (2007). Body image, hauora and identity: Experiences of Māori girls in sport. *Childrenz Issues, 11*(2), 12–19.

Peak, L. (1989). Learning to become part of the group: The Japanese child's transition to preschool life. *Journal of Japanese Studies, 15*(1), 93–123.

Peak, L. (1991). *Learning to go to school in Japan: The transition from home to preschool life.* Berkeley: University of California Press.

Phillips, J. (1996). *A man's country: The image of the Pākehā male—A history.* Auckland, New Zealand: Penguin Books.

Pulvers, Roger (2012, August 19). Monster parents make matters worse for their children. *The Japan Times.* Retrieved from www.japantimes.co.jp/opinion/2012/08/19/commentary/monster-parents-make-matters-worse-for-their-children-and-teachers/#.U_FbAcWSx8E

Rayner, S. (1992). Cultural theory and risk analysis. In S. Krimsky & D. Golding (Eds.), *Social theories of risk* (pp. 83–116). Westport, CT: Praeger.

Rohrmann, B. (1996). *Perception and evaluation of risks: Findings for New Zealand and cross-cultural comparisons.* Lincoln, Canterbury, New Zealand: Lincoln University.

Severs, J., Whitlam, P., & Woodhouse, J. (2003). *Safety and risk in primary school physical education: A guide for teachers.* London, NY: Routledge.

Sixth grader kills her classmate, 12. (2004, June 2). *The Japan Times.* Retrieved from www.japantimes.co.jp/2004/06/02/announcements/sixth-grader-kills-her-classmate-12/#.U_FcgsWSx8E

Smith, A. B. (1998). *Understanding children's development* (4th ed.). Wellington, New Zealand: Bridget Williams Books.

Standards Association of New Zealand. (1986). *New Zealand standard specification for playgrounds and playground equipment (NZS 5828: Parts 1–3: 1986).* Wellington, New Zealand: Standards Association of New Zealand.

Stearns, P. N. (2003). *Anxious parents: A history of modern child-rearing in America.* New York: New York University Press.

Sutherden, E. (1998). Catching on to the carpentry groove. *Playcentre Journal,* (101), 8–10.

Tansey, J., & Rayner, S. (2009). Cultural theory and risk. In R. L. Heath & H. D. O'Hair (Eds.), *Handbook of risk and crisis communication* (pp. 53–79). New York, NY: Routledge.

Motive key for teen in school rampage. (2005, September 25). The Japan Times. Retrieved from www.japantimes.co.jp/news/2005/09/25/national/motive-key-for-teen-in-school-rampage/#.U_FflsWSx8E

Thomas, G., & Hocking, G. (2003). *Other people's children.* London, UK: Demos.

Tobin, J. J., Wu, D. Y. H., & Davidson, D. H. (1989). *Preschool in three cultures: Japan, China and the United States.* New Haven, CT: Yale University Press.

Walsh, D. J. (2002). The development of self in Japanese preschools: Negotiating space. In L. Bresler & A. Ardichvili (Eds.), *Research in international education: Experience, theory and practice* (pp. 213–245). New York, NY: Peter Lang Publishing.

Walsh, D. J. (2004). Frog boy and the American monkey: The body in Japanese early schooling. In L. Bresler (Ed.), *Knowing bodies, moving minds: Towards embodied teaching and learning* (pp. 97–109). Dordrecht, The Netherlands: Kluwer Academic.

Whiting, J. W. M. (1941). *Becoming a Kwoma*. New Haven, CT: Yale University Press.

Wilkinson, P. F., & Lockhart, R. S. (1980). Safety in children's formal play environments. In P. F. Wilkinson (Ed.), *Innovation in play environments* (pp. 85–96). New York, NY: St Martin's Press.

Wood, D. (1977). Free the children! Down with playgrounds! *McGill Journal of Education, 12*(2), 227–242.

Wynne, B. (1996). May the sheep safely graze?: A reflexive view of the expert-lay-knowledge divide. In S. Lash, B. Szerszinski, & B. Wynne (Eds.), *Risk, environment and modernity: Towards a new ecology* (pp. 44–83). London, UK: Sage.

Zelizer, V. A. (1994). *Pricing the priceless child: The changing social value of children*. Princeton, NJ: Princeton University Press.

5

THE BODY AS A SITE
OF DISCIPLINE

[Japanese children are] expected to be loud and wild—their spirit is not to be quashed.

(Walsh, 2004, p. 105)

Excessive noise of the type found in [New Zealand] early childhood education centres is now well recognized as having major consequences on the health and learning of young children.

(McLaren, 2005, p. 9)

Introduction

The previous chapters have discussed the ways in which children's bodies reflect the structures of the centres and the communities in which they are based. In the same way, how teachers try to maintain order, and the ways in which children subvert or submit to these measures, provides an interesting lens through which to gain an insight into implicit practices in the early childhood sector. From birth, the bodies of children are subject to the civilising controls of adults (Elias, 2000). Foucault (1975/1995) has focussed on the body as a site of discipline, exposing the civilising power of modern institutions such as prisons, hospitals, and schools. According to Foucault, the foundations for change in society were laid during the seventeenth and eighteenth century. During this period, new mechanisms of power began to emerge "whose operation [was] not ensured by right but by technique, not by law but by normalization, not by punishment but by control, methods that [were] employed on all levels and in forms that go beyond the state and its apparatus" (Foucault, 1981, p. 89). The body is rendered docile through the micro-physics of bio-power and the normalisation of rational control. Through a process of assessment, coordination, and ultimately, surveillance, emerges the "disciplinary individual" who has been created by these techniques of power (Foucault, 1975/1995, p. 227).

This chapter argues that the ways in which these techniques of power operate to control and regulate children's bodies is culturally mediated. The chapter presents key points for discussion. The first section looks at how noisy environments are not only regarded as disorderly, but they are seen as detrimental to children's learning in New Zealand. This view contrasts with both research and teacher opinion in Japan, which does not regard noise as impinging on a positive early childhood experience for children. The second section discusses notions of conflict and confrontation through an analysis of the kinds of behaviour deemed inappropriate in each context and the approaches used to manage it. Finally, an examination is made of the ways time and space are managed to create the kind of environment favoured by the early childhood sector in New Zealand and Japan.

Deconstructing Noise

Holliday and Hassard (2001) argue that the Foucauldian disciplined and docile body is accorded high status in Western culture. The idea of the mind as symbolically significant, rather than the body, stems from the writings of Descartes, which have strongly influenced Western philosophy. Connected intimately with the mind, the disciplined body can therefore subdue bodily excesses. Within this framework, strong minds are manifest in disciplined bodies. The following discussion on the aversion to noise, noted in the New Zealand context, appears to normalise the Cartesian aspirations for a disciplined body under the control of the mind. In contrast to the Cartesian mind/body dichotomy, Japanese philosophy is regarded as constructing the whole being as a holistic entity (Picone, 1989). The Japanese approach to children's noise can be understood through the terms *genki* (lively) and *kodomo-rashi* (childlike), which do not carry a pejorative meaning. Rather, noise is intrinsically linked to childhood. The presence or absence of noise can, therefore, be seen as symptomatic of the normalising process at work (Foucault, 1975/1995). In New Zealand, the absence of noise becomes a tool for reproducing the social order. In Japan, the presence of noise serves the same purpose.

As the video of the Japanese kindergarten wound to a close, following its screening to Kaimai Kindergarten teachers, the viewers commented excitedly about the riotous scenes interspersed with periods of controlled calm. Putting themselves in the position of the Japanese staff, the New Zealanders found it hard to believe that either the teachers could be effective or that the children would be able to learn. At the crux of their discussions was the constant noise that reverberated across the centre during periods of free play, singing, and group activities:

It's the noise that got me!
It's not just little voices. It's the fact that . . . I didn't realise until I watched the video that it's like a huge great hall and it's got classrooms off this hallway

and the noise must be just be [incredible]! I was watching something else in this class and you can hear this other class down the hall. God, I would go mad!

For example, it is quiet here but it's the next door classrooms making noise. If I was a teacher here, I'd be wanting to go "Can you just be quiet!"

The New Zealand teachers felt that the Japanese kindergarten's environment obviously contributed to excessive noise levels with its wooden floors and open plan classrooms, in contrast with their own centre's thick carpet and sound proofed walls. They also noted that the Japanese teacher seemed to be encouraging the children to raise their voices even further through her praise of the class's exuberant singing. They felt this act to be completely counter to achieving a harmonious result:

It's like they are being promoted to yell throughout the song. They're not singing.

That's the other thing. She tells them, if I remember rightly, to do it loud and we tell the children here to sing. We actually tell them that they all need to sing but she almost encourages them to shout it and we would stop the song if they were shouting. There's a difference between singing and putting a bit of effort into the song and screaming which is what I saw some of the children do.

Noise as Counterproductive

But why were these teachers so disturbed by noise levels that Japanese viewers described as unexceptional? It would seem that noise in Japanese centres is counter to New Zealand expectations that children's bodies be civilised (Elias, 2000) or made docile (Foucault, 1975/1995). Research supports the view that excessive noise is inappropriate in New Zealand settings such as the home and the classroom (McLaren, 2008; Ministry of Education, 2011; Ritchie & Ritchie, 1997). In their portrait of an "ordinary mother" in the 1960s, Ritchie and Ritchie (1970, p. 95) found there was little tolerance for spiritedness in the house. Speaking with a woman, they call Sheila, they asked, "How about making noise in the house—how much of that do you allow?" Sheila replies, "Less than most people, believe me. You get three children of two stone[1] each flinging themselves around, it's too much". Although the authors note that "noise and 'charging about' is curbed in the house", Sheila is described by the Ritchie and Ritchie (1970, p. 107) as "a little more relaxed" than most of the mothers they spoke with. When interviewing New Zealand mothers of four-year-olds, Ritchie & Ritchie (1997) found that noisy behaviour was treated with disapproval. "High spirits, excited squeals, verbal expressions of anger or injustice, loud laughter frequently earned parental rebuke" (Ritchie & Ritchie, 1997, p. 37). This concern with noise and general disorder has become more pronounced in recent decades as expectations for groomed homes have risen (Eyles-Bennett & Baker-Shreeve, 2007; Ritchie & Ritchie, 1997).

The detrimental effects of noisy surroundings on the health and development of young children in New Zealand has been the focus of research by McLaren (2005) who cites a number of studies linking children's poor performance to noisy learning environments (Bronzaft, 1981; Bronzaft & McCarthy, 1975; Hambrick-Dixon, 1985; Maxwell & Evans, 2000 cited in McLaren, 2005). While McLaren suggests that all children are at risk of impaired learning in a noisy environment, he argues that most affected are children with sensory integration dysfunction. McLaren (2005) found that many of the centres in his study lacked quiet spaces, making it an issue of frustration and inadequate planning for teachers. He determined that 18% of children in sessional centres, and 43% in all day centres are being exposed to sound levels higher than the maximum specified for adults in the workplace (McLaren, 2008).

A combination of revisions to the *NZ Education (Early Childhood) Regulations 1998* (Ministry of Education, 2012) and McLaren's study has resulted in a new clause being added to the criteria, which specifically refers to the potential damage of noise and seeks to minimise it (McLaren, 2008). To assist with this aim, a new piece of equipment known as the Safe Sound Indicator has begun to be marketed to early childhood professionals. The purpose of the indicator is to monitor noise levels in settings such as the early childhood centre. Designed to look like a traffic light, the monitor flashes from green to yellow and finally to red as noise escalates above acceptable thresholds.

New Zealand teachers interviewed as part of this study overwhelmingly supported the view that noise is not only an obstacle to children's learning, but it has the potential to do great damage to young ears. They also acknowledged that the issue has recently gained greater attention in the early childhood sector. However, teachers seemed to be less united on exactly why noise is so undesirable. In Napier, teachers commented that

> [t]here was a bit of squealing outside, you know, and we stop the squealing.
>
> We are constantly trying to limit noise.
>
> Because it damages their ears and it is just . . . it increases. You know, noise makes more noise, doesn't it?
>
> And there are children that don't like the noise in their environment. The quiet little ones deserve just as much right to play as those who like the noisy, boisterous play.

At Kaimai Kindergarten, teachers were less concerned with the rights of children's access to a quiet play area, but instead directed their attention to the negative impression noisy spaces conveyed and its potential to impede learning:

> Noise is a measure of lack of control here.
>
> I think noise goes with size, group size and where is the learning when there's a whole lot of noise? How does a child relax?

So what do these comments indicate about the unacceptable nature of noisy early childhood environments in New Zealand? In the first instance, noise links to discourses which depict the child in need of protection from damaging forces. High levels of noise are viewed as damaging to the body and a source of stress for both children and adults. In fact, government criteria for early childhood centres describe noise as a potential health and safety hazard (Ministry of Education, 2011).

In the minds of these teachers, noise also symbolises a lack of control. Children are not seen to be respecting the authority of teaching staff if they are running about the centre, shrieking and yelling. There also seemed to be the view that this kind of behaviour also does not display respect to other children at the centre. Then there is the issue of children's rights, which call for all members of the centre to have equal access to play and learning opportunities (Te One, 2005). Teachers admitted that it was challenging to balance the rights of the individual with those of others. However, most expressed the belief that children who wished to play in a quiet space needed to be supported. In centres, which are mainly of open plan design, this is difficult unless high noise levels are curbed. Children are often encouraged to conduct noisy activities outside which leaves the indoor area available for quieter activities. But as teachers in both this study and McLaren's (2008) pointed out, this is not necessarily an option when the weather turns nasty. Teachers also linked large class sizes with noisy settings and a subsequent lack of learning opportunities.[2]

Noise as Organic

The views expressed by the New Zealand teachers resemble those of American teachers interviewed as part of Fujita and Sano's (1988) comparative study of early childhood settings in the United States and Japan. The American teachers found the Japanese centre noisy and chaotic, which they attributed to lack of teacher control within the structure of large classrooms. However, New Zealand and American opinions surrounding noise and disorder contrast with the Japanese early childhood context, which is punctuated by high levels of noise and boisterous classes. In fact, many anthropologists (Hendry, 1986; Lewis, 1995; Peak, 1991; Tobin, Wu, & Davidson, 1989) look at a schedule dominated by free play, little apparent disciplinary action by teachers, and consequently deafening noise levels as a defining feature of Japanese early childhood centres. But rather than seeing disorder and noise as detrimental to children's development and learning as New Zealand teachers might, Japanese teachers can see the benefits of periods of unstructured, noisy chaos. A kindergarten teacher in Tokyo explained that while it is not desirable for children to interact in a constant state of white noise, during times such as the lengthy free play periods, lively verbal or physical exchanges are not curtailed by the staff.

Of course, play-time is very noisy. But in the classroom with fifty-four children, sixty children, if they use loud voices with each other, they may start to develop hearing problems. So we point this out to them so they can understand. But during play-time it's fine. During play-time nobody says "Sshh" in Japan. So you can be very, very noisy, and that's fine.

Tobin et al. (1989) have specifically identified lower expectations for children's noise levels and rowdy behaviour as one of several pedagogical strategies that teachers use to socialise children towards the goal of *shūdan seikatsu*. Ben-Ari (2008, p. 256) has stated that children's "vibrancy and liveliness often ends up in noisy, messy, and frenzied activity". Like others before him he suggests that the chaotic, disordered nature of Japanese centres actually contributes to children's development. He argues that the 'mischief' such as name-calling, obscenity, and irony, which is common in Japanese centres, actually serves to conceptualise how the socialisation of self occurs. Through critical play children learn to develop 'role distance' or an ability to distance oneself from structured social situations. Ben-Ari suggests that this capacity for detachment is necessary for children, and later adults, to interact successfully in group-oriented Japanese society. LeVine and White (2003) note that primary school classrooms are just as chaotic as kindergartens, which might lead visitors to wonder who is in control of the room. They point out that teachers are not concerned by the noise, which is often indicative of children excitedly debating over the content of the lessons. They even suggest that a noisy classroom may be seen as a measure of success. Walsh (2004) discovered that teachers saw the raucous scenes as encouraging children to be *genki*, the highly valued quality that denotes strength, physicality, health, and vitality.

In our study too, the word *genki* (lively) often came up during the course of the day at Oka Kindergarten, and especially during morning greetings and singing, such as the exuberant episode that was so roundly criticised by the New Zealand teachers at the beginning of this chapter. Yet most of the Japanese viewers at focus groups felt the noise levels were appropriate, even admirable, as this comment from Hokkaido suggests:

> The children all used really, loud clear voices throughout that whole session. They were really using their voices.

However, a kindergarten teacher, in Tokyo, reflected that although the Japanese teacher in the video often called on children to use their *genki* (lively) voice, she personally encouraged children to use their beautiful voices (*kirei na koe*) instead which produced more gentle results. While individual teachers may take steps to reduce their contribution to the noise levels, children who run about the Japanese centre shrieking and yelling are not regarded as problematic, but seen as expressing energy and enthusiasm conducive with being a child. Japanese teachers at both the centre where fieldwork took place and at the focus groups regularly used the word *kodomo-rashi* (childlike) to describe this kind of behaviour. Scholars have also mentioned the positive connotations of this term when linked to the noisy behaviour of children (Peak, 1991).

FIGURE 5.1 At Kaimai Kindergarten, a teacher mediates in a conflict in the sandpit

In Japanese preschools, active, boisterous behaviour is even believed to contribute to strength of character in later years. Japanese teachers cheerfully tolerate high levels of noise and activity and avoid direct use of their authority to discipline individual children, preferring instead to ignore inappropriate behaviour or to encourage the class to govern their own actions. This contrasts with views expressed in New Zealand which supported adult intervention as part of conflict resolution, especially during disputes of a physical nature (see Figure 5.1). Teacher intervention in disputes is not only seen as a feature of a quality programme, but it is held up as an opportunity to scaffold children's learning and social development. The following section discusses how the video screenings and focus groups in each country revealed differing perceptions of what constitutes social disorder in the early childhood setting, as well as the accepted means of dealing with children's inappropriate behaviour.

Conflict and Confrontation

Conflict and confrontation are a normal part of the interactions between children in early childhood settings, just as they are regular features in the lives of adults. This section discusses how teachers react to disturbances to routine and considers the different methods of social control and conflict resolution normalised in each setting. It is this normalising gaze, which informs how individuals are classified, judged, and punished (Foucault, 1975/1995). At Kaimai Kindergarten in New Zealand, there are several conflicts which occurred during the course of the video.

In one of them, the beginnings of a dispute can be heard in the distance with first one child, then a group, chanting for another child to go away. Out of shot, the teacher states "Stop! What's going on here?" The camera fixes on Ben who is sitting on the couch clutching a toy. Other children begin to drift over towards the couch where the teacher has established that Ben has taken a toy off another child whom she believes to be Jake. Although the teacher speaks calmly to Ben to relinquish the toy, he refuses to cooperate and as she reaches in to take it, Ben lashes out and kicks her. The teacher moves swiftly to contain the flailing limbs and awkwardly lifts Ben off the couch to the floor. She wraps her arms around him and says firmly, "Stop. I want you to stop". Ben wriggles free from her grasp and throws the toy across the room, shouting "I'm giving it to Jake". The teacher asks him, "Are you going to give it to Jake? Listen, this is what I want you to do. When Jake is around, you use your words". Another little girl, Anna, comes over and retrieves the toy off the floor. The teacher looks up and asks, "Oh, is it yours, Anna?" When Anna replies in the affirmative the teacher turns her attention back to Ben, saying, "You need to calm down. Do you want some time out by yourself? OK?" Ben pushes free and climbs defiantly back on the couch.

At an American centre, Tobin et al. (1989) have described a similar scene where the teacher intervenes in a dispute in order to identify the innocent and guilty parties, and to administer appropriate punishment. Tobin et al. viewed this approach as being linked to American views of fairness and justice. Just as adults in the society regularly deal with litigation and arbitration, American children are learning to resolve conflict in the same way. In New Zealand too, there is a strong sense of fairness, but also a desire for equity. Throughout the fieldwork early childhood staff regularly discussed egalitarian beliefs about children's access to resources and play opportunities. These discussions were framed within the wider historical context of New Zealand society, which scholars have claimed to be almost 'classless' in comparison to the stratified British society that many immigrants left from during the colonial period (Sinclair, 2000). Although class issues in New Zealand have come under closer scrutiny in recent decades, there remains an underlying idealism about living in an egalitarian society despite the reality that suggests otherwise (Black, 2005; Howland, 2002).

Rights Discourses in New Zealand

New Zealand teachers have also been influenced by rights-based discourses which lead them to believe that all children are entitled to a relatively harmonious play and learning space. This contrasts with the Japanese context where children are unfamiliar with the notion of rights, and take few opportunities to exercise them (Goodman, 1996; Kita, 2008). In New Zealand, support for rights-based discourses can be seen in the words of the early childhood curriculum, which states that children's "rights to personal dignity, to equitable opportunities for participation, to protection from physical, mental, or emotional abuse and injury, and to opportunities for rest and leisure must be safeguarded" (Ministry of Education, 1996, p. 40). A strong belief in children's rights was also evident in comments made by focus group participants:

> There was that girl walking over the plank and the boys just pushed her off and then she was just gone. She wasn't encouraged to talk to them about how she didn't like that because she has a right to play. Even if she gets hurt, she still has a right to play, and it was like no one was helping her to say "you have a right to play, so play".

Fighting is not encouraged at Kaimai Kindergarten, and when conflict does occur, resolution is most often achieved through verbal exchanges between the children or with the teacher acting as a mediator. Children are encouraged to verbally negotiate resolutions to disputes, and teachers are regarded as important role models through the provision of appropriate language. They are also expected to offer help if children appear to need assistance. Elias (2005) argues that intervention in conflict is a mark of civilisation. Within this framework, "every form of physical violence not licenced by the state calls for an intervention of state authorities" (Elias, 2005, p. 97). Elias's argument is challenged by the Japanese early childhood context, where teachers frequently elect not to intervene in conflict, but to take a more organic approach to violence, as discussed later in this chapter.

Teachers at the New Zealand centre were specific about the ways in which verbal communication was vital to the development of young children in their care. Not only did they see their roles as modeling appropriate communicative behaviour, but as providing positive examples for children to practically implement during their interactions within the centre:

> It's helping children articulate and there are certain times when they can't articulate those deep feelings of conflict, if you like. So if a child is just working with paint, or playdough or paper and glue they know what they are doing. You don't need to extend or sit next to them, you can just leave them alone but in a situation where [children are fighting] that's where they need to learn that conflict stuff.
>
> I think it's also to reinforce, to make sure they are being heard, as in to acknowledge that they have something important to say and it's important that the other person listens to them and to give them that confidence and to clarify it for the other person.

Teachers did not just see themselves as providing a model for children's communicative competency, but also felt responsible for predicting and minimising conflict in the early childhood setting, as this Wellington teacher explains:

I think pre-empting issues is a big part of a teacher's role. If you see something is going to be a problem, you don't have just one bike because you
know it's going to cause conflict unless it's there for a purpose like learning
to take turns. I think a big part of the whole conflict thing is minimising
reasons the children will have conflict and then from there, figuring out
how to deal with it. I think because children are developing their social
skills it is important in early childhood to give them the opportunities to
learn how to express themselves and that's generally done verbally. That's
how you communicate.

The curriculum, *Te Whāriki* (Ministry of Education, 1996) recommends that
"the environment and routines are planned to minimise confrontation and conflict, for instance, from crowding and queuing" (p. 63). It also asks teachers to
reflect on how much importance should be placed on sharing as opposed to
ensuring there are enough resources to prevent conflict. *Te Whāriki* advises that
all children have an opportunity to access the equipment and if there are discrep-
ancies teachers should mediate in those conflicts (Ministry of Education, 1996).
McLaren (2005) has argued that an inability to communicate effectively verbally
due to impediments such as a noisy environment often leads children to resort to
physical force or other non-verbal means of communication to resolve conflicts.
Through these texts it becomes implicitly clear that physical conflict is seen as
undesirable behavior, which is not supported in the New Zealand early childhood
sector.

The notion that conflict between young children is to be avoided has gained
currency in a world consumed by risk analysis as discussed in the previous chapter.
Guldberg (2009) argues that as contemporary society has increasingly moved to
protect children within a safety-first culture, young people have become unable
to place minor altercations in perspective or to resolve their own conflicts. Rather
than being encouraged to address problems within their peer groups, contemporary children are taught to seek assistance from teachers and adults. In New
Zealand, there is a hesitancy to allow conflicts to escalate, especially if they are of a
physical nature. But in Japan, it became apparent from the ethnographic observations that disorder can provide the chance for children to learn important social
lessons without the intervention of adults.

The Lessons of Conflict

At Oka Kindergarten, there were also regular skirmishes that broke out during the
course of fieldwork. However, they were of quite a different nature to the New
Zealand conflict, and resolved in another manner. In one of these episodes, Joji, a
four-year-old boy, is milling about the washbasin near a group of children when
Kota suddenly comes across and starts to push him. Joji pushes back, then as Kota
begins to twist his opponent's shirt up around his neck, Joji kicks Kota hard in

the shins. Throughout the altercation, they don't appear to exchange words. After receiving another firm kick from Joji, Kota turns abruptly and rushes back to his desk where he sits with his head in his hands. Joji walks across and places his hand on Kota's arm, saying "I'm sorry" (*gomen ne*). Kota glances up to give Joji a disdainful look and puts his head back down again. Joji tries one more time then drifts off back to where the other children are playing. Eventually, Kota also rejoins the group without expressing any residual malice. At the locus of this confrontation was the child's body.

The first thing that struck Kaimai Kindergarten teachers about this scene was the absence of the Japanese teacher during the conflict. With a large class of thirty-three children to manage, the teacher was still outside finishing a post-assembly ritual, which involved quizzing each child individually. She had instructed the children to independently return to the classroom as each one completed the task. The New Zealand viewers were also perturbed by the sudden and seemingly unprovoked nature of the attack and the way that hitting seemed to be the first course of action rather than a last resort. However, upon viewing the video the Japanese teacher was relaxed about the images before her, commenting that those two boys seemed to have a particular aversion to each other that would take time to resolve. She was concerned neither about the physical contact between the boys nor her supposedly neglectful supervision as identified by the Kaimai Kindergarten teachers.

In the original *Preschool in Three Cultures* (*PS3C*) study, Tobin et al. (1989) also found that similar scenes of violence and unruly behaviour between Japanese children were shocking to American and Chinese viewers. However, a Japanese principal explained that fighting, especially among boys, served an important developmental purpose for them. He commented that

> [i]f there were no fights among four-year-old children, that would be a real problem. We don't encourage children to fight, but children need to fight when they are young if they are to develop into complete human beings. When children are preschool age, they naturally fight if given the chance, and it is by fighting and experiencing what it feels like to hit someone and hurt them and to be hit and be hurt that they learn to control this urge to fight, that they learn the dangers of fighting and get it out of their system.
>
> *(Tobin et al., 1989, p. 33)*

Children who provoke fights are seen by Japanese teachers as giving other children a valuable opportunity to practice resolving conflicts themselves, and to assist in mediating disagreements between their classmates. Teachers may even employ more direct strategies in order to provoke conflict, such as putting out fewer toys or crayons than there are children, forcing them to learn to cooperate and share the limited resources (Tobin et al., 1989).[3]

Learning Communicative Competency

Viewing the New Zealand video, the Oka Kindergarten teachers identified verbal communication as a skill that appeared to them to be both encouraged and developed within the New Zealand early childhood setting. A number of scholars have discussed the Western propensity to prioritise verbal communication over non-verbal methods as well as the problems that may occur when diverse cultural groups encounter this expectation (Lancy, 2008; Rogoff, Mosier, Mistry, & Göncü, 1998; Tough, 1977). Farquhar and Fleer (2007) point out that New Zealand teachers not only expect children to be competent in communicating when entering the early childhood education environment, they place stress on verbal interactions.

Informal sources support the notion that language and verbal communication are given prominence in New Zealand. A website dedicated to informing parents about raising children in New Zealand had this to say about what to expect at kindergarten:

> Children are encouraged to use language to communicate. They are taught to let others know how they are feeling and what their needs are by talking to them. The expression "Use your words" will be commonly heard— especially when encouraging youngsters not to hit or get frustrated. Your child will also be taught to stand up for themselves verbally, by learning phrases such as "Stop it, I don't like it" ("Kindergarten", 2007).

Indeed, during the New Zealand video the phrase "use your words" occurred several times as teachers dealt with conflict situations or tried to encourage children to express how they were feeling. The very fact that "use your words" cannot be easily translated into Japanese is a strong indication about the preferred style of communication in each country. As discussed in chapter three, remaining unstated in New Zealand, yet implicitly clear is the message: 'use your words *and not your body*'.

Rather than seeing their role as modelling oral competency and appropriate responses, Japanese parents and teachers work on children's ability to implicitly interpret what is going on. Clancy (2008) notes that verbal expression and those who rely on it are seen negatively in Japanese culture to the extent that verbosity is linked to insincerity and shallowness of character. When verbal communication does occur, it is often ambiguous and indirect. Clancy identifies the way in which Japanese communicate as a point of difference compared to other cultures. In Japan, the emphasis is on the listener to correctly interpret the nuances of speech, rather than on the speaker to make clear his or her point. This contrasts with patterns of expression where speakers are urged to effectively clarify their thoughts (Reddy, 1979). Upwardly mobile parents recognise that oral fluency is linked to future success in school where children will be expected to analyse, explain, discuss, report, and respond to testing (Martini, 1995). With this aim in mind, Western parents are not only tolerant of children's interruptions to adult conversations, but they expect even very young children to form opinions and express them (Portes, Dunham, King, & Kidwell, 1988).

Developing Empathy

Clancy (2008) found that Japanese mothers spend a great deal of time and effort ensuring that their children develop the skill of empathy. In the same way, Japanese teachers appeal to children's emotions by highlighting the feelings of all involved in the conflict, rather than assuming an authoritarian role or identifying a perpetrator. Teachers make more use of peer-group approval and condemnation and less of their own positive or negative opinions to influence children's behaviour (Tobin, 1997). Fujita and Sano (1988) also found that Japanese teachers preferred to demonstrate appropriate behaviour or activities, rather than explain it as American teachers were prone to do. This thinking extended to disciplining children for fighting. While the American teachers liked to discuss the issue and suggest rules prior to disputes breaking out, the Japanese teachers were inclined to wait for a fight to occur to take action.

During Rachael's fieldwork, the Oka teachers also indicated that they dealt with fighting by taking a 'wait and see' approach, or *mimamoru* in Japanese. Instead of intervening immediately in children's disputes, they preferred to allow the conflict to play out unless children were in danger of becoming physically injured. Tobin et al. (2009, p. 133) have identified this as a common strategy, which is part of a larger pedagogical approach known as *machi no hoiku* or 'caring for children by waiting'. Although this strategy does not feature in either the curriculum or as part of teacher preservice education programmes, it is accepted by early childhood teachers as valuable for children's social development. Teachers also recognise that it is not an easy strategy to implement which is why it takes several years of practical experience before teachers can become comfortable with the levels of self-control required to allow children's fights to continue uninterrupted. As Tobin et al. have pointed out, this can look like neglect or passivity to the outsider but is in fact a deliberate strategy.

In Japan, hitting is treated as relatively inconsequential by teachers who will generally ignore fights and intervene only if the incident has gone on for a protracted length of time. As Peak (1989) explains, "Japanese teachers do not consider hitting a 'crime' or a demonstration of anti-social tendencies. Rather, it indicates social immaturity and frustration at an inability to verbalize one's feelings" (p. 108). Play fighting or *tatakau-gokko* is one of the most popular games for children at kindergarten, especially boys. While it may sound harmless enough, the Japanese word comes from the verb *tataku,* which actually means to strike, hit, or knock, and encounters can be very rough. While hitting in a New Zealand context is tantamount to disorderly behaviour, in a Japanese context, this is not necessarily so. As Walsh (2002) and Tobin (1992) have discussed, the early childhood centre is made up of structured periods followed by almost chaotic frenzy. Children learn to tolerate the organised formality of their day as they know it won't be long before they will be free to be spontaneous. In the same way, teachers are not disturbed by disorder as they know the class will soon resume a sense of orderliness.

The Use of Time and Space

In both the New Zealand and Japanese early childhood contexts, time, and space are used to create a sense of order, and to discipline children's bodies. Foucault (1975/1995) sees the control of time and space as central to his theory of a disciplinary society because they are at the crux of all human interaction. He links the regulation of time and space to monastic and military life, arguing that "disciplinary space tends to be divided into as many sections as there are bodies or elements to be distributed" (Foucault, 1975/1995, p. 143). This idea can be seen most clearly in the Japanese context where children at Oka Kindergarten are divided into classes, then again into timetabled sessions, and are constantly required to line up in a pre-determined order during assemblies, medical inspections, and events. Members of different classes are instantly identifiable by their matching coloured class caps. Within the highly literate Japanese society, documents pertaining to early childhood education are generally produced by 'experts' in Tokyo, and present parameters of 'normal' childhood development which both inform and construct children's behaviour (Goodman, 2002). As the majority of teachers are constantly referring to these texts, they come to structure their day around official definitions of what is desirable or necessary for becoming a 'good' Japanese child (White & LeVine, 1986).

In New Zealand, Kaimai Kindergarten's practices reflect more fluid structures of time and space. With the exception of the fencing around the grounds, the physical structure of the centre resembles a home in many ways. Whereas in Japan, the entry into early childhood education represents a break with the family environment, in New Zealand the emphasis is more on continuity. Planning and routines stem from "observations of the children's interests, strengths, needs, and behaviours" (Ministry of Education, 1996, p. 28). Although the doors of the centre open at 8.30 am, children are not required to arrive exactly on time and will not be disadvantaged if they miss all or part of a session. Unlike Oka Kindergarten, where children are not only arranged by class and then again by small groups, there are few overt classifying structures in place at Kaimai Kindergarten. On a macro level, however, the centre still works to regulate children's bodies to routine daily patterns, but this is challenged by rights-based discourses that increasingly form an integral part of New Zealand's early childhood landscape.

Time and Space as Disciplinary Techniques
in the Japanese Kindergarten

Tobin (1992) has discussed how spaces in Japanese centres contribute to children's understanding of inside (*uchi*) and outside (*soto*) contexts. Unlike in New Zealand, where parents are encouraged to enter the centre and spend time settling their children, Japanese centres are notable for the formal spaces that mark *uchi* and *soto* worlds. Teachers ask parents to remain in the foyer (*genkan*) while saying good-bye. This is a unique space, which incorporates both the *uchi* and *soto* worlds. Just as the family home represents an *uchi* (inside) context, so does the kindergarten or childcare centre. Once children cross alone into the centre, they have again entered the *uchi* world, which is marked by acts such as placing their shoes in their cubby hole and stowing their bag. While New Zealand parents may frequently be present at the centre conducting parent help or observing their children, Japanese parents' time past the threshold of the *genkan* is limited to special events or open days. In observing this division of space, Japanese teachers maintain that they can most effectively keep control of their classrooms and facilitate children's socialisation.

In the same way, time is assigned a more formal meaning in the Japanese centre as "children learn to punctuate their lives and record their development less according to their birthdays . . . than according to their year in school" (Tobin, 1992, p. 34). Hendry (1993) has shown how the use of time in the Japanese context acts as a form of temporal wrapping. She points out that early childhood settings are spaces where beginnings and endings become both more pronounced and more complex. This can be seen in how the day is divided into ritual events such as opening sequences before the daily activities begin. At Oka Kindergarten, an example of this kind of ritual event is the assembly, which takes place every morning following the free play session. Children are alerted to the impending gathering by music pumped out over the loudspeaker following the ritualised clean-up time. Teachers impress upon children to make their way hastily to the designated meeting spot, as if the assembly is an eagerly awaited event. From the beginning of the academic year, children learn to line up quickly and efficiently according to height, all the while clapping or stamping in time to the duty teacher's actions at the front of the stage. At Oka Kindergarten, assemblies are held in the hall in winter and outside during the summer months, but despite the venue, the routine does not vary (see Figure 5.2).

For some of the Japanese focus groups, this attention to protracted embodied rituals is associated with a traditional style of early childhood education, which is less popular in today's more liberal centres. Despite this difference, the temporal structures obvious in the video are familiar, as academics from Hiroshima explain:

> For example, now it's time to arrive at kindergarten, for free play, assembly, group activity, lunchtime, then free play again, then leave, that's a typical [kindergarten] schedule. So everything is structured one after the other.

FIGURE 5.2 Oka Kindergarten children listen to the morning talk at assembly

Hendry (1993) has discussed the routines which punctuate activity sequences, break times, meals, and leaving times. She gives the example of a principal formally greeting each child as they arrive in the morning as evidence of yet more temporal wrapping, as well as individual class greeting rituals, which are regular features of Japanese early childhood settings. Oka Kindergarten again strongly resembled the descriptions given by Hendry. Each morning, the principal awaits the arrival of the brightly painted kindergarten buses, and as he assists each child down the steps, he offers a hearty *"ohayo gozaimasu"* ("good morning") and expects the same in return. Meal times at the kindergarten are not just marked by spoken greetings, but children are expected to stand and sing a dedicated song for each event including lunch, arrival, and departure, as well as during the roll and English class. Observations by the Japanese focus groups suggest that while this is familiar territory, there is a move away from such defined and lengthy rituals, towards a shorter, streamlined version of these temporal wrappings. But still at the crux of these rituals are the familiar 'body techniques' (Mauss, 1936/1973) that serve to internalise Japanese values.

Children's Bodies as Objects of the Medical Gaze

The way in which time is given, or withheld, to both the individual and the group, in the early childhood setting can reveal deeper cultural assumptions. This idea is illustrated by a scene from the Japanese video where Oka children are visited by the local doctor. Foucault (1973) has traced the development of the medical gaze which places the body as an object to be observed, and then compared to a norm of corporeality. This process of observation and normalisation of the body is a common feature of Japanese centres where importance is given to children's health checks and visits by health professionals (Duncan, 2006). All Japanese children are expected to undergo routine medical examinations during their time at the kindergarten and as the doctor is afforded an elevated social status, it is expected that everyone is ready to greet him once he arrives.

Half an hour before the check, the children are instructed to remove all their clothing, except for their underpants, to ensure that everything is folded neatly in their bags. The teacher then instructs them to line up according to gender and, finally, to sit down and wait for the doctor to arrive. She reminds all the children that they need to be quiet during the visit and show the doctor the respect he deserves. The bare-chested children squirm a little on the wooden floor, but most peer silently down the corridor as they wait for the doctor to arrive from the previous classes. Once he comes in, the teacher and the class greet him formally and he begins examining each child one by one by pressing his stethoscope to their chests and checking their ears and throats (see Figure 5.3). As the children are individually dismissed by the doctor, they are allowed to move back to their desks and begin getting dressed. Those who finish before the others are required to wait quietly until the all the children have completed their check and a farewell greeting has been issued to the doctor.

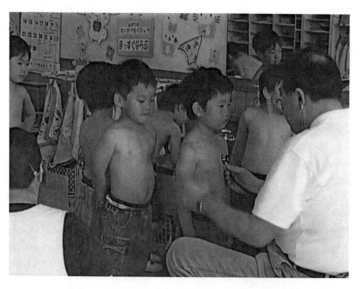

FIGURE 5.3 Children take part in a medical check at Oka Kindergarten

Kaimai Kindergarten teachers were critical of this scene due to the Japanese teachers' inefficient use of time and unfair approach:

> You know how here all the children are sitting in one place, lined up, waiting to be seen by the doctor, well, we wouldn't do that. We would individually call them up. You know, the children would be free playing and we would just go and grab them, or you know, we might get a couple.
> So they don't have to wait.
> That's right. This is a lot of waiting for some of these children. Especially the last person. We just wouldn't expect that children would do that. The most that we would do, sometimes with the Hearing and Vision lady she comes here and we call a few. So we might have two or three children just so she doesn't have to wait all the time, and there's a nice flow going. But we certainly wouldn't make the whole lot of them sit there with their clothes off all ready to go!
> See that's not fair on the child.

The New Zealand teachers felt it was important that children did not give up their valuable play and learning time to wait unproductively for others. This idea is supported by the curriculum, which encourages teachers to minimise unnecessary wait times for children (Ministry of Education, 1996). However, a Japanese analysis of the same situation would not necessarily see the time spent waiting as unproductive or unfair. Benedict (1946) has argued that self-discipline, such as that displayed by the Japanese children while waiting for the doctor, is linked to individual sacrifice in the West. For the Japanese, however, self-discipline may require practice, but it also makes one's life more enjoyable through the social system of reciprocity. Benedict identifies a two-pronged concept of Japanese selfhood, which emphasises both interdependence but also individual accountability and self-reliance. While waiting for others might be seen as giving up one's time in a New Zealand context, in Japan, the waiting is merely a way of working with the group, which ultimately leads to greater rewards than serving the purposes of the individual. Reflecting on these texts, it becomes clear that temporal structures can be manipulated in the same way, but have different outcomes depending on the cultural lens they are viewed through.

Reflecting on the Body as a Site of Discipline

According to Foucault (1981), the 'normal' body can be seen as a site of bio-power. Bio-power can be defined as a technology of power which works to manage people as a group through regulation and subjugation of their bodies. In a disciplinary society, the mechanical body is supplanted by the 'natural body' created by training and the control of activity, time, and space. The body is rendered docile through the micro-physics of bio-power and the normalisation of rational control

(Foucault, 1975/1995). This chapter has discussed some of the ways in which New Zealand and Japanese early childhood settings reflect concepts of the 'normal' child's body and those whose bodies present a challenge to these constructs.

While McLaren's (2008) study is fairly recent, it is clear from research such as the Ritchies' (1997) that many New Zealanders have found the noise of small children bothersome for quite some time. While no longer fashionable, the expression 'children should be seen and not heard' was often uttered in post-war homes in an attempt to subdue unruly children who were noisy and disruptive. The perception that noise corrupts order was also common to other European societies and continues today (Cohen, 2004; Hastings, 2008; Levarie, 1977; Majumdar, 2010). In the New Zealand early childhood context, the issue of noise brings together the 'three bodies' (Scheper-Hughes & Lock, 1987). For the individual, 'physical body', noise is seen as damaging to hearing, and indicative of loss of control when considering the 'social body'. For the 'body politic', noise is regulated by health and safety requirements.

It does however appear to be a particularly European influenced viewpoint. Within New Zealand, Rameka (2009) has drawn on the characteristics of mythological hero, Maui, to create an assessment framework for Māori early childhood services. Maui displayed both positive and less desirable traits, all of which were equally essential to his success. For example, the trait of *whakatoi* or spiritedness may be seen as undesirable in a New Zealand European context, but it is considered favourably according to a Māori world view. The positive view of this characteristic bears many similarities to the Japanese notion of *genki,* which also can be translated as lively or spirited. Rather than interpreting noise as a manifestation of disorder, Japanese early childhood settings reflect the view that children are naturally active, boisterous, and above all, noisy. With this view accepted, there is no conflict between learning and noise—the two quite easily go hand in hand.

This leads to the next issue, which is inappropriate conduct. Just as boisterous behaviour may not be indulged in the New Zealand early childhood setting, hitting is judged inappropriate by the New Zealand teachers that took part in this study. It is notable that while less hitting actually took place in the New Zealand centre compared to the Japanese kindergarten, it was tolerated less and regarded more seriously. At Oka Kindergarten, regular physical contact occurred between the children, but hitting was not seen as a threat to social stability. Children are left to resolve conflicts themselves as part of a pedagogical approach practised by teachers across the country. In most cases, this means that Japanese children will eventually exchange verbal apologies and move on with their play without the intervention of an adult. New Zealand teachers were compelled not only to find the perpetrator but to assist in meting out justice so that children would feel that they had been listened to, and that justice had been served.

In both the Japanese and New Zealand contexts, order is restored through implicit expectations shared by children and teachers but by contrasting means. In the New Zealand early childhood context, children's individual bodies have rights and boundaries that need to be respected and protected. When a child transgresses the rights of another, teachers seek to remove the offending body. The isolation of the individual body, in the form of disciplinary techniques such as 'time out', differs from the Japanese approach where teachers look for ways to incorporate the individual body back into the fold of the collective body. Strategies such as *mimamoru* (wait and see) allow a degree of physicality not sanctioned in the New Zealand context.

In the same way, concepts of appropriate behaviour are shaped as the children and teachers negotiate each day at their respective centres. Foucault (1975/1995) claims that "discipline is a political anatomy of detail" (p. 139). For children at Oka Kindergarten, there is a certain amount of inevitability to the way each day is divided into ritualised periods such as organised class sessions, lunch time, assembly, and greeting routines. This contrasts with time spent in free play, which is striking for its complete lack of structure. Peak (1991) provides a good observation of this:

> Many times each day, the tempo and tenor of activity fluctuates between a tight and a loose structure. Chaotic periods of free play are followed by silent, formal ritual. In Japanese preschools the measure of good discipline is not an overall low level of noise and controlled activity but a quick and precise maintenance between two radically different levels of order.
>
> *(p. 78)*

She adds that an uninformed visitor could mistakenly categorise the very same centre as either extremely rigid in structure or totally chaotic. In fact, Japanese children learn to change their behaviour quickly according to the changing context in preparation for adulthood, where it is essential to understand the appropriate conduct for various social situations (Hendry, 1990).

At Kaimai Kindergarten in New Zealand, order was much less defined by periods of structure. For the Japanese viewers, without any familiar ritualised activities, there seemed little that marked the New Zealand centre as recognisable to them. As one Oka teacher remarked, "There's so much free play going on. It's difficult to see where the curriculum comes in". In fact, the New Zealand early childhood curriculum, *Te Whāriki,* (Ministry of Education, 1996) does not follow a traditional content- or activities-based structure or prescribe subject-based learning areas, which are the basis of the school system. It takes a sociocultural approach to curriculum based on the desire to foster children's natural dispositions to learn (Carr, 2001). Both the way time is managed, and the way the centre space is arranged, supports this aim. While children may be restrained from fighting or excessively yelling, they are given ample opportunities to explore, create, and discover with minimal interruptions from adults unless they ask for assistance. New Zealand children are also required to learn appropriate social conduct, but there is less stress placed on this than in the Japanese environment. More important is the hope that children will grow up confident in their own abilities, be prepared to tackle new challenges and be a contributing member of society (Ministry of Education, 1996, p. 9). Despite differences in approach, both the New Zealand and Japanese early childhood contexts reflect the ways in which children's bodies are subject to diffuse uses of disciplinary power to render them docile (Foucault, 1981).

Notes

1 At the time of the Ritchie's research, New Zealand was still using the imperial measurement system. Two stone in weight equates to approximately twelve and a half kilos.
2 While in the New Zealand early childhood context, scholars such as Smith, McMillan, Kennedy, and Ratcliffe (1989) and Smith (1999) suggest that small groups of around fourteen children are ideal in order to meet quality standards, Tobin (1992) has argued that Japan's large class sizes are a deliberate strategy to promote a group ethos and peer interactions. Burke (2007) found that most Japanese teachers believe one teacher to twenty children to be the optimal size group.
3 While this strategy may still be employed in relatively traditional centres, such as the kindergarten where the fieldwork took place, there are signs that approaches to conflict are changing as Japanese parents become more anxious about their shrinking numbers of offspring. At an elite private Japanese childcare centre in Hokkaido, the principal did not condone the way the teacher handled the boys' squabble, noting that she preferred to reconstruct the event so that children could understand the feelings of all involved.

References

Ben-Ari, E. (2008). Formal caring alternatives: Kindergartens and day-care centers. In J. Robertson (Ed.), *A companion to the anthropology of Japan* (pp. 247–260). Malden, MA: Blackwell.

Benedict, R. (1946). *The chrysanthemum and the sword: Patterns of Japanese culture*. Boston, MA: Houghton Mifflin.

Black, J. (2005). Show a bit of class. *The Listener, 198*(3394), 16–21.

Burke, R. (2007). *Changing times for young minds: Declining class size and shudan seikatsu ideology in Hokkaido preschools*. Unpublished Master's Thesis, Massey University, Auckland, New Zealand.

Carr, M. (2001). *Assessment in early childhood settings: Learning stories*. London, UK: Paul Chapman.

Clancy, P. M. (2008). The acquisition of the communicative style in Japanese. In R. A. LeVine & R. S. New (Eds.), *Anthropology and child development: A cross-cultural reader* (pp. 165–181). Malden, MA: Blackwell.

Cohen, L. (2004). The history of noise. *Proceedings of the SPIE, 5473*, 85–109.

Duncan, J. (2006). Aspiring to quality—Culturally constructed. *Early Childhood Folio, 10*, 32–36.

Elias, N. (2000). *The civilizing process: Sociogenetic and psychogenetic investigations*. Oxford, UK: Blackwell.

Elias, N. (2005). Civilization and psychosomatics. In M. Fraser & M. Greco (Eds.), *The body: A reader* (pp. 96–99). London, UK: Routledge.

Eyles-Bennett, J., & Baker-Shreeve, A. (2007). Dress for success. *New Zealand Property Magazine, 45*, 33–35.

Farquhar, S., & Fleer, M. (2007). Developmental colonisation of early childhood education in Aotearoa/New Zealand and Australia. In L. Keesing-Styles & H. Hedges (Eds.), *Theorising early childhood practice: Emerging dialogues* (pp. 27–49). Castle Hill, NSW, Australia: Pademelon Press.

Foucault, M. (1973). *The birth of the clinic.* New York, NY: Pantheon Books.

Foucault, M. (1975/1995). *Discipline and punish: The birth of the prison* (A. Sheridan, Trans.). New York, NY: Vintage Books.

Foucault, M. (1981). *The history of sexuality, Volume 1: An introduction.* Harmondsworth, UK: Penguin.

Fujita, M., & Sano, T. (1988). Children in American and Japanese day-care centres: Ethnography and reflective cross-cultural interviewing. In H. T. Trueba & C. Delgado-Gaitan (Eds.), *School and society: Learning content through culture* (pp. 73–97). New York, NY: Praeger.

Goodman, R. (1996). On introducing the UN Convention of Rights of the Child into Japan. In R. Goodman & I. Neary (Eds.), *Case studies on human rights in Japan* (pp. 109–140). Richmond, UK: Japan Library.

Goodman, R. (2002). Anthropology, policy and the study of Japan. In R. Goodman (Ed.), *Family and social policy in Japan: Anthropological approaches* (pp. 1–28). Cambridge, UK: Cambridge University Press.

Guldberg, H. (2009). *Reclaiming childhood: Freedom and play in an age of fear.* Abingdon, Oxon, UK: Routledge.

Hastings, C. (2008, September 6). Anti-terrorism laws used to spy on noisy children. *The Telegraph.* Retrieved from www.telegraph.co.uk/news/uknews/2696031/Anti-terrorism-laws-used-to-spy-on-noisy-children/html

Hendry, J. (1986). *Becoming Japanese: The world of the pre-school child.* Honolulu: University of Hawaii Press.

Hendry, J. (1990). Humidity, hygiene, or ritual care: Some thoughts on wrapping as a social phenomenon. In B.-A. Eyal, B. Moeran, & J. Valentine (Eds.), *Unwrapping Japan: Society and culture in anthropological perspective* (pp. 18–35). Manchester, UK: Manchester University Press.

Hendry, J. (1993). *Wrapping culture: Politeness, presentation, and power in Japan and other societies.* Oxford, UK: Oxford University Press.

Holliday, R., & Hassard, J. (2001). *Contested bodies.* New York, NY: Routledge.

Howland, P. (2002). *Lotto, long-drops & lolly scrambles: The extra-ordinary anthropology of middle New Zealand.* Wellington, New Zealand: Steele Roberts.

Kindergarten. (2007). *Kiwi Families.* Retrieved from www.kiwifamilies.co.nz/Topics/Education/Early+Childhood-Education/Kindergarten.html

Kita, A. (2008). Child rights education in Japanese schools. *Human Rights Education in Asia-Pacific* Retrieved from www.hurights.or.jp/archives/asia-pacific/section1/12%20Akihito%20Kita.pdf

Lancy, D. F. (2008). *The anthropology of childhood: Cherubs, chattel, changelings.* Cambridge, UK: Cambridge University Press.

Levarie, S. (1977). Noise. *Critical Inquiry, 4*(1), 21–31.

LeVine, R., & White, M. (2003). Educational mobilization: The case of Japan. In R. LeVine (Ed.), *Childhood socialization: Comparative studies of parenting, learning and educational change* (pp. 159–186). Hong Kong: The University of Hong Kong, Comparative Education Research Centre.

Lewis, C. C. (1995). *Educating hearts and minds: Reflections of Japanese preschool and elementary education.* Cambridge, UK: University of Cambridge.

Majumdar, S. (2010, 6 October). Kicking off against noisy kids. *Word of mouth blog*. Retrieved from www.guardian.co.uk/lifeandstyle/wordofmouth/2010/oct/06/children-restaurants

Martini, M. (1995). Features of home environments associated with children's school success. *Early Child Development and Care, 111,* 49–68.

Mauss, M. (1936/1973). Techniques of the body. *Economy and Society, 2,* 70–88.

McLaren, S. J. (2005). Noise and at-risk children in early childhood education centres. *Early Childhood Folio, 9,* 39–43.

McLaren, S. J. (2008). *Noise in early childhood education centres: The effects on the children and their teachers.* Unpublished PhD thesis, Massey University, Wellington, New Zealand.

Ministry of Education. (1996). *Te Whāriki: He Whāriki Mātauranga mō ngā Mokopuna o Aotearoa. New Zealand early childhood curriculum.* Wellington, New Zealand: Learning Media.

Ministry of Education. (2011). Noise levels. *Welcome to early childhood education: ECE lead.* Retrieved from www.lead.ece.govt.nz/ServiceTypes/CentreBasedECEServices/HealthAndSafety/HazardsAndOutings/HS15NoiseLevels.aspx

Ministry of Education. (2012). Information about ECE regulations. *Early childhood education: ECE lead.* Retrieved from www.lead.ece.govt.nz/ManagementInformation/RegulatoryFrameworkForECEServices.aspx

Peak, L. (1989). Learning to become part of the group: The Japanese child's transition to preschool life. *Journal of Japanese Studies, 15*(1), 93–123.

Peak, L. (1991). *Learning to go to school in Japan: The transition from home to preschool life.* Berkeley: University of California Press.

Picone, M. (1989). The ghost in the machine: Religious healing and representations of the body in Japan. In M. Feher (Ed.), *Fragments for a history of the human body: Part two* (pp. 466–489). New York, NY: Zone.

Portes, P., Dunham, R. M., King, F. J., & Kidwell, J. S. (1988). Early age intervention and parent-child interaction: Their relation to student achievement. *Journal of Research and Development in Education, 21*(4), 78–86.

Rameka, L. (2009). Kaupapa Māori assessment: A journey of meaning making. *Early Childhood Folio, 13,* 32–36.

Reddy, M. (1979). The conduit metaphor: A case of frame conflict in our language about language. In A. Ortony (Ed.), *Metaphor and thought* (pp. 284–320). Cambridge, UK: Cambridge University Press.

Ritchie, J., & Ritchie, J. (1970). *Child rearing patterns in New Zealand.* Wellington, New Zealand: A.H. & A.W. Reed.

Ritchie, J., & Ritchie, J. (1997). *The next generation: Child-rearing in New Zealand.* Auckland, New Zealand: Penguin.

Rogoff, B., Mosier, C., Mistry, J., & Göncü, A. (1998). Toddlers' guided participation with their caregivers in cultural activity. In M. Woodhead, D. Faulkner, & K. Littleton (Eds.), *Cultural worlds of early childhood* (pp. 225–249). London, UK: Routledge.

Scheper-Hughes, N., & Lock, M. (1987). The mindful body: A prolegomenon to future work in medical anthropology. *Medical Anthropology Quarterly, 1*(1), 6–41.

Sinclair, K. (2000). *A history of New Zealand.* Auckland, New Zealand: Penguin Books.

Smith, A. B. (1999). Quality childcare and joint attention. *International Journal of Early Years Education, 71*(1), 85–98.

Smith, A. B., McMillan, B. W., Kennedy, S., & Ratcliffe, B. (1989). The effect of improving preschool teacher/child ratios: An "experiment in nature". *Early Child Development and Care,* (41), 122–138.

Te One, S. (2005). Children's rights and early childhood policy: Impacts and influences. *New Zealand Annual Review of Education, 14,* 171–193.

Tobin, J. (1992). Japanese preschools and the pedagogy of selfhood. In N. R. Rosenberger (Ed.), *Japanese sense of self* (pp. 21–39). Cambridge, UK: Cambridge University Press.

Tobin, J. (1997). Playing doctor in two cultures: The United States and Ireland. In J. Tobin (Ed.), *Making a place for pleasure in early childhood education* (pp. 119–158). New Haven, CT: Yale University Press.

Tobin, J., Hsueh, Y., & Karasawa, M. (2009). *Preschool in three cultures revisited: China, Japan and the United States.* Chicago: University of Chicago Press.

Tobin, J. J., Wu, D. Y. H., & Davidson, D. H. (1989). *Preschool in three cultures: Japan, China and the United States.* New Haven, CT: Yale University Press.

Tough, J. (1977). *Talking and learning: A guide to fostering communication skills in nursery and infant schools.* London, UK: Ward Lock Educational.

Walsh, D. J. (2002). The development of self in Japanese preschools: Negotiating space. In L. Bresler & A. Ardichvili (Eds.), *Research in international education: Experience, theory and practice* (pp. 213–245). New York, NY: Peter Lang Publishing.

Walsh, D. J. (2004). Frog boy and the American monkey: The body in Japanese early schooling. In L. Bresler (Ed.), *Knowing bodies, moving minds: Towards embodied teaching and learning* (pp. 97–109). Dordrecht, The Netherlands: Kluwer Academic.

White, M. I., & LeVine, R. A. (1986). What is an ii ko (good child)? In H. Stevenson, H. Azuma, & K. Hakuta (Eds.), *Child development and education in Japan* (pp. 55–62). New York, NY: W.H. Freeman.

6

THE BODY AS NATURAL SYMBOL

Reflection on dirt involves reflection on the relation of order to disorder, being to non-being, form to formlessness, life to death.

(*Douglas, 1966, p. 16*)

Introduction

The previous chapter discussed the ways in which teachers seek to maintain order in the early childhood education setting in New Zealand and Japan. While at first glance it may seem that concepts of order and pollution are not closely connected, Douglas (1966) has argued that dirt is essentially symbolic of disorder, in that its existence offends against order. Therefore, the removal of dirt cannot be a negative act, but rather a positive means of restoring order. Douglas goes on to show that rituals of purity and impurity actually serve to create unity through their experience. She writes that "dirt . . . is never a unique, isolated event. Where there is dirt there is system. Dirt is the by-product of a systematic ordering and classification of matter, in so far as ordering involves rejecting inappropriate elements" (Douglas, 1966, p. 48). Douglas perceives dirt as an ambiguity positioned at the boundary of categories, which then becomes the source of anomaly. Anomalies may be managed by ignoring the ambiguity, destroying the cause, by avoidance or by being labelled dangerous.

In this chapter, differing instances of issues related to dirt and pollution are discussed using Douglas's framework to inform the analysis. The first section, on dirt and the body, is a consideration of the body as a site that inevitably becomes polluted, yet may be purified both in a physical and ritual sense through cultural practices. The second section interrogates the issue of polluted spaces and the ways in which the anomaly of dirt can be mitigated. The final section focuses on prohibitions and rituals around food, which, according to Douglas, centre on notions of the ordered versus that which is out of place.

Dirt and the Body

As discussed in earlier chapters, the body can be seen as a site where cultural constructions meet, a place where curricula may be reflected and a tangible example of children's physicality. The body is also regarded as a major site for rituals and practices, which pertain to beliefs relating to pollution and purity (Douglas, 1966; Namihira, 1987; Norbeck, 1952). The same can be said of the organs of the body, as well as the body's excreta and fluids (Turner, 2003). This section looks at the meanings that New Zealand and Japanese teachers bring to dirt, concepts of pollution and purity, and how these might intersect with the body. This is undertaken through an analysis of a scene from the New Zealand video, which provoked comment and discussion from teachers in both countries.

In the New Zealand video, Peter, a four-year-old boy comes crying to the teacher, Jody (see Figure 6.1). He is upset about a cut on his knee, which is the result of chasing some bigger boys around the playground and then tripping during the exhilarating chase. Jody is sympathetic to his plight, and after looking at all the 'lovely blood' trickling out of the wound, she suggests that they head inside to put a sticking plaster on it. Once inside, another teacher takes over. She seats Peter in a chair and kneels down to take a look at the scraped

FIGURE 6.1 Peter's bleeding knee

knees. She asks him which knee he would like dealt with first, then tucking her hair back from her face, she peels the backing from a sticking plaster and presses it firmly over the cut.

This scene elicited a great deal of surprise from the Japanese viewers at Oka Kindergarten. Comments such as this one were typical:

> When the little boy falls over and gets a bleeding knee, I was very surprised to see that the teacher didn't put any disinfectant (*shōdoku*) on his wound. What about bacteria or infection? Are the teachers not worried about that?

At first impression, it seems that the Japanese teachers, like early childhood professionals all over the world, are concerned that the New Zealand teachers did not follow well-known policies relating to cleaning the body after injury. However, we would suggest that the major difference in the reading of the scene is the cultural meanings New Zealand and Japanese teachers bring to it. For the Japanese teachers, the scene revealed the strong association Japanese have with the outside and dirt (Ohnuki-Tierney, 1984). Simply placing a sticking plaster over an unsterilised wound seemed abhorrent on a personal level as well as a professional one. Several of the New Zealand focus group participants also reacted in surprise to the teacher's failure to clean the wound. Unlike the Japanese viewers, their reaction did not come from notions of bodily pollution or from a deep, internalised belief that lack of sterilisation would lead to an unfortunate result, such as infection. Instead, they were motivated more by centre policy and rules, which require them to respond appropriately to children's injuries. The following section discusses these two approaches in greater detail through an analysis of teachers' comments and examples from the literature.

The Physical Body as a Microcosm of Society

Foucault's (1973) theories about bio-medicine show how practices are deemed appropriate according to new forms of knowledge. In the New Zealand early childhood context there are clear procedures that must be followed in the case of children getting injured, especially those involving blood or bodily fluids being spilled or exchanged. Many of these changes occurred as a result of the 1980s HIV global epidemic which culminated in centres becoming more aware of potential infection through blood or saliva (Ministry of Education, 1999). Current policies instruct teachers to minimise risks and exposure to disease by using standard infection control precautions such as disposable latex gloves, hand washing, and disinfectant (Frith, Kambouris, & O'Grady, 2003). While these policies have been put in place to protect children's bodies from bacteria and infection, they are also equally informed by a need to safeguard the bodies of teachers. McGrath and Huntington (2007) suggest that those working with young children are particularly at risk from infectious diseases.

This risk is recognised by teachers in Napier who pointed out that they, like the Japanese teachers, would have chosen to clean the wound before applying a bandage. This approach was not only related to policy, but reflected an awareness that the fluid seen on the child's knee could, in fact, have been a mixture of dirt, blood, or even some other foreign substance. In any case, it required cleaning before a barrier was placed over it:

> We would wash the wound. The sticking plaster was just put on top of the "beautiful blood". It may not have been blood.
>
> It looked like blood. I took it she was trying to put a positive spin on "Yes, you've hurt yourself, but it's really quite fascinating, isn't it, because that's your blood and there's nothing to be worried about. It's all perfectly natural, just a flesh wound. Let me come inside and fix it for you".
>
> If you go running around saying, "Oh, get the plaster", it can go a bit over the top really.

Teachers in Wellington expressed the same sentiments:

> It wasn't all-dramatic. I like the example of the teacher looking at the wonderful blood!
>
> I think that was her attitude too, you know, "Oh well, you'll be alright, it's just a bit of blood".

These comments show that the teachers felt it was important not to overly dramatise incidents, which involved injuries, by downplaying cuts and grazes as a regular part of childhood. Scholars suggest that New Zealand national identity is strongly linked to key stoic values (Wevers, 1980), which are manifested in characteristics shown by the first pioneers such as flexibility, resilience, and self-reliance. Phillips (1996) has shown how the denial of pain is one of the most admired traits in rugby players, who themselves symbolise the pinnacle of New Zealand masculine identity. Studies also indicate that New Zealanders have a tendency to take risks (Adams, 2011) and to endeavour to cope with pain without complaining (Madjar, 1991). The belief that one should stoically endure pain as well as a 'laidback' attitude to dealing with injuries appears common.

In contrast to the low key New Zealand reaction to the scraped knee, injuries were dealt with very seriously in the Japanese kindergarten. Children would often come to the staffroom complaining of cuts and grazes, and yet the actual site of the wound could not be found. Nonetheless, the staff would take time to thoroughly examine each child and detergent would be administered, as well as a sticking plaster. For those cuts where blood was actually visible, the teachers would rush about with a great sense of urgency, applying pressure and dabbing on lotions. For a skinned knee, there was a procedure that was assiduously followed: the site would be gently washed with warm water, then detergent wiped over, followed by an antiseptic cream, and finally some form of bandage or sticking plaster would be applied. The whole process gave the impression of an important kind of ritual. Ohnuki-Tierney (1984) has argued that Japanese notions of germs (*baikin*) and hygiene have less to do with actual risks to one's health but rather are cultural concepts located within a framework of pollution and purity.

While the New Zealand teachers tended to dismiss minor injuries as relatively insignificant and encouraged children to continue with their activities, the Japanese teachers were more likely to make quite a fuss of children. On a personal level, Rachael can recall several times during her time working at a Japanese kindergarten when she had sent children with minor scratches back outside to play, only to have them called back by the Japanese teacher to undergo the procedure described above. On their return to New Zealand, Rachael's own children were very disappointed to discover that a scraped knee garnered concern in Japan but received little attention back home. Ohnuki-Tierney (1984) suggests that illness, and we would add injuries, such as those described above, are legitimised in the Japanese culture. Rather than equating pain and illness with deviant behaviour as described in other countries such as the United States (Jackson, 2011), the Japanese take an opposing view and believe that indulgent pampering of the sick facilitates recovery. Responses to injury and views of illness are factors which have contributed to scholars labelling the Japanese as tending towards hypochondria (Haring, 1949; La Barre, 1945). Ohnuki-Tierney (1984) has said that the Japanese characteristically like to portray themselves as somewhat sickly. Although Ohnuki-Tierney's views may seem to contradict earlier descriptions of feverish children attending kindergarten, Benedict (1946) argues that such paradoxes are a feature of Japanese psychology. While in a New Zealand context, men especially, may be reluctant to portray themselves as physically weak, Ohnuki-Tierney argues that there is no conflict between a masculine image and illness in Japan. In fact, a sickly body is often regarded as a sign of intellectual ability and sensitivity. Therefore, it can become a source of pride.

The Symbolism of Protective Barriers

Another difference in the readings of the scene concerns the issue of wearing gloves. While the Japanese teachers were concerned that the New Zealand teacher in the video did not use disinfectant to clean the wound, they did not enquire about the absence of gloves. In the New Zealand early childhood context, gloves are now an essential part of every centre's first aid kit, and teachers are expected to don them when dealing with bodily fluids such as blood, faeces, and vomit. In reality, however, this is not always practical and teachers seem to take a haphazard approach to this policy. Focus group participants indicated that they would only use gloves if the injury is serious enough to warrant it. However, the way teachers evaluated the severity of the wound depended on how they viewed the body on a social, medical, and political level, as these comments from Napier teachers indicate:

> They looked to be fairly significant grazes, didn't they? From the distance that it was videoed you could see the little round circles [of blood] and I would probably put a glove on.
>
> If we knew that there was a video camera there we would certainly put a glove on!
>
> I would regardless [of the camera] and it's certainly what is advised, but in practice I don't think it always happens 100% of the time.

These statements point to Foucault's (1975/1995) notions of surveillance at work. It appears that the teachers do not really believe that neglecting to wear gloves will negatively affect either their own or the child's health. The motivation behind wearing gloves seems to be more a measure of compliance and a way of fulfilling expectations around appropriate practice. Foucault (1975/1995) has argued that the principles of panopticism can only be effective if those being watched believe that they could be being observed at any time by a central, unseen observer. As one of the teachers points out, if a video camera was fulfilling the role of the panopticon, the staff would feel compelled to comply with the rules regarding gloves. In reality, without the threat of a constant observer, donning gloves is not regarded as medically or culturally necessary enough for staff to regulate their own behaviour.

Piper and Stronach (2008, p. 81) have argued that in British early childhood settings rubber gloves act more like a "moral contraceptive", than a practical means of preventing the spread of disease. In other words, the gloves inhibit any form of intimacy between the teacher and child in situations where touch is expected as a sign of caring. However, in the cases observed by the authors, trying to administer plasters or change children wearing gloves often resulted in the teacher ripping gaping holes in the rubber barrier. In contrast, doctors and nurses games, which involved children poking spatulas in each other's mouths, were not seen as unhygienic. Piper and Stronach see this as evidence of a staff protection agenda rather than concerns over guarding children from infection. Tobin (1997) found that American teachers tended to view children's play that involved intimate touch, such as kissing games, through the lens of medical and psychological symptomology. This kind of play was seen as endangering children through its association with germ transmission, contagious illnesses, and even sexual disease.

At this point, it is worth thinking about the symbolism of the rubber glove in the New Zealand early childhood setting. What is its underlying role or purpose? Does it function to protect the injured child from becoming infected, to prevent the spread of disease to the teachers, or to act as a "moral contraceptive" as suggested by Piper and Stronach (2008, p. 81)? Although the rubber glove is touted as a way of keeping children safe, New Zealand teachers' comments indicate that it is predominantly for the protection of staff, rather than for the children's benefit. Inconsistent use of the glove implies that teachers take a personal view of the risks involved when dealing with bodily fluids. These fluids represent potential danger both in a microbiological sense and metaphorically through their symbolic link to disorder (Douglas, 1966; Turner, 2003). To neglect to use a glove is then, both to subvert state policies regarding hygiene, and to allow an anomaly to remain. But it is clear that these fluids are not enough of a cultural anomaly for all New Zealand teachers to regard them as a potent source of danger.

Although the rubber glove is not a regular feature of the Japanese early childhood context, it is common to see children and staff wearing face masks. Like the glove, the mask can be culturally revealing. Outside of Asia, masks are generally worn by surgeons or patients in hospital settings, whereas Japanese people wear masks outside in public. Ohnuki-Tierney (1984) suggests that the difference lies in the purpose of the mask. In non-Asian contexts, the mask is used to prevent a person spreading their germs to someone else in situations, such as the operating theatre. In Japan, the mask serves to prevent one from inhaling the germs of others. It can also signify a person's polluted state. In this case, the mask functions as a boundary between the polluted and unpolluted, but it allows a person to remain in society through this clear demarcation (Lock, 1980).

Bodily Fluids as Metaphors of Disorder

In the same way, the rubber glove can serve as a metaphor for opposing agendas in the early childhood centre. For the New Zealand teachers, it is a tangible reminder that centres have become places where physical touch is discouraged and bodily fluids represent a threat (Turner, 2003). MacLure (2010) has gone further and argued that such fluids are often given symbolic meaning by both teachers and researchers. She gives the example of a child whose repeated vomiting at perceived inopportune moments was interpreted by staff at the centre as signifying something. She writes that

> the vomiting is not, therefore, seen just as a bodily process, but as representational—that is, as *a sign of* something else. But notice also that *we*, as researchers, were trying to do the same thing: that is, asking what the vomiting *means*.
>
> *(MacLure, 2010, p. 10, emphasis in original)*

MacLure notes that the child who vomits, along with those who "poo and pee in the 'wrong' place" generates strong feelings of disgust in adults. MacLure's ideas resonate with Ohnuki-Tierney's (1984) belief that illness in Western contexts is somehow deviant, as well as symbolic of an underlying cause that needs to be exposed. This view can influence the way in which teachers respond to children who disrupt the order of the classroom through the "irruption" (MacLure, 2010, p. 10) of the body into the early childhood setting.

In their study of moral panics in British early childhood settings, Piper and Stronach (2008) have discussed inconsistencies in teacher responses to injured children. In many of the cases that they observed, teachers were unwilling to assist the children directly. Instead, children were encouraged to deal with the injury themselves by following teachers' instructions regarding cleaning the wound and plaster application. Piper and Stronach suggest this policy is not motivated by issues of possible infection or a desire to instil independence, but fear of being accused of inappropriate touching. At Kaimai Kindergarten, it did not appear that teachers allowed these concerns to completely overwhelm them when dealing with children who had suffered an injury or an accident. Yet, comforting hugs and kisses still appear to be fraught with potential implications as one Wellington teacher succinctly acknowledged:

> I'm all for ECE being professional, but I also believe that early childhood has a large element of care and, for lack of a better word, love, involved in it. I think that's a difficult dilemma because emotional well-being, a sense of belonging, all of those sorts of things are part of our curriculum and something we value but in some ways we are restricted to develop those sorts of relationships and feelings.

However, in Japan, the large amount of attention directed towards children who were sick or injured seemed to indicate a deliberate desire to show love and concern. These kinds of interactions were typified by a lot of touching and hugging, which created the feeling of pampering described by Ohnuki-Tierney (1984). The personalised attention given by teachers to sick children is at odds with the regular practice of group socialisation which emphasises children's self-reliance over teacher involvement. Illness or injury appears to permit the suspension of the usual kindergarten routine to delve into the *amae* (dependency) based practices of the home (Lock, 1980). In this way, illness in the Japanese early childhood setting fits with Douglas's (1966) notion of disorder. In the New Zealand setting too, the 'irruption' of bodily fluids such as blood, vomit, and urine represent something out of place.

Purification of the Body

It is useful again to return to Douglas' (1966) theories when considering another scene from the New Zealand video. In this case, a group of children are preparing to take part in a baking session. The teacher asks if they have washed their hands, and while all the children claim that they have, there is no evidence to suggest that this is true. Later in the day, children are seen sitting down to lunch, again, without having obviously washed their hands before eating. The Japanese teachers considered the attitude to hand washing to be very lax in the New Zealand centre and were concerned about the dirt that might be present on some fingers, but not others. They were also shocked by barefoot children running freely from the outside, which they perceived as very dirty, to the inside area which in their minds represented an unpolluted space. As Douglas (1966) has shown, rituals of purity and impurity are less about eliminating all bacteria but more about creating unity through their experience.

The body is a site of both pollution and purification and therefore appropriate action needs to be taken to ensure cleansing has occurred. In the Japanese early childhood setting, the purity of the body is maintained by washing of the hands and feet, and gargling. While these acts are certainly linked to hygienic practice, their real value lies in the belief that washing and gargling removes perceived impurities from the body (Lock, 1980). Ohnuki-Tierney (1984) argues that while washing may exist in most cultures, the Japanese are unusual in their emphasis on cleansing certain body parts. These parts, hands, feet, and throat, are given particular attention as they are where the body comes into contact with the outside. The hands are used to touch things, the feet touch the ground, and air enters the body through the throat. Even after washing, the hands are still seen as vulnerable to dirt. Ohnuki-Tierney gives a number of examples to illustrate this belief such as the absence of Japanese finger food, the ubiquitous hot towel (*oshibori*) used to wipe one's hands before a meal, chopstick etiquette which prevents the exchange of saliva, and the pristine white gloves worn by employees like taxi drivers, door attendants and elevator operators who primarily work with their hands. As Kawano (2005) notes, "dirty things are not purely "mental" phenomena. They are embodied and emplaced—and are therefore deeply experiential" (p. 43).

At Oka Kindergarten, gargling with cold water was also a regular part of a daily ritual, which the principal explained would prevent ill health. At the time, Rachael was skeptical that gargling could be effective as a cold-prevention strategy, but the teachers around her insisted on its validity. Other foreigners living in Japan have expressed the same doubts, and while it appears there is little medical evidence to support the idea that gargling with water prevents infection, using tea may show some results due to its anti-microbial properties (Gordenker, 2003). Yet the claim of gargling for antibacterial purposes appears particularly tenuous when one considers that the cups used are hung above the basins to be communally shared and just given a quick rinse with cold water in between users (see Figure 6.2). Clearly, the real value of gargling lies in its symbolic value which sees water remove the impurities that may have been inadvertently inhaled from the outside.

This same interpretation can answer an issue raised by the New Zealand viewers who noted the absence of soap in the wash basins at Oka Kindergarten. While the New Zealanders saw this as contrary to providing sufficient resources for hygienic practices, the Japanese teachers felt washing with just water to be

FIGURE 6.2 Cups for gargling hang above the basins at this Hiroshima kindergarten

perfectly appropriate. As Clark (1994) has described, the Japanese do not see soap as essential when washing their hands, as the purpose of the act is to symbolically purify by splashing water over the area rather than to thoroughly clean it. This is also why there is often no soap in public toilets, which may come as a surprise to foreign visitors. While advocating that hand washing should be carried out prior to eating and activities involving food, New Zealand teachers were relatively relaxed about enforcing this policy and certainly avoided the type of lengthy speeches on the topic favoured by the Japanese principal.

As the section on the body explored, New Zealand attitudes to dirt appear to be more nonchalant than those of the Japanese. While cleanliness was once next to godliness in colonial New Zealand (Wood, 1977), in recent years dirt has come to be associated positively with nature, freedom, and physical strength rather than a symbol of impurity. For example, Mulgan's (1999) article explores the belief that modern society's obsession with cleanliness has negatively affected children's immunity systems by reducing their capacity to fight germs. In the early childhood setting, this ideology is reflected in the provision of messy play activities, sandpits, and natural outdoor areas. In the media, it can be seen in advertisements such as the one with the by-line 'dirt is good', which is naturally sponsored by a washing powder company ("Why Do We Think Dirt Is Good", 2011). In Rachael's local community, a popular summer event for children is a mudslide built by the Scouts group. A Japanese visitor staying with Rachael during this time was both horrified and confused as to why New Zealanders would consider this activity to be enjoyable. While chapter three describes Japanese teachers who similarly encouraged children to get dirty as a counterpoint to sanitised modern lifestyles, in Japan, the outdoors is widely regarded as an inherently dirty place, which explains children's reluctance to engage with it. The following section looks at those spaces which are deemed impure or pure in the New Zealand and Japanese early childhood settings.

Polluted Spaces

Ohnuki-Tierney (1984) notes that the way that Japanese children are socialised reveals the strong association Japanese have with the outside and dirt.[1] One of the first words children learn is *bacchi*, or dirty, which is taught by adults repeatedly identifying objects that are unclean and therefore should not be touched. The concept of polluted objects and spaces become so ingrained by early childhood, that children sometimes exploit this fear of 'cultural germs' or 'people dirt' by starting to sit down on a dirty surface so adults will carry them. The belief that the outdoors is a dirty space is also reflected in objects that mothers are expected to purchase as part of their children's essential kindergarten equipment. For example, every child is required to own a colourful square of plastic sheeting that compactly folds away. This *re-ja sheeto* (leisure sheet) is used to spread over the ground and sit upon when the children go on trips to the local park or gardens. One Japanese mother Rachael met, who was living in Auckland, became quite distraught when she realised that the New Zealand version of a spontaneous picnic meant that she and the children were going to have to sit directly on the grass. After riffling desperately through her handbag, she finally retrieved some handkerchiefs and spread them over the ground so that everyone could safely perch atop the cloth.

These views of the outdoors as an impure space can be seen in a vignette from the Japanese video, which depicts the children preparing to go outside for a water play session. The teacher stands at the front of the class and gives detailed instructions related to the removal of clothing. When she instructs the children to remove their shoes and socks, a notable cry of resistance erupts from the class. The children begin to chatter among themselves about the implications of the teacher's words. Their voices convey both excitement and some anxiety about traversing the bare ground without the protection of footwear. Ohnuki-Tierney (1984) claims that in regards to hygiene, Japanese daily behaviour is connected to spatial classifications that regard the outside and below as dirty. One of the most potent symbols of dirt from below is footwear, along with the feet, the floor, and the ground. In order to prevent the dirt from both outside and below from entering the clean space of the early childhood setting, children are required to make a number of changes to their footwear during the course of the day. At Oka

Kindergarten, children exchange outside shoes for an inside pair as soon as they arrive in the morning. If children go back outside to play or take part in class activities, they must again exchange their shoes. This ritual occurs many times a day, and most children are so adept at it that they barely pause while conducting it. When children need to use the toilet, they slip off their inside shoes at the entrance to the ablutions area, and put on a pair of slippers used exclusively in this space. If children decide to select a book from the carpeted library corner, they must remove their indoor shoes and step into the area in socked feet. The same action is required if children tread on *tatami* mats which have been laid either outside or inside the kindergarten.

The only time the children are permitted to alter these rituals around footwear are during the regular evacuation drills when the emphasis is on hastily exiting the building. During these moments, the teachers often have to remind children not to pause to change their shoes, even it makes them feel strange and uncomfortable. Just as the drills prepare for a rare event such as an earthquake or fire, forgoing the regular rituals around footwear reflect a unique, irregular break with order. It is only during these moments of disorder, these ruptures in the regular structure, that feet are permitted to come into contact with the dirt of the ground.

For the Kaimai Kindergarten teachers, the Japanese children's reaction to going barefoot prior to water play was quite incomprehensible. Without the same absolutist views governing the realm of outside as dirty and the inside as clean, the meaning attached to a bare foot was lost on them:

> They're all worried about taking their shoes off. They're not sure if they want to go. I mean our kids in the middle of winter stand outside barefoot. [In regards to shoes] it's all about comfort and choice here.

Others recognised that while the wearing of shoes might not be an issue in their own centre (see Figure 6.3), there are early childhood contexts in New Zealand where cultural rituals around footwear are also a feature of the setting, such as *kōhanga reo*.[2]

From the Japanese point of view, scenes of barefoot New Zealand children freely wandering between the outside, the inside, and the toilet at the centre were shocking on multiple levels. Several teachers commented that while the New Zealand centre looked attractive and clean on a superficial level, in reality there was an invisible layer of impurities lingering around the space due to the constant cross-contamination occurring by both children and staff. The sandpit was another area labelled as potentially polluting by Japanese viewers, who admired the pit as a resource, but had many questions about adequate cleaning of the space:

> The sandpit in the New Zealand video looks wonderful, especially being right next to the class like that. We would also love to have a sandpit like that, but you're not allowed in Japan because cat and dog poo might get

FIGURE 6.3 It is quite common to see New Zealand children playing barefoot both inside and outside

into it. It might get all dirty. It's not allowed due to the germs. You're only allowed one if you have a lid and you spray disinfectant on it every single day. But sandpits are so wonderful for children's imagination.

In the Japanese video, Oka Kindergarten did feature a small sand and mud area, but it was covered every evening and doused with disinfectant each morning, along with the toys used in it. In a reflection of the hand washing practices, cleaning the sandpit with disinfectant in Japan seems to serve the purpose of ritual purification, rather than effective sterilisation. In New Zealand, the Ministry of Health (1997) advises that the sand and soil of the sandpit serves to neutralise disinfectant, rendering it ineffective. They recommend alternative strategies such as raking, exposing the space to heavy rainfall, hosing it down, and periodically replacing the sand. The sandpit at Kaimai Kindergarten was one of the most popular spaces for children's play, and teachers seemed quite unconcerned about its capacity to harbour dangerous bacteria. They were far more interested in the way that the Japanese teacher allowed children's hands to delve into a communal jar of candy, as well as the free exchange of foodstuffs, that occurred during lunchtime. In their minds, this appeared to be much more of a violation of the rules relating to dirt and hygiene. The following section explores the prohibitions and rituals around food and its consumption as articulated by the teachers.

Food In and Out of Place

Near the end of the day at Oka Kindergarten, the children are preparing to go home. After they pack their bags and stack their chairs, they sing the farewell song in loud voices before filing up to the front of the room where the teacher has put out three glass jars that appear to contain candy. As the teacher explains that each jar contains a different flavor, she tips a few of the jelly-like drops on to each of the three lids. She then asks for a show of hands to choose the most popular flavor of the day before allowing children to come forward, a group at a time, to take a drop of their choice. Some children pause over their selection, putting their chosen drop back and choose another flavor. The small quantity on the lids is soon exhausted, so some children need to put their hands inside the jar and scrabble round to reach the object of their desire. The teacher tells the children to hold the drop in their hand until all their classmates are ready, then to proceed as a group to pop the drops into their mouths after uttering the greeting of *itadakimasu*.

This scene was surprising to the New Zealand viewers for the way in which it appeared to violate implicit rules relating to both external hygiene, in the form of the hands, and internally, in the form of the mouth. Allowing a large group of children to touch the displayed drops while they made their choice seemed the antithesis of clean handling practices concerning food. The viewers also felt the teacher's role modelling of suitable food choices to be inappropriate. This is because the Kaimai Kindergarten teachers identified the drops as sugar-laden 'lollies'[3] which are not permitted in their centre. Then there was the further question of why the teacher would choose a food product with such strong connotations to reward systems:

> The lolly thing!
> The children put all their hands in. That's dirty.
> I don't think there's any law against it, but it's just one of those things we don't do.
> It would be served so they could perhaps take something without touching anything else but not in that sort of format.
> We wouldn't give it out to them in the way she's doing it anyway. What's that for? I don't know what that's for. A reward?
> We wouldn't do that. Not for no reason. Also it would be against our food and nutrition policy.

As these Kaimai teachers articulated, there is no specific policy, which prevents children from retrieving food with their hands from a communal vessel, yet it is inherently abhorrent to them. The consumption of sugary foods is, however, actively discouraged through state guidelines for early childhood education services. These guidelines have been designed to help centres develop food and nutrition policies and practices, which tacitly deem certain foodstuffs as either acceptable or unacceptable (Ministry of Education, 2009). Lollies fall squarely into the category of a food 'out of place' (Douglas, 1966) in the New Zealand early childhood setting.

In reality, the drops that the Japanese children were consuming were not lollies but *kanyu*, fruit-flavoured jelly vitamins made from cod liver oil. *Kanyu* were first produced in Japan in 1911 and remain a popular dietary supplement for children due to their pleasant taste. Adults are attracted by the claims that regular consumption of *kanyu* can increase children's bone density, promote physical growth, and boost immunity. Japanese viewers in the focus groups took a nostalgic view of the *kanyu* distribution, as these comments from Kutchan teachers suggest:

> When I was a child at kindergarten I also received *kanyu* just before going home.
>
> Well, it's really only meant to be if you're not receiving enough nutrients from your regular food and the children are all eating packed lunches these days so I'm a little surprised.
>
> I noticed she put it out on lids rather than leaving the jar open for everyone.
>
> That's because *kanyu* is very expensive.

Although the *kanyu* is not fact regarded as a sweet/candy, Japanese teachers in the focus group sessions indicated that the occasional dispensing of candy was not a problem in their centres. Lock (1980) has described how candy is frequently given to Japanese children in order to restore balance. At Oka Kindergarten, lollies were given to children following periods of intense physical exertion such as the sports day practice or the swimming lesson. These same teachers dismissed the notion that candy might lead to concerned mothers complaining about cavities in their children's teeth. In New Zealand, however, the teacher who regularly dishes out lollies is seen as contravening 'healthy food' policies, which ban such food products from the early childhood setting. These kinds of teachers are implicitly regarded as somewhat neglectful in the same way that mothers who frequently include sugary foods in their children's lunchboxes or diets are labelled by other mothers as inferior (Albon & Mukherji, 2008).

For Japanese viewers, the scene of the *kanyu* distribution could be read quite differently. Rather than a violation of physical and oral hygiene, it was interpreted as continuing a traditional practice that was common in the post-war years, but has become less prevalent with rising standards of living and nutrition. Placing the *kanyu* on lids was seen as a means of elevating the drops from simple candy, which could be taken straight from the container, to a food product that deserved its own ritual in the form of a simple serving platter, the lid. More surprising for these viewers, was the fact that the children in the video did not show enough respect for the *kanyu* that they were about to consume:

> I was most surprised about the fact that the children just grabbed the *kanyu*, put it in their mouths, and were chewing away right before they said their farewell greetings. I thought they would sit down first and then eat before leaving for home.

Rituals around Food

The display of good table manners is an integral part of Japanese culture (Ohnuki-Tierney, 1993). To neglect to observe the rituals around food is regarded as a major break with expected behaviour in the Japanese early childhood setting. Hendry (1993) describes the routines that surround mealtimes at kindergartens as examples of temporal wrapping. They are a way of dividing up time to make an event clear by separating it from others around it through an obvious beginning and ending. Mealtimes follow a structured routine in homes, kindergartens, schools, and organisations over all Japan. The beginning of the meal consumption must always be preceded by *itadakimasu*, to express receipt of food, and end with the phrase *gochisōsama deshita*, which indicates thanks. As Hendry points out, this routine is so familiar to children by the time they start kindergarten that they will wait patiently for everyone to be ready and the greeting to be given before touching their food. Likewise, children learn to remain seated at the table until the end of the meal has been formally announced. This routine is even more elaborate in many early childhood settings as children, acting in the role of duty monitors, run through a series of questions before giving the call to begin. Rituals around meal times serve an important socialising role, as a kindergarten teacher from Yokohama explains:

> It's important for the children to become sincere, good members of society and we try and teach that here at our kindergarten. We learn to do that all together. Maybe when foreigners see us learning that kind of thing together (*go issho ni*) it might look a bit strange, but those words such as *itadakimasu* are the same all over the country and its comforting for us to have that solidarity and familiarity. Also, once children are interacting in society they need to know how to act appropriately and use the correct greeting and actions. Our kindergarten equips them with that knowledge.

In the Japanese setting, emphasis is placed not only on children participating fully in rituals at mealtimes but attention is given to how the food is served, its aesthetic presentation, and the creation of a positive atmosphere in which to enjoy it. Teachers are responsible for providing positive role models for children and in order to fulfil this role, they are required to consume their lunch together with their class. This contrasts with the New Zealand centre where one staff member is responsible for the small group of children who eat lunch outdoors at the centre. The other staff members are free to prepare a meal in the staffroom or consume food there that they have brought from home. Lunchtime at Kaimai Kindergarten is seen as time for staff to take a break from the demanding job of working with young children, and an opportunity to converse with the other adults. Although the children are theoretically supposed to give thanks for their food before they eat, the whole process has quite a haphazard manner about it, and the video depicts a group of boys ripping wrappings off cheese and sandwiches before the teacher approaches to sit with them. Although she gently chides them with, "You're supposed to say thanks for your food", the group does not pause eating and her manner is joking rather than authoritarian. As the children finish, one by one, they pack up their lunchboxes and wander off to play for the rest of the break time.

This contrasts with lunchtime at the Japanese kindergarten where preparations and consumption of the midday meal take over an hour. The children are required to first lay out their equipment for lunch: napkin, chopsticks, cup, lunch box *(bentō)*. Each object has a specific place and must be neatly arranged a certain distance along the table from one's neighbour. The duty monitors help the teacher bring in the large teapot full of barley tea and pour a little into the upturned cups. Then the duty monitors lead the class in the lunch-time greeting rituals which consist of a special song sung each day, as well as a prayer which is chanted as a group. Only when all of these rituals have been completed are the children allowed to begin eating. However, as the focus groups pointed out, the class at the centre of the video was a particularly large and boisterous group, which did not always conform to expectations. This is regarded as a serious breach of etiquette, as a kindergarten teacher from Kutchan, Hokkaido explained:

> In the case of my classroom, greetings such as 'good morning' are very important. Straight after the water play finished, the children went inside to eat lunch and even though the duty monitors respectfully commenced the lunchtime greeting rituals there were still some children who were getting their lunches out, while others were standing up and others were still getting ready. However the teacher still carried on. She didn't stop the children or show the food or the lunch rituals the respect that it deserves. I thought it was really a shame. It's so important to correctly demonstrate to children how important food is and what the proper behaviour should be when we are about to eat it.

These comments reflect Japanese assumptions that food habits are intrinsically linked to national character as well as a reflection of social and cultural values (Cwiertka, 2008). However, it is not just the routines, which link to deeper social meanings. At the Japanese kindergarten, notions of purity and pollution are externalised in the form of the lunchbox or *bentō*. As Bestor (1999) writes,

> concerns about seasonality—and hence, freshness and purity—are normal parts of any food culture. In the Japanese case, however, purity and pollution both have multiple meanings, and the ideal of perfect external form—*kata*—adds an extra dimension to assessing foodstuffs.
>
> *(p. 166)*

In his analysis of the Tsukiji fish market, Bestor notes that the Japanese consumer is apprehensive about purchasing products with any perceptible flaws. Suppliers must therefore be careful to select products, which are perfect as external blemishes may be a sign of internal imperfection. Bestor links these concerns both with folk wisdom and with the very real health threats from famous pollution cases in the 1970s. More recently, the Japanese government has failed to act promptly following cases of 'mad cow disease' (Kingston, 2004), and the country has been rocked by a series of food scares involving products imported from China ("Fears Made in China", 2007) as well as internal corruption scandals (Pulvers, 2008). These fears are reflected in a preference for domestically produced food products but also show the desire for the perfect form, *kata*, which foreign producers often cannot satisfy (Bestor, 1999).[4]

The Lunchbox as a Reflection of Cultural Ideology

The result of this ideology can be seen in the production of the Japanese child's lunchbox, which also plays a role in ensuring mothers are socialised into 'good wives and wise mothers' (Uno, 1993). Teachers at Oka Kindergarten often noted poorly assembled lunchboxes, and attributed them to inadequate mothers. This did not go unnoticed by mothers, and there was keen competition to produce the most admired lunchbox which would be judged, photographed, and pinned to the wall each week by the staff. For those mothers who are unsure of how to perfect their craft, help is at hand in the form of child-rearing and food magazines, which carry articles on the topic of the lunchbox. These are accompanied by glossy photographs of beautiful, nutritious *bentō*, such as rice balls adorned with seaweed or sesame patterns, delicate vegetable flowers, and sausages cut into the shape of an octopus. Not only is the mother judged on her ability to produce an aesthetically pleasing, wholesome *bentō*, but the child is expected to consume it in its entirety during the ritualised lunch time. At times, teachers would resort to spoon-feeding children the remains of their lunch (see Figure 6.4). For just as it is the mother's responsibility to make a delicious lunch, and the child's job to consume it completely and cheerfully, it is up to the teacher to ensure that this operation is correctly carried out. In their cross-cultural study, Fujita and Sano (1988) showed how approaches to food consumption in early childhood settings

FIGURE 6.4 A Japanese kindergarten teacher spoon feeds a reluctant child the remains of his lunch

differ. While Japanese teachers were happy to help slow eaters, American teach-ers felt it was important that young children learn to feed themselves in order to become independent. Allison (1997) argues that *bentō* not only serves to keep Japanese children culturally and ideologically attached, but it is "a representation of what the mother is and what the child should become" (p. 302).

In the New Zealand context, the Japanese teachers were surprised by children's decision not to eat some foods despite the fact that their mothers had prepared it for them. It was immediately clear, however, that the same level of preparation had not gone into the New Zealand lunchboxes. At one point, a child tips all of his yoghurt into the rubbish bin, and the teacher asks him, "Aren't you going to eat that? That's a waste" but does not try to prevent the child's act. While the children do sit down as a group, consumption of the food is marked more as an individual act rather than linked explicitly to that of others around them. This contrasts with Japanese cultural approaches, which see meal times as governed by rituals which identify children as part of a group.

James, Curtis, and Ellis (2009) have suggested that parents link their child's willingness to eat the same food as others in the family with a "commitment and identification with the family" (p. 45). Viewed through this lens, family food thus takes on a symbolic importance that can reveal the depth of a child's engagement and obligation to the family group. The child who rejects this symbolic offering, that is the fussy child, can therefore also be seen as refusing to identify as a member of that group. James et al. (2009) point to the practice of mothers persevering to make reluctant children eat, even if it is just a tiny amount, as a sign of "the importance of demonstrating family membership through food sharing" (p. 45). In contrast, children who have consistently consumed home-cooked food without a fuss are revered as dutiful members of the family unit. These practices seek to teach children the value of 'family' through sharing and consumption of family food. In the Japanese early childhood setting, the same can be said for rituals around food, which teach children to become members of a group through the sharing of food. That is why it is important that everyone consumes their meal, and why the teacher will persevere in feeding those children who resist this ideology.

During the lunch scenes at the New Zealand centre, another contrast becomes apparent when a child in the group offers a piece of cheese to his friend who quickly swallows it, just as the teacher tries to intervene with, "Oh no! We don't share our food because you might not be allowed to eat that. That's why we only eat our own food". At a policy level, the sharing of food is prohibited at Kaimai Kindergarten due to fears that children with allergies might inadvertently swallow something that could make them ill, or worse, be fatal. The strong reaction of the teacher in the video clip also gives the sense that food shared is somehow food that has become polluted or unfit for consumption. Again, this is food that is out of place (Douglas, 1966). As Murcott (1988) has pointed out,

> Food is used to signify not just people's relation to objects, but also to their own bodies. It displays something of our ideas about what is acceptable and safe to take into the body—it betrays the meanings we attach to our bodies in their objective aspect. And our use of food reveals into the bargain concepts of closeness and acceptability in our relationships with one another.
>
> *(p. 12)*

Yet, sharing food is a large part of Māori culture and practices as Ritchie (2001) points out in her description of 'fruit time' in early childhood settings. Inspired by Māori values, fruit time involves children gathering as a group to listen to a story while consuming a variety of fruits brought from home. However, government policies relating to food now require children to bring their own individual piece of fruit rather than a selection to share with others. In other areas of the New Zealand curriculum, Māori values around food have been retained such as respect for the cultural belief that it is inappropriate to use food in play (Dudding, 2011). In Japan, there are no cultural prohibitions of this kind, and it is common to use cut potatoes to make prints, to scatter and glue rice to create textual paintings, and to use onion skins for dyeing.

FIGURE 6.5 Meal times are the focus of protracted rituals at Oka Kindergarten

Douglas (1972) has argued that food occupies a symbolic order, which is reflected in its preparation, cooking, and consumption. She believes that the pattern of meal times, and the way in which each meal is consumed, conceals deeper cultural meanings. With this in mind, consider meal times at the Japanese kindergarten replete with lunchbox contents which are designed to be shared (see Figure 6.5). Each day the children would delight in presenting their lunch to others around them, and often asked their peers, the teacher or visitors to taste the food. This expectation is equally apparent at kindergarten events such as the excursion (*ensoku*). Hendry (1999) has described her embarrassment at arriving at one of these events with some bread and packets of meat only to be greeted by mats loaded with elaborate creations prepared by the other mothers. As Hendry points out, these foodstuffs, such as *sushi*, could be shared amongst the other families present unlike her own meal.

Reflecting on Constructions of Dirt, Pollution, and Purity

This chapter has interrogated the ways in which constructions of dirt, pollution, and purity are expressed in the early childhood settings of New Zealand and Japan. As a site of rituals and practices of purification, the body appears a logical place to begin despite its earlier neglect by scholars (Lock, 1987; Turner, 2008).

Douglas (1999, p. 111) claims that the "idea of dirt implies system", therefore the avoidance of dirt can be seen as a means of ensuring order is restored. Pollution rules are an extension of this process in the way they impose order on experience, support clarification of forms, and minimise dissonance. Pollution rules are most often applied to functions or products of the human body. Contact with blood, vomit, excreta, and food are commonly regulated through these rules, but the actual rules themselves vary according to cultural context. An analysis of New Zealand and Japanese teachers' reactions to treatment of a child's bleeding knee shows these constructions in evidence. The scene concludes with the New Zealand teacher placing a plaster over a child's wound without administering disinfectant. Reactions by both Japanese viewers and New Zealand focus groups participants show the clear links between dirt as mediated through conceptions of the individual and the social body.

Foucault's (1973) theories about bio-medicine show how health practices evolve according to new forms of knowledge. In the New Zealand early childhood setting, approaches to the body are framed by pervasive health and safety discourses, which dictate the level of physical and microbiological contact between teachers and children's bodies. This ideology is symbolised by the rubber glove, which is supposed to be worn by teachers, yet they regularly subvert this regulation since there is little which culturally resonates with its relevance in many instances. We believe that a large part of teachers' reticence to slavishly conform to wearing gloves and disinfecting all wounds is informed by the belief that dirt is not always polluting. In the New Zealand context, dirt has been repositioned as an expression of freedom, and this is realised in children's outdoor play, which frequently results in minor scrapes and soiled bodies. Injuries, even those which involve the spilling of blood, are dealt with in a matter of fact way that minimises drama or individual attention. This kind of reaction serves to reinforce characteristics of New Zealand identity that are viewed favourably, such as stoicism and humility. New Zealanders prefer to distance themselves from characteristics such as flamboyance and pride that they perceive to be traits of more confident cultures such the United States (MacDonald, 2004).

In the Japanese setting, disinfectant is seen as an essential means of purifying wounds or bloody scrapes. Yet, unlike the New Zealand context, gloves are neither required nor worn. The emphasis is firmly on preventing dirt from entering the body of the child rather than preventing bacteria emanating from the child's wound to penetrate the skin of the adult. This approach links to the Japanese fear of inhaling or absorbing dirt from the outside, which is perceived as an inherently polluted space. It also shows why gloves may be commonly used in occupations or activities which call for contact with "people dirt" (Ohnuki-Tierney, 1984, p. 26) in the outside, but why gloves are not deemed necessary in the sanctity of the unpolluted inside of the kindergarten. While New Zealand approaches to the body and dirt may be symbolised by the rubber glove, in Japan it is the mask, which provides the most useful metaphor. The mask is used to protect the body when it is necessary to traverse from the context of the (dirty) outside world to a (clean) inside space and back again. That is why it is not common to see Japanese wearing masks inside their homes, as they believe there is little or no threat of inhaling germs in this space. In the same way, it would be unusual to see a New Zealand parent pulling on a rubber glove to deal with a cut knee in the backyard, as the glove is linked to institutional health and safety discourses in the New Zealand context.

There are also differences in the way that early childhood teachers in New Zealand and Japan treat cases of illness and injury. While New Zealand children may be implicitly admired for enduring pain with a minimum of fuss, Japanese children are expected to call attention to their plight. In contrast to the regular approach of benign neglect usually taken by Japanese teachers, illness represents an accepted opportunity to disrupt the order of socialisation processes. Sick children are pampered and indulged in a reflection of adult society which views illness as a legitimate chance to enjoy the care and concern (*amae*) of others beyond the family group.

Concepts of polluted spaces seem straightforward as most people, for example, would classify the toilet area as dirty. However, in the Japanese kindergarten the division of potentially polluting and clean spaces is more clearly defined by ritual and practice than in the New Zealand centre. It is very important that Japanese children follow the correct rituals around appropriate footwear in the corresponding spaces. To fail to do so is not only socially inexcusable, it puts others at risk of contamination. Ohnuki-Tierney (1984) has described a child who played with hospital slippers as an extremely disturbing anecdote because the act concerned three potent symbols of dirt and pollution: footwear, the floor, and the hospital. In Rachael's first year of living in Japan, a British friend recounted an incident, which had left him shocked by the Japanese people's unsympathetic response to injury. During a health check at the hospital, he had been asked to take a urine sample and was told to change out of the slippers he had donned (after previously leaving his shoes in the foyer) and put on toilet slippers at the toilet door. Once inside the toilet area, however, he found the generic slippers far too small and he tripped and fell, dislocating his jaw and badly gashing his head. As he lurched out of the toilet bleeding profusely, the nurses rushed over, only to try and pull his toilet slippers off his feet and exchange them for hospital slippers. What Rachael's friend had mistaken for unkindness was in fact a genuine horror that he was about to pollute the whole ward.

For New Zealand children, there is less to internalise when it comes to rituals concerning the feet or polluted spaces. In New Zealand early childhood settings, concepts of pollution centre more on hygiene practices, which require children to wash their hands before eating and after using the toilet, or health and safety guidelines which prevent the sharing of food or drinking vessels. Policy has increasingly required food to be individually consumed in light of rising allergy cases and as a result food that is shared has become undesirable in the eyes of teachers, but quite possibly more coveted in the minds of children. For the children at the Japanese kindergarten, the sharing of food does not break with any rituals or prohibitions, therefore it does not warrant any special attention, much in the same way that going barefoot is unexceptional in the New Zealand context. Instead, the focus is on the food itself, which must conform to exacting aesthetic and nutritional standards in order to banish any thoughts of imperfection. Labour intensively prepared food is complemented by structured meal-time rituals which Japanese children are expected to perfect during their time at kindergarten.

This chapter has used the theories of Douglas (1999) and Foucault (1973) to discuss the differing ways dirt and pollution are dealt with in the early childhood context. Children's bodies inevitably become polluted, but can be physically and ritually purified through cultural acts. Polluted spaces can be addressed in the same way. Finally, the way food is approached in each of the two centres reflects cultural prohibitions related to the anomaly of dirt out of place. The next, and final, chapter synthesises the discussion and reflects on the themes of the book.

Notes

1 The notion that the outside is associated with dirt and fear has been rejected by some radical sectors of Japanese society such as supporters of the 'back-to-nature' movement studied by Knight (1997).
2 At *kōhanga reo*, which literally translates as Māori language nest, appropriate cultural protocol is followed including removing footwear inside.
3 Lolly, or its plural form, lollies, is the New Zealand expression for sweets (England) or candy (United States). In Japan, the word *kyandii* (candy) is also often used in place of the original Japanese word *ame*.
4 In the wake of the March 2011 earthquake, tsunami and nuclear tragedy in Northern Japan, this ideology may well be under threat. With domestic food products facing repeated safety scares ("Stop Claiming Food Is Safe", 2011) Japanese consumers may be forced to look to other countries to satisfy their needs.

References

Adams, G. (2011). She'll be right: The risky business of being a New Zealander. *North and South*, (300), 85–91.

Albon, D., & Mukherji, P. (2008). *Food and health in early childhood: A holistic approach*. London, UK: Sage.

Allison, A. (1997). Japanese mothers and obentos: The lunch-box as state apparatus. In C. Counihan & P. Van-Esterik (Eds.), *Food and culture: A reader* (pp. 296–314). London, UK: Routledge.

Benedict, R. (1946). *The chrysanthemum and the sword: Patterns of Japanese culture*. Boston, MA: Houghton Mifflin.

Bestor, T. C. (1999). Constructing sushi: Culture, cuisine, and commodification in a Japanese market. In S. O. Long (Ed.), *Lives in motion: Composing circles of self and community in Japan* (pp. 151–190). New York, NY: Cornell East Asia Program.

Clark, S. (1994). *Japan: A view from the bath*. Honolulu: University of Hawaii Press.

Cwiertka, K. (2008). Culinary culture and the making of a national cuisine. In J. Robertson (Ed.), *A companion to the anthropology of Japan* (pp. 415–428). Malden, MA: Blackwell.

Douglas, M. (1966). *Purity and danger: An analysis of concepts of pollution and taboo*. Harmondsworth, UK: Penguin Books.

Douglas, M. (1972). Deciphering a meal. *Daedalus, 101*(1), 61–81.

Douglas, M. (1999). *Implicit meanings: Selected essays in anthropology*. London, UK: Routledge.

Dudding, A. (2011, April 17). Tapu taboos. *Sunday Star Times*. Retrieved from www.stuff.co.nz/sunday-star-times/features/4894377/Tapu-taboos

Fears made in China. (2007, July 9). *The Japan Times*. Retrieved from www.japantimes.co.jp/opinion/2007/07/09/editorials/fears-of-made-in-china/#.U_GEScWSx8E

Foucault, M. (1973). *The birth of the clinic*. New York, NY: Pantheon Books.

Foucault, M. (1975/1995). *Discipline and punish: The birth of the prison* (A. Sheridan, Trans.). New York, NY: Vintage Books.

Frith, J., Kambouris, N., & O'Grady, O. (2003). *Health and safety in family day care: Model policies and practices* (2nd ed.). Sydney, Australia: University of New South Wales.

Fujita, M., & Sano, T. (1988). Children in American and Japanese day-care centres: Ethnography and reflective cross-cultural interviewing. In H. T. Trueba & C. Delgado-Gaitan (Eds.), *School and society: Learning content through culture* (pp. 73–97). New York, NY: Praeger.

Gordenker, A. (2003, June 5). National hygiene begins in the classroom. *The Japan Times*. Retrieved from www.japantimes.co.jp/life/2003/06/05/lifestyle/national-hygiene-begins-in-the-classroom/#.U_GEnsWSx8E

Haring, D. G. (1949). Japan and the Japanese, 1868–1945. In R. Linton (Ed.), *Most of the world* (pp. 814–875). New York, NY: Columbia University Press.

Hendry, J. (1993). *Wrapping culture: Politeness, presentation, and power in Japan and other societies*. Oxford, UK: Oxford University Press.

Hendry, J. (1999). *An anthropologist in Japan: Glimpses of life in the field*. London, UK: Routledge.

Jackson, J. (2011). Pain: Pain and bodies. In F. E. Mascia-Lees (Ed.), *A companion to the anthropology of the body and embodiment* (pp. 370–387). Chichester, UK: Wiley-Blackwell.

James, A., Curtis, P., & Ellis, K. (2009). Negotiating family, negotiating food: Children as family participants? In A. James, A. T. Kjorholt, & V. Tingstad (Eds.), *Children, food and identity in everyday life* (pp. 35–51). Basingstoke, UK: Palgrave Macmillan.

Kawano, S. (2005). *Ritual practice in modern Japan: Ordering place, people, and action*. Honolulu: University of Hawaii Press.

Kingston, J. (2004). *Japan's quiet transformation: Social change and civil society in the twenty-first century*. London, UK: RoutledgeCurzon.

Knight, J. (1997). The soil as teacher: Natural farming in a mountain village. In P. J. Asquith & A. Kalland (Eds.), *Japanese images of nature: Cultural perspectives* (pp. 236–256). Richmond, UK: Curzon Press.

La Barre, W. (1945). Some observations on character structure in the Orient: The Japanese. *Psychiatry, 8*, 319–342.

Lock, M. (1980). *East Asian medicine in urban Japan*. Berkeley: University of California Press.

Lock, M. (1987). Introduction: Health and medical care as cultural and social phenomena. In E. Norbeck & M. Lock (Eds.), *Health, illness, and medical care in Japan: Cultural and social dimensions* (pp. 1–23). Honolulu: University of Hawaii Press.

MacDonald, G. G. V. (2004, November 24). Abused by anti-Americanism. *The Press*, A19.

MacLure, M. (2010, December). *Qualitative inquiry: Where are the ruins?* Paper presented at the New Zealand Association for Research in Education Conference, University of Auckland, Auckland, New Zealand.

Madjar, I. (1991). *Pain as embodied experience: A phenomenological study of clinically inflicted pain in adult patients.* Unpublished PhD thesis, Massey University, Palmerston North, New Zealand.

McGrath, B. J., & Huntington, A. D. (2007). The health and wellbeing of adults working in early childhood education. *Australian Journal of Early Childhood, 32*(3), 33–38.

Ministry of Education. (1999). Education circular 1999/21: HIV/AIDS and other blood-borne diseases. *Education Circulars.* Retrieved from www.minedu.govt.nz/NZ Education/EducationPolicies/Schools/PublicationsAndResources/Circulars/ Circulars1999/Circular199921.aspx

Ministry of Education. (2009). Food and nutrition for healthy, confident kids. *Promoting healthy lifestyles.* Retrieved from http://healthylifestyles.tki.org.nz/National-nutrition-resource-list/Food-and-nutrition-for-healthy-confident-kids

Ministry of Health. (1997). *Nga Kupu Oranga: Healthy Messages: A health and safety resource for early childhood services.* Retrieved from www.arphs.govt.nz/healthy_environments/ downloads/Nga/20Kupu/20Oranga/20HealthyMessages.pdf

Mulgan, R. (1999, March). Dishing the dirt. *Grace: New Zealand, 102*–103.

Murcott, A. (1988). Sociological and social anthropological approaches to food and eating. *World Review of Nutrition and Diet, 55,* 1–40.

Namihira, E. (1987). Pollution in the folk belief system. *Current Anthropology, 28*(4), S65–S74.

Norbeck, E. (1952). Pollution and taboo in contemporary Japan. *Southwestern Journal of Anthropology, 8*(3), 269–285.

Ohnuki-Tierney, E. (1984). *Illness and culture in contemporary Japan: An anthropological view.* Cambridge, UK: Cambridge University Press.

Ohnuki-Tierney, E. (1993). *Rice as self: Japanese identities through time.* Princeton, NJ: Princeton University Press.

Phillips, J. (1996). *A man's country: The image of the Pākehā male—A history.* Auckland, New Zealand: Penguin Books.

Piper, H., & Stronach, I. (2008). *Don't touch!: The educational story of a panic.* Abingdon, UK: Routledge.

Pulvers, R. (2008, October 19). Is anyone watching over Japan's official food-quality watch-dogs? *The Japan Times.* Retrieved from www.japantimes.co.jp/opinion/2008/10/19/ commentary/is-anyone-watching-over-japans-official-food-quality-watchdogs/#.U_ GGv8WSx8E

Ritchie, J. (2001). Reflections on collectivism in early childhood teaching in Aotearoa/ New Zealand. In S. Grieshaber & G. S. Cannella (Eds.), *Embracing identities in early child-hood education: Diversity and possibilities* (pp. 133–147). New York, NY: Teachers College Press.

Stop claiming food is safe. (2011, August 9). *The Japan Times.* Retrieved from www. japantimes.co.jp/news/2011/08/09/national/stop-claiming-food-is-safe-ministry-told/#.U_GJtsWSx8E

Tobin, J. (1997). Playing doctor in two cultures: The United States and Ireland. In J. Tobin (Ed.), *Making a place for pleasure in early childhood education* (pp. 119–158). New Haven, CT: Yale University Press.

Turner, B. S. (2003). Social fluids: Metaphors and meanings of society. *Body and Society, 9*(1), 1–10.

Turner, B. S. (2008). *The body and society: explorations in social theory* (3rd ed.). Los Angeles: Sage.

Uno, K. (1993). The death of "good wife, wise mother"? In A. Gordon (Ed.), *Postwar Japan as history* (pp. 293–322). Berkeley: University of California Press.

Wevers, L. (1980). Pioneer into feminist: Jane Mander's heroines. In P. Bunkle & B. Hughes (Eds.), *Women in New Zealand society* (pp. 244–260). Auckland, New Zealand: George Allen and Unwin.

Why do we think dirt is good. (2011, September). *Persil.* Retrieved from www.persil.co.nz/dirt-is-good/why-do-we-think-dirt-is-good

Wood, D. (1977). Free the children! Down with playgrounds! *McGill Journal of Education, 12*(2), 227–242.

7

BODIES IN CONTEXT

Introduction

Using the body as a focal point, we have argued that implicit cultural understandings not only shape most of the interactions taking place in the New Zealand and Japanese early childhood contexts, but many of these practices often go unnoticed or unrecognised as being culturally informed. In both New Zealand and Japan, the policies and structures of early childhood education are the focus of ongoing state attention (Aoki, 2010; Davison & Mitchell, 2008; May, 2009; Takahara, 2010) resulting in a climate of uncertainty and change. However, many of the cultural assumptions underpinning the early childhood sector in each context remain fundamentally consistent.

Although the body was once neglected as an object of scholarly study (Fraser & Greco, 2005; Lock, 1987; Turner, 2008), it has now become a significant site for anthropological analysis. Inspired by Foucault (1975/1995), scholars have come to acknowledge that "the body is socially and culturally produced and historically situated, it is both a part of nature and society but, at the same time, a representation of the way that nature and society are conceived" (Lock, 1987, p. 8). While Foucault (1975/1995) regarded the body as a site of discipline, domestication, and training by the state, Douglas (1970/1996) viewed the individual, physical body, and the social body as reciprocally symbolic. Douglas builds on Mauss' (1936/1973) assertion that the human body be treated as an image of society. In other words, every natural symbol originating from the body contains and conveys a social meaning, and every culture selects its own meaning from the myriad of potential body symbolisms. We have called on the theories of these scholars, resulting in an examination of what Scheper-Hughes and Lock (1987) term "the three bodies" (p. 7).

Bodies from the Beginning

To address New Zealand and Japanese notions of the body in early childhood education, it is necessary to start at the very beginning of a child's life. In New Zealand, children's bodies have been the object of political attention, most powerfully in the form of the early childhood welfare Plunket ideology, which sought to regulate child-rearing through a pattern of limited physical contact and strict routine. In many families, discipline took the form of physical punishment, although this has now been outlawed and consideration has turned towards strong support of children's rights discourses (Te One, 2005). In Japan too, the body has been the focus of state agendas such as pro-natal campaigns, which have been revived in the current climate of the low birth rate (Suzuki, 2006). Rather than taking a disciplinary approach in the home, Japanese mothers indulge their children to promote dependence. The cultural ideology of *skinship* prevails, which sees the bodies of mother and child linked through embodied practices such as co-sleeping and extensive physical contact.

For both the New Zealand and Japanese child, entry into the early childhood setting marks a period of transition. In order to facilitate this path smoothly, New Zealand centres strive to foster and acknowledge links between the family and the wider community in order to create a shared sense of belonging (Ministry of Education, 1996). However, in Japan, the transition from home to kindergarten is marked by the separation of the bodies of mother and child. While Japanese centres seek to order and regulate children's bodies as a part of socialisation goals, New Zealand centres favour rituals that replicate the home environment. In reality, these ideals have to be tempered with the cultural, social, and political realities of each country.

Constructing the Body

Children's bodies have come to occupy a culturally contested space in the early childhood arena. A scene from the Japanese video, which depicts naked children in the playground, became a catalyst for teachers' discussions on how the bodies of children and early childhood teachers intersect. In Western contexts, the child's body has become a site for fear and anxiety in the light of political and scholarly debate over appropriate policy and practice (Tobin, 1997). Like other centres across New Zealand, children's bodies at Kaimai Kindergarten have come under increasing surveillance and regulation following high profile cases of child sexual abuse (Duncan, 1998; Jones, 2001). In his exploration of power, Foucault (1975/1995) suggests that observation is a key mechanism for achieving disciplinary control. The perfect disciplinary institution, therefore, is one in which everything, and everyone, can be simultaneously viewed. Foucault drew on the concept of the *panopticon* to show how human behaviour can be modified through constant monitoring of actions, work habits, physical appearance, right through to moral beliefs. Originally designed by Bentham for use in prisons, the goal of the panopticon was never simply limited to organising the deprivation of liberty, but instead dedicated to transforming individuals. The concept of the panopticon was extended to military garrisons, factories, hospitals, and schools, although discipline could not be seen to originate from a central social authority or ruling class, since it permeated the entire social body and manifested itself in innumerable structures.

Operating within an environment of constant surveillance renders all those within the gaze as permanently visible. Foucault (1975/1995) argues that through this process human beings can be coerced to change their behaviour without the threat of physical violence to the body. We have argued that teachers in the New Zealand early childhood context have internalised the idea that unclothed children's bodies deviate from the "norm" (Foucault, 1975/1995, p. 199). Other sensory and physical interactions between teacher and child, once common two or three decades ago, have also been branded dangerous according to Foucault's binary divisions of power. Within this environment of surveillance, the bodies of children have also become more visible as doors are removed and mirrors installed, ostensibly to protect the children themselves. For many teachers, interviewed as part of this research, diminished opportunities for sensory interactions between themselves and children have been met with regret, but also with relief. New Zealand teachers are extremely aware of the way young children's bodies politically intersect with sexuality, and they steer away from the precarious position intimate contact with children may put them in.

For teachers in the Japanese context, a group of naked children does not hold the same threat. Children's bodies continue to be viewed in terms of a nostalgic or remembered past (Robertson, 1988) in spite of challenges to this (re)imagined ideal. Concepts of privacy are creeping into the early childhood environment, and the pleasures of communal nakedness are increasingly being replaced by modesty. In recent years, Japan has been rocked by a number of threats to children's safety, in the form of violence, abuse, natural disasters, and viral diseases (Kita, 2008). As a result of these events, Japanese teachers are increasingly aware of the potential for children's bodies to be harmed. While New Zealand early childhood centres may literally be tearing down the doors to ensure children are safe, Japanese centres are looking to build fences for the same reason. In many of the urban areas where focus group sessions were conducted, fences and security systems are already a reality. Despite fears that the child's body may be under threat, Japanese centres continue to offer opportunities for intimate bodily contact in the form of communal bathing, naptime, and sleepovers. The cultural ideology of *skinship* remains a pervasive influence in the lives of young children, and the importance attached to these activities reflects that.

The Body and Its Products

Japanese philosophy is regarded as constructing the whole being as a holistic entity (Picone, 1989). We saw evidence in our research that the Japanese context also reflected a more organic view of the body and its products. These approaches contrasted with Western philosophy where a dualism of mind and body, as articulated by Descartes, dominates critical thought (Grosz, 2005). Within this dichotomy, consciousness is elevated above corporeality. Connected intimately with the mind, the disciplined body can therefore subdue bodily excesses. In the New Zealand early childhood setting, bodily functions are subject to European civilising processes (Elias, 2000) that render them repugnant. However, Japanese early childhood education frames the body and its products as useful metaphors for educating children. This does not mean that these 'social fluids' are not classified as dirty in Japan, but rather that these findings reflect Douglas' (1970/1996) claims that the extent to which bodily fluids and excretions are classified as polluting is culturally constructed. In other words, it is not a matter of considering objects or fluids themselves as dirty, but asking where they stand within a system of categories.

While approaches to the body as a site of excretion may vary in New Zealand and Japan, both contexts reflect a belief in the body as key means of extending children's learning through physical and sensory opportunities. There are many similarities in the way that New Zealand and Japanese centres embrace dirt and totally embodied play as a means of compensating for the limits of modern society. For example, in New Zealand, messy play is seen as an iconic part of the early childhood scene. Children are encouraged to make sense of their world through tactile interactions with substances such as slime, mud, paint, and clay. Messy play makes links to the ideals of freedom and creativity—seen as important components of New Zealand national identity. These experiences have become all the more valued as New Zealand children are increasingly forbidden to create mess in pristine homes. Japanese children also have fewer chances to experience an unsanitised play environment due to factors such as the shrinking family size and urbanisation. In an effort to mitigate these issues, Japanese teachers see the provision of vigorous, embodied play opportunities as part of their role. However, a difference can be found in the way the dirty or wet body is treated in each context. At Kaimai Kindergarten, soiled clothing and bodies do not represent a breach of the purity rule (Douglas, 1966), but at Oka Kindergarten, the body is unwrapped and rewrapped in line with Japanese concepts of cleanliness and pollution (Hendry, 1993).

Internalising Techniques of the Body

Mauss (1963/1973) has shown how each culture has its own special bodily habits, which he identifies as techniques. Children learn to master these techniques in order to become integrated into society. In the Japanese early childhood context, there is an emphasis on repetitive body techniques such as bowing, chanting, sitting, and lining up. While these techniques were interpreted as regulating by New Zealanders, they are seen as an integral part of learning to embody being Japanese. The body plays a vital part in internalising key Japanese characteristics, such as perseverance (*gambaru*) and liveliness (*genki*) through physically arduous training and challenging, risky play. At a macro level, New Zealand, children's bodies are not subject to the same kinds of repetitive techniques, but they are still regulated by health and safety discourses in the early childhood environment.

In each context, culturally constructed approaches to bodily risk can be seen (Douglas & Wildavsky, 1982), and this study has focussed on the playground as a means of locating a pedagogy of risk (Smith, 1998). At Kaimai Kindergarten, the play space is the focus of stringent regulations which dictate how fencing, fall surfaces, climbing apparatus, and equipment should be used. High teacher-to-child ratios also serve to ensure all children are "permanently visible" (Foucault, 1975/1995, p. 201) in order to meet with cultural expectations concerning adequate supervision. Yet, these risk-averse measures have been waived when it comes to the use of real tools in the carpentry area. Identified by teachers as an iconic part of New Zealand early childhood education, the hammers, saws, and vices link back to New Zealand's pioneering past, seen as a vital piece in the construction of national identity (Phillips, 1996; Wevers, 1980). The meaningful learning opportunities children can gain from using real objects in a context of play and work are contrasted favourably against any risks they may pose.

Douglas and Wildavsky (1982, p. 14) maintain that every culture has a unique set of shared values and social institutions that support and maintain it. These values and institutions are inherently biased towards accentuating particular risks and minimising others. At Oka Kindergarten, the benefits of real tools are overwhelmed by the risks to the body that they present, making hammers, saws, and nails unavailable for children's play. Yet, in the Japanese context, there is a fatalistic attitude to children flirting with risk as reflected in the stony, hard grounds, towering slides, and minimal fencing. Japanese children learn to challenge their bodies through vigorous play that would be deemed dangerous elsewhere (Walsh, 2004). With less direct supervision by their teachers, peer support and control instead contribute towards keeping children physically and emotionally safe. In both the Japanese and New Zealand context, attitudes towards the embodiment of risk reflect the intersection of the cultural, social, and the political.

Order and the Body

The ways in which children's bodies are disciplined and regulated in overt, and implicit, ways can reveal deeper cultural values. Foucault (1975/1995, 1981) sees the body as a site of bio-power through a process of regulation and control. Through the micro-physics of bio-power, the body is rendered docile in order to become 'normal'. The disciplined body is held in high esteem in Western culture (Holliday & Hassard, 2001) where Descartes's ideas of mind-body dualism still prevail. A disciplined body can therefore be seen as a manifestation of a strong mind. In the New Zealand early childhood setting, noisy bodies are constructed as undisciplined through their challenge to notions of normal behaviour in this context. Children are discouraged from yelling, squealing, or rushing boisterously about the centre as these acts are counter to Western concepts of civilised behaviour (Elias, 2000).

In Japanese philosophy, the Cartesian mind-body dichotomy is disregarded in favour of a more holistic view of the body as a system of mutually interdependent parts (Lock, 1980; Picone, 1989). At Oka Kindergarten, the noisy acts of children are not seen as disorderly, but regarded as naturally childlike (*kodomo-rashi*) behaviour. Japanese constructions of boisterous play do not render it disorderly, but place it as a valuable expression of childhood within a holistic world view. For example, boisterous play is believed to contribute to strength of character and good health. Tobin (1992) has suggested that modern Japanese perceive the world of the child to be shrinking, and, regardless of whether this belief is supported in reality, it has affected the evolution of early childhood education. This may be another reason why Japanese teachers are reluctant to impose order during the free play periods. There is a desire to allow children to experience the kind of unconstrained, unmediated interactions they once would have enjoyed while roaming their local neighbourhoods, even if the chaotic results are quite surprising to outsiders (Smith, 1995). The presence or absence of noise can, therefore, be seen as an expression of the normalising process at work (Foucault, 1975/1995). While in New Zealand the absence of noise becomes an instrument for reproducing the social order, in Japan, the presence of noise serves the same function.

In the same way, how inappropriate behaviour is constructed and conflict is resolved can be seen as reproducing cultural norms. In the New Zealand context, fighting is not condoned due to the importance placed on children's rights. Physical violence and verbal attacks are viewed as direct violations of those rights. When a child transgresses the rights of another, teachers seek to remove the offending body through methods such as time out. Children are encouraged to solve disputes verbally, rather than with their bodies. While New Zealand teachers may look to isolate the individual body in the pursuit of calm, Japanese teachers seek ways to incorporate children back into the collective body. An organic approach to children's bodies can be seen in the way Japanese teachers allow children to resolve conflicts themselves, even if this sometimes results in a physical skirmish. The act of hitting another child is not seen as a threat to social stability, but rather an inevitable part of childhood. Although Japanese approaches to discipline may appear relaxed, it is part of a pedagogical approach practised by early childhood teachers throughout the country (Tobin, Hsueh, & Karasawa, 2009).

Foucault (1975/1995) claims that "discipline is a political anatomy of detail" (p. 139). The control of time and space are fundamental to the disciplinary society. Timetables, exercise routines, rows of desks and classrooms all serve to regulate the body through activity. At Oka Kindergarten, children's bodies are subject to disciplinary techniques in numerous ways. Daily classes are meticulously planned and events are entered up to a year in advance on an annual calendar. Classes are divided both spatially, through the groups of desks, and temporally, through the periods of quiet, formal ritual interspersed with chaotic free play. Routines for lunch time, assembly, arrival, and departure are all internalised through repetitive practice. Children become adept at lining up at a moment's notice and take part in group exercise drills each morning, ostensibly for the good of their health. However, Foucault (1975/1995, p. 155) would argue that rather than benefitting the individual, these acts actually serve to control and discipline the collective body.

At Kaimai Kindergarten, the kinds of disciplinary techniques described above are much less prevalent. The day is dominated by free play, with only a handful of structured rituals in the form of 'mat time', morning, and afternoon tea. Unlike in Japan, where teachers plan their day according to standardised texts which present parameters of 'normal' childhood behaviour (Goodman 2002), the New Zealand early childhood curriculum does not follow a content- or activities-based structure. Children are not required to line up in rows, sit at desks, or take part in morning callisthenics. While the children at Kaimai Kindergarten may be discouraged from fighting or screaming, there is little other structure explicitly imposed on them by adults. Implicitly, however, the centre is still the site of unseen power which governs much of children and teachers' days at the centre. Rather than emanating from a person, Foucault (1975/1995) sees power as "a certain concerted distribution of bodies, surfaces, lights, gazes; in an arrangement whose internal mechanisms produce the relations in which individuals are caught up" (p. 202). Kaimai Kindergarten may lack many of the rituals of Oka Kindergarten, but children and teachers' bodies are still subject to normalising forces as seen in the discussion above of unclothed bodies.

Approaches to Dirt and Pollution

In both New Zealand and Japan, health and safety discourses are located within this normalising framework. While it may seem that ideas about dirt, pollution, and bodies are due to modern understandings of pathogenic organisms, Douglas (1999) points out that concepts of dirt predate contemporary medicine. Defined by Douglas as "matter out of place" (p. 109), dirt can therefore only exist within a set of ordered relations. The presence of dirt contravenes that order. It is common to see pollution rules applied to functions or products of the human body, and early childhood settings are no exception to this. Contact with blood, vomit, excreta, and food are regulated through these rules. While teachers at Oka Kindergarten were shocked by a New Zealand teacher not applying disinfectant to a bleeding knee, Douglas (1966) would see their concerns less as stemming from a fear of pathogens than as a rupture of pollution constructs. In Japan, spaces are symbolically defined as either 'outside' and therefore dirty and possibly dangerous, or the sacred, clean 'inside'. This idea is central to the way the body, social relationships, and physical spaces are constructed (Lock, 1980). The scene of the bleeding knee reveals the strong association Japanese have with the outside and dirt (Ohnuki-Tierney, 1984). Failure to thoroughly clean the wound implies a confusion of these two constructs, potentially allowing the outside dirt to enter the inside of the body. The Japanese fear of absorbing or inhaling dirt from the outside (seen as an inherently polluted space) is the reason that masks and gloves continue to be worn. It explains why children are stripped naked to be thoroughly washed off after a period of water and sand play, as described above. It can also be seen in the rituals around appropriate footwear in different spaces. This is not only a feature of early childhood settings, but the most ubiquitous example of Japanese pollution rules.

In the New Zealand early childhood setting, approaches to pollution and the body are increasingly being framed by pervasive health and safety discourses. This ideology is symbolised by the rubber glove, which has become a standard fixture in kindergarten medical kits. New Zealand analysis of the bleeding knee scenario focused less on the issue of potential pollution and more on the context of surveillance in which the injury occurred. As one New Zealand teacher articulated, "If we knew that there was a video camera there, we would certainly put a glove on". Douglas (1999) defines pollution beliefs as cultural phenomena, "institutions that can keep their forms only by bringing pressure to bear on deviant individuals" (p. 114). For the New Zealand teachers interviewed in this research, the symbolism of dirt is not wholly constructed according to notions of pollution. Dirt has been repositioned as an expression of freedom and creativity embodied through children's soiled bodies and clothing. Aside from the fear of being caught subverting hygiene policies, there is little to compel teachers to religiously apply disinfectant and don gloves. Although the potential pathogenicity of dirt is well understood, dirt does not represent the same symbolic threat to children's bodies that it does in Japan.

Just as an analysis of dirt may reflect notions of pollution, Douglas (1966, 1972) maintains that rituals around food and the sharing of meals express social relations. These rituals "work upon the body politic through the symbolic medium of the physical body" (Douglas, 1966, p. 128). Treating food sharing as a code can reveal "hierarchy, inclusion and exclusion, boundaries and transactions across the boundaries" (Douglas, 1999, p. 231). Food can also be constructed as polluting when the external boundaries of the society are under pressure. At Kaimai Kindergarten, policy dictates that children are to consume only their own food during the shared lunch-time. This rule has arisen due to the growing number of children with food allergies. As a result, food that is shared has been reclassified as potentially polluting, both in a biological sense and symbolically. Like lollies, it has become food 'out of place' in the New Zealand early childhood setting (Douglas, 1966). At Oka Kindergarten, notions of purity and pollution are externalised in the form of the lunchbox or *bentō*. Lunches made by the children's mothers not only reflect the ideal of the perfect form (Bestor, 1999), but serve to keep Japanese children culturally and ideologically attached (Allison, 1997). Children are expected to consume the entire contents of their lunchbox both to show their understanding of this construct and to demonstrate their commitment and identification with the group (James, Curtis, & Ellis, 2009). Meal times and special events such as the annual picnic demonstrate how the identity of the wider kindergarten family (children, parents, and teachers) are linked through the sharing of food. As Douglas (1966) shows, "one cannot share the food prepared by people without sharing in their nature" (p. 126).

Coming Full Circle

This research journey began in a very personal way, with Rachael's family's experience of early childhood education in Japan and New Zealand, and Judith's professional interactions with early childhood in New Zealand and Japan. As we explained in the introduction, Rachael's family's return to New Zealand from Japan had very different outcomes for her children. While her older son felt lost without the rituals that anchored him at his Japanese kindergarten, her middle son felt freed from structure and repetition. Early in this research journey, many of the New Zealand teachers confessed to stereotypical views of the Japanese early childhood system as rigid, controlling, and repressive of children's creativity. Just as the New Zealand teachers held preconceived ideas about Japan, the Japanese teachers envisaged New Zealand centres as individualistic, ritual-poor, and lacking in structure. Knowing that Rachael was conducting research in the two countries, and that her three children had experienced both settings, people often asked her, "but which system do *you* think is the best?" What has become evident is that both settings (re)produce cultural practices which are valued in each country and designed to socialise children to become fully functioning members of their own society. Yet, in a globalised world, where cultural identity is not discretely located within geographic national boundaries, the relevance of this work lies in its ability to uncover and interrogate implicit cultural practices, and to discuss and understand them. This process opens the way for constructive reflections of traditional and embedded practices, as well as to avoid the creation of stereotypes, while challenging our assumptions about everyday practices in early childhood education.

References

Allison, A. (1997). Japanese mothers and obentos: The lunch-box as state apparatus. In C. Counihan & P. Van-Esterik (Eds.), *Food and culture: A reader* (pp. 296–314). London, UK: Routledge.

Aoki, M. (2010, February). *Preschool education in Japan today: From the viewpoint of the child-care worker training.* Paper presented at the Asia Pacific Week, The Australian National University, Canberra.

Bestor, T. C. (1999). Constructing sushi: Culture, cuisine, and commodification in a Japanese market. In S. O. Long (Ed.), *Lives in motion: Composing circles of self and community in Japan* (pp. 151–190). New York, NY: Cornell East Asia Program.

Davison, C., & Mitchell, L. (2008). The role of the state in early childhood care and education: Kindergartens as a case study of changing relationships. *New Zealand Annual Review of Education, 18,* 123–141.

Douglas, M. (1966). *Purity and danger: An analysis of concepts of pollution and taboo.* Harmondsworth, UK: Penguin Books.

Douglas, M. (1970/1996). *Natural symbols: Explorations in cosmology.* London, UK: Routledge.

Douglas, M. (1999). *Implicit meanings: Selected essays in anthropology.* London, UK: Routledge.

Douglas, M., & Wildavsky, A. (1982). *Risk and culture: An essay on the selection of technological and environmental dangers.* Berkeley: University of California Press.

Duncan, J. (1998). *I spy: Sexual abuse prevention polices: Protection or harm?* Wellington, New Zealand: Institute for Early Childhood Studies, Victoria University of Wellington.

Elias, N. (2000). *The civilizing process: Sociogenetic and psychogentic investigations.* Oxford, UK: Blackwell.

Foucault, M. (1975/1995). *Discipline and punish: The birth of the prison* (A. Sheridan, Trans.). New York, NY: Vintage Books.

Foucault, M. (1981). *The history of sexuality, Volume 1: An introduction.* Harmondsworth, UK: Penguin.

Fraser, M., & Greco, M. (Eds.). (2005). *The body: A reader.* London, UK: Routledge.

Goodman, R. (2002). Anthropology, policy and the study of Japan. In R. Goodman (Ed.), *Family and social policy in Japan: Anthropological approaches* (pp. 1–28). Cambridge, UK: Cambridge University Press.

Grosz, E. (2005). Refiguring bodies. In M. Fraser & M. Greco (Eds.), *The body: A reader* (pp. 47–51). London, UK: Routledge.

Hendry, J. (1993). *Wrapping culture: Politeness, presentation, and power in Japan and other societies.* Oxford, UK: Oxford University Press.

Holliday, R., & Hassard, J. (2001). *Contested bodies.* New York, NY: Routledge.

James, A., Curtis, P., & Ellis, K. (2009). Negotiating family, negotiating food: Children as family participants? In A. James, A. T. Kjorholt, & V. Tingstad (Eds.), *Children, food and identity in everyday life* (pp. 35–51). Basingstoke, UK: Palgrave Macmillan.

Jones, A. (2001). Introduction. In A. Jones (Ed.), *Touchy subject: Teachers touching children* (pp. 9–13). Dunedin, New Zealand: University of Otago Press.

Kita, A. (2008). Child rights education in Japanese schools. *Human Rights Education in Asia-Pacific.* Retrieved from www.hurights.or.jp/archives/asia-pacific/section1/12%20 Akihito%20Kita.pdf

Lock, M. (1980). *East Asian medicine in urban Japan.* Berkeley: University of California Press.

Lock, M. (1987). Introduction: Health and medical care as cultural and social phenomena. In E. Norbeck & M. Lock (Eds.), *Health, illness, and medical care in Japan: Cultural and social dimensions* (pp. 1–23). Honolulu: University of Hawaii Press.

Mauss, M. (1936/1973). Techniques of the body. *Economy and Society, 2,* 70–88.

May, H. (2009). *Politics in the playground: The world of early childhood in New Zealand* [Revised ed.]. Dunedin, New Zealand: Otago University Press.

Ministry of Education. (1996). *Te Whāriki: He Whāriki Mātauranga mō ngā Mokopuna o Aotearoa. New Zealand early childhood curriculum.* Wellington, New Zealand: Learning Media.

Ohnuki-Tierney, E. (1984). *Illness and culture in contemporary Japan: An anthropological view.* Cambridge, UK: Cambridge University Press.

Phillips, J. (1996). *A man's country: The image of the Pākehā male—A history.* Auckland, New Zealand: Penguin Books.

Picone, M. (1989). The ghost in the machine: Religious healing and representations of the body in Japan. In M. Feher (Ed.), *Fragments for a history of the human body: Part two* (pp. 466–489). New York, NY: Zone.

Robertson, J. (1988). Furusato Japan: The culture and politics of nostalgia. *Politics, Culture and Society, 1,* 494–518.

Scheper-Hughes, N., & Lock, M. (1987). The mindful body: A prolegomenon to future work in medical anthropology. *Medical Anthropology Quarterly, 1*(1), 6–41.

Smith, A. B. (1998). *Understanding children's development* (4th ed.). Wellington, New Zealand: Bridget Williams Books.

Smith, H. W. (1995). *The myth of Japanese homogeneity: Social-ecological diversity in education and socialization.* Commack, NY: Nova Science.

Suzuki, T. (2006). Fertility decline and policy development in Japan. *The Japanese Journal of Population, 4*(1), 1–32.

Takahara, K. (2010, 17 November). Kindergartens, day care centers may merge. *The Japan Times.* Retrieved from www.japantimes.co.jp/news/2010/11/17/reference/kindergartens-day-care-centers-may-merge/#.U-1ux-OSx8E

Te One, S. (2005). Children's rights and early childhood policy: Impacts and influences. *New Zealand Annual Review of Education, 14,* 171–193.

Tobin, J. (1992). Japanese preschools and the pedagogy of selfhood. In N. R. Rosenberger (Ed.), *Japanese sense of self* (pp. 21–39). Cambridge, UK: Cambridge University Press.

Tobin, J. (1997). Introduction: The missing discourse of pleasure and desire. In J. Tobin (Ed.), *Making a place for pleasure in early childhood education* (pp. 1–37). New Haven, CT: Yale University Press.

Tobin, J., Hsueh, Y., & Karasawa, M. (2009). *Preschool in three cultures revisited: China, Japan and the United States.* Chicago, IL: University of Chicago Press.

Turner, B. S. (2008). *The body and society: Explorations in social theory* (3rd ed.). Los Angeles, CA: Sage.

Walsh, D. J. (2004). Frog boy and the American monkey: The body in Japanese early schooling. In L. Bresler (Ed.), *Knowing bodies, moving minds: Towards embodied teaching and learning* (pp. 97–109). Dordrecht, The Netherlands: Kluwer Academic.

Wevers, L. (1980). Pioneer into feminist: Jane Mander's heroines. In P. Bunkle & B. Hughes (Eds.), *Women in New Zealand society* (pp. 244–260). Auckland, New Zealand: George Allen and Unwin.

AUTHOR INDEX

SUBJECT INDEX